PENGUIN BOOKS
RABINDRANATH TAGORE

Sabyasachi Bhattacharya, former professor of history at Jawaharlal Nehru University, New Delhi, and chairman, Indian Council of Historical Research (ICHR), has served as vice chancellor of Visva-Bharati University, Santiniketan. He has also held research and teaching positions at St Antony's College at Oxford University, the University of Chicago and El Colegio de México. His recent publications are *The Colonial State: Theory and Practice* (2016), *The Defining Moments in Bengal, 1920–1947* (2014), *Vande Mataram: The Biography of a Song* (2013), *Talking Back: The Idea of Civilization in the Indian Nationalist Discourse* (2011), and now in seventh imprint, *The Mahatma and the Poet: Letters and Debates Between Gandhi and Tagore, 1915–1941* (2008).

PRAISE FOR THE BOOK

'A balanced, sensitive, objective, impeccably written short biography . . . Admirable, lucid, non-hagiographical'—William Radice, *Frontline*

'Brilliant . . . Tagore who in his day—and for our day too, through his writings—had all the characteristics of what we would nowadays call a "public intellectual"'—*Statesman*

RABINDRANATH
TAGORE
AN INTERPRETATION

SABYASACHI BHATTACHARYA

PENGUIN BOOKS

An imprint of Penguin Random House

PENGUIN BOOKS

USA | Canada | UK | Ireland | Australia
New Zealand | India | South Africa | China | Singapore

Penguin Books is part of the Penguin Random House group of companies
whose addresses can be found at global.penguinrandomhouse.com

Published by Penguin Random House India Pvt. Ltd
4th Floor, Capital Tower 1, MG Road,
Gurugram 122 002, Haryana, India

Penguin
Random House
India

First published in Viking by Penguin Books India 2011
Published in Penguin Books by Penguin Random House India 2017

10 9 8 7 6 5 4 3 2

The views and opinions expressed in the book are the author's own and the
facts as reported by him which have been verified to the extent possible,
and the publishers are not in any way liable for the same.

ISBN 9780143440307

Typeset in Adobe Garamond by InoSoft Systems, Noida

Printed at Repro India Limited

www.penguin.co.in

This is a legitimate digitally printed version of the book and therefore might not
have certain extra finishing on the cover.

Contents

Acknowledgements

I am deeply indebted to several generations of Tagore scholars who have documented his life and illuminated his works. I would like to send a special word of thanks to the archivists of the Tagore papers at Rabindra Bhavan who helped me explore unpublished documents whenever I turned to them, in between my other commitments while I worked as vice chancellor at Visva-Bharati University in Santiniketan in 1991–95. In the years since then, as the project to write this book took shape, I drew upon the intellectual generosity of some of my colleagues at Jawaharlal Nehru University and a few scholars I came in touch with while I was at the Indian Council of Historical Research. I thank Penguin India for bringing the long gestation period to a closure when they asked me to write this book. Kamini Mahadevan of Penguin India helped enormously with editorial suggestions in respect of presentation. I would like to thank Richa Burman and Indrani Dasgupta of Penguin Random House for being immensely helpful while the present paperback edition was being prepared. Professor Sankha Ghosh has opened up in recent decades new windows into Tagore studies and I am grateful that he meticulously went through my text and improved it in many ways. Like other students of Tagore literature, I am indebted to Professor Sukanta Chaudhuri who has brought about a revolution in Tagore studies as the leader of a team that created the electronic aid, Bichitra, an online Tagore variorum. I also owe thanks to the vice chancellor, Rabindra Bharati University, Kolkata, for kindly according permission to use a self-portrait sketched by Tagore, now in the possession of the university museum. I chose this self-portrait because I thought it was appropriate for a book which, on the basis of my reading of Tagore's writings and letters and self-reflective remarks on his 'inner life', aims to capture Tagore's portrayal of his own self. Finally, my debt to Malabika, Ashidhara and Aditya is of a different order from any of the debts I acknowledge above and I give this book to them.

Abbreviations in References

C.P.:   Rabindranath Tagore, *Chithi Patra*, Visva-Bharati, Calcutta, vols. I–XIX. (Letters written by Tagore, selected by editors), 1993, new ed; 1942; 1943; 1945; 1957; 1960; 1963; 1964; 1967; 1974; 1986; 1992; 1995; 1998; 2000; 2002; and 2004.

EWRT: Rabindranath Tagore, *English Writings of Rabindranath Tagore*, (ed.) S.K. Das, Sahitya Akademi, New Delhi, 1994–96, vols. I–III.

J.S.:   Rabindranath Tagore, *Jiban Smriti,* in *R.R.*

L.F.:   Rabindranath Tagore, *Letters to a Friend,* in *EWRT.*

N.A.I.:   National Archives of India, New Delhi.

R.B.:   Archives: Rabindra Bhavan Archives, Visva-Bharati, Santiniketan.

R.R.:   *Rabindra Rachanabali*, Visva-Bharati, Calcutta, I–XVIII, (1393 BS). I preferred using this edition rather than the older series of volumes (thirty-one in number) commonly cited by Tagore scholars; the later edition I have used is more handy and it contains more recent data in the bibliographic notes at the end of each volume.

R.R.A.:   *Rabindra Rachanabali Achalita Sangraha* , vols. I–II, Visva-Bharati, Calcutta, 1940–41.

R.T.:   Rabindranath Tagore.

Sel. Letters: Krishna Dutta and Andrew Robinson (eds.), *Selected Letters of Rabindranath Tagore*, Cambridge University Press, Cambridge, 1997.

W.B.S.A.:   West Bengal State Archives, Kolkata.

Rabindranath Tagore. Self-portrait, ink and brush sketch, signed and dated 1935, 22.3 cm × 34 cm, Rabindra Bharati University Museum, Calcutta. Courtesy of the Vice Chancellor of the university.

Introduction

It is curious how sceptical Rabindranath Tagore was of his fame. Would it stand, he asked anxiously over and over again, the test of time? Not that he did not aspire to be read by generations to come. 'A hundred years from now, / Who are you reading this poem of mine?' He wrote that when he was barely thirty-five years of age and a relatively obscure poet.[1] But he doubted the habit of mind which encourages in men 'pretensions to immortality—for an instant'.[2] His self-doubt seemed to increase with his fame. And with it the thought, how would history remember him? 'When I shall cease to be / should you wish to remember me'[3]—thus begins one of his famous poems. At the peak of his success, he saw all his achievements turning some day into dust 'under the wheel of time',[4] gnawed away into nothingness by the remorseless 'ocean waves of time'.[5]

In putting together and thus conflating what might be looked upon as discrete pieces of writing from different points of time, are we exaggerating a tendency of his mind? Perhaps not. An acute consciousness of his 'place in history', in the memory of his people, seems to be a trait marking out Tagore from many other authors. As he became an icon in his country, he repeatedly asked himself the question, could 'this image (*putuli*) that has been made', escape the 'hunger of the dust'?

Today when we look back upon Tagore's life and work, his question seems to have been answered. He has not been forgotten.

But is he remembered just as a national icon, with only fading remnants of his fame in the public mind and steadily fading knowledge of his place in history? The Bengali-speaking community in India and elsewhere may like to believe that this is not true. But those who cannot access his works in Bengali—given the fact that only a small fraction of his writings have been translated into English, and still less into Indian languages—may think otherwise. It seems worthwhile, therefore, to attempt a brief interpretative account of Tagore's life and work.

I think that there are many aspects of Tagore's life which remain unexamined. These are 'Frequently Unasked Questions' about him. An inventory of them would show how they converge in particular on one aspect—the evolution of his intellectual life. This theme is addressed in the first chapter of this book and foregrounded in the narrative as a whole.

In pursuing that theme my method has been to draw from Tagore's own statements about the ideas and experiences which drove his creative and intellectual life. Tagore himself provides us the sources: in his autobiography, in his reminiscences and occasional self-analysis, and in over twenty-five hundred letters which have been archived. Read with his published literary works, these sources throw light on what the poet called his 'inner life'. I have deliberately avoided citing learned literary critics—the vast amount they have produced takes us to a different terrain altogether and I have preferred to depend upon Tagore's own testimonies and self-reflective observations. As such, I have depended on Tagore's own translations of his writings and, of course, what he wrote in English, given that few translations do justice to Tagore as a poet. The problem is not so great as far as prose works, particularly essays, are concerned. As regards his poetic works, even Tagore's own translations have been questioned on stylistic grounds; but translations by the original author are presumably more dependable, so far as authorial intention is concerned. Since there are not many translations by Tagore himself out of his vast corpus of writings, occasionally I have had to make do with renderings by others, or myself. To my mind that is acceptable so far as his prose works, an ideologue. In the evolution of the reformist ideology of the Brahma Samaj, later in the anti-partition or Swadeshi movement 1905–09, and in his writings supporting and sometimes differing from Gandhi from 1919 onwards, Tagore was a political thinker of consequence, addressing issues that were facing the emerging nation and the incipient freedom struggle, right from the beginning of the twentieth century. In the following pages a good deal of attention is paid to Tagore's social and political essays; few of them have been translated. No complete appreciation of Tagore's mind and activities can be arrived at if one excludes those writings.

Thirdly, it needs to be underlined that, given the constraint of the poverty in the quality as well as the quantity of translation and the consequent difficulty of access to a good deal of Tagore's writings for those not acquainted with his language, we have focused in the following pages on the *ideas* at the core of his writings. Needless to say, this involves an interpretation of the trends of Tagore's thinking. Fortunately, as we shall see, Tagore often took up the role of his own critical interpreter. In the task of interpretation, one is helped by those commentaries. Nevertheless, there will always remain the possibility of interpretations other than that offered in the following pages. It is worthwhile to recall what Tagore himself had said of the interpretation of literature: different readings of creative writings are possible and admissible.[8] If the interpretation in the present work raises new questions about Tagore's life and work, if it leads to further explorations, the aims of this biography will have been met.

Tagore's Intellectual Evolution

When the University of Oxford conferred the degree DLitt *honoris causa* on Tagore in 1940, among the many beautiful words in the citation, one phrase is memorable: 'Here before you is the myriad-minded poet and writer' ('*poeta et scriptor myrianous*'). That was an appropriate description of the vast range of Tagore's literary creations in the form of poetry, dramatic works, songs, essays, novels and short stories, which have been published in the thirty-one bulky volumes of his 'Collected Works'. What is more, he not only produced a vast corpus of writings but recreated his language, so that the Bengali in use today is the language of Tagore. And with historical hindsight to aid us, it is possible to add that it is given to very few to reshape the aesthetic sensibilities of an entire people and Tagore's creative writings brought about a cultural change of that order. It is necessary to convey all this to our readers, though that is not easy. The present intellectual biography thus seeks to be different from some other biographies of Tagore.

In our attempt to understand his life and work, Tagore's self-reflections are of great significance. In the following chapter we have extensively used these statements made at different points of his life, first at the age of forty-three and again at fifty-one, fifty-six, seventy, seventy-eight and eighty. Particularly important has been his 'Introduction' to the *Rabindra Rachanabali*.

> My writings have taken twists and turns and various forms due to changing environment and the state of things around me, some signature of unity marks them as writings related to one another. It is discerned in the analysis of those who look at it and study it from outside. But the author is unaware of it. To the author the moments of creation, the seasons of flowering and fruit-gathering are what matters; that is what touches him emotionally.[9]

In this statement Tagore applied the metaphor of the river to the flow of creative writing and he speaks of the twists and turns, the new direction it takes now and then. Elsewhere, as we have seen, he uses the imagery of the seasons of nature.[10] Any biography seeking to present the course of his intellectual life should thus try to highlight on the one hand the overarching unity of his thinking and the changes that occurred in different phases of his life and work.

The structuration of this book is inseparable from my interpretation of the trends in Tagore's life and work. Judging by Tagore's own reflections on his literary life and the historical context in which we may situate him, we can propose some major turning points, each of which marks the beginning of the five phases in Tagore's intellectual life. Is it presumptuous to cut up a man's creative endeavour into phases as perceived by us today? It need not be. This book offers an interpretation and alternative approaches remain open.

The Inner Life

The first chapter is about what Tagore often called his 'inner life'. He used this term to distinguish the quotidian life from the life of the mind. In part, this term also reflected his sense of isolation. Needless to say, there are many instances in history which suggest that intellectual solitude is very often the destiny of great minds. But Tagore seems to have specially suffered from an intense feeling of loneliness right from his childhood. He wrote of this quite often. For example he writes from New York to his confidant Charles Freer Andrews in 1921: 'I am afraid I shall be rejected by my own people when I go back to India. My solitary cell is awaiting me in my motherland.'[11] As we shall see in the following chapter there are many other statements of this kind. There is bitterness in them, but it suggests fear of rejection, not the isolation of arrogance. And Tagore did not nurture his isolation in his inner life to keep himself away from his public duties. 'It is not by meticulous care in avoiding all contaminations that we can keep our spirit clean and give it grace,' he wrote in another letter in 1918, 'but by urging it to give vigorous expression to its inner life in the very midst of all the dust and heat' of public life.[12] I consider the first chapter on 'inner life' an essential introduction to our attempt to understand Tagore's intellectual evolution.

The Enchanted Garden: 1861–1890

The second chapter, on the first thirty years of Tagore's life, is called 'The Enchanted Garden'. The garden in his ancestral home always figured prominently in his memories—that was his window into the world outside. The garden was almost a metaphor for the isolated and privileged life he led during these years. He was the grandson of an exceptionally wealthy entrepreneur of the early nineteenth century; a favourite son of the patriarch of a front-rank family of Bengal; had an elder brother who was the first Indian ICS officer; was gifted with a talent for versifying in Bengali, and was lucky to escape the mind-deadening schooling which his generation received, and sent away to acquire polish in England at age seventeen. He was the precocious author of contributions to journals owned by the family, and several slender books of poems by the time he was thirty. Tagore later wrote that the book of poems he published in 1890, *Manasi* (an approximate translation might be 'She Who Dwells in Imagination'), was his first work worthy of recognition as a literary work.[13] That publication, at the age of twenty-nine, perhaps may be regarded as the beginning of a new phase in his creative life.

Into the World: Tagore in the Public Sphere: 1891–1908

What is the next phase about? This is when Tagore emerged into public life from the private and privileged life he led earlier. He assumed the role of a landlord over the Tagore estates, and in the 1890s, he became the literary editor of more than one journal; he produced a stream of essays on social and political issues of the day; and finally he assumed the cultural leadership of the Swadeshi movement from 1905. Of these aspects of Tagore's presence in the public domain, the most important was the fame he acquired as the author of national songs during the Swadeshi agitation against the partition of Bengal. And the songs of that genre were also some of his most enduring creations. Two of such songs were destined to become the national anthems of two countries in the subcontinent, India and Bangladesh.

A number of events in Tagore's life in 1890–1891 mark the year as a turning point. He returned from Europe in November

1890 and produced a travel diary which departed from tradition and marked a new turn, in that it was not written in 'chaste' Bengali but in the Bengali that is spoken. This later became a distinguishing feature of the Tagorean style. A big change in his personal life came in 1891. The Tagore estates needed his constant supervision and hence he undertook frequent visits to fragments of them lying between north Bengal and Orissa. He also took over as the literary editor of a new journal *Hitabadi* (1891) and later another monthly called *Sadhana*. Tagore in his journalistic writings began to engage in controversies with contemporary spokesmen of Hindu orthodoxy. In December 1891 the Santiniketan prayer hall was inaugurated in his presence and this was the place which was to become the centre of his life in future.

In the 1890s Tagore wrote a number of short stories—no doubt partly due to his editorial task of 'feeding the monster', i.e. filling up his journal—which are memorable as his first attempt to imagine the life of the ordinary folk in Bengal, people he met in course of his travels as a landlord. His old muse of poetry continued to receive his tributes in a series of books of verse (*Chitra*, 1896; *Kanika*, 'A Fragment', 1899; *Katha o Kahini*, 'Tales and Legends',1900; *Kalpana*, 'Imagination', 1900; *Kshanika*, 'Momentary', 1900; *Naibedya*, 'Offerings',1901; and *Kheya*, 'Crossing', 1906).

From 1905 the anti-partition movement drew upon his creativity and he produced a series of essays, first giving expression to the initial spirit of the Swadeshi movement and later looking at it from a distance critically: collections of essays (*Atma-sakti*, 'Self-empowerment', 1905; *Bharatvarsha*, 1906; *Raja Praja*, 'Rulers and Subjects', 1908; *Samuha*, 'The Many', 1908; *Swadesh*, 'Our Land', 1908; *Siksha*, 'Education', 1908). This phase also produced a series of essays of literary criticism (*Prachin Sahitya*, 'Ancient Literature', 1907; *Loka-sahitya*, 'People's Literature', 1907; *Sahitya*, 'Literature', 1907;, *Adhunik Sahitya*, 'Modern Literature', 1907). And in the middle of it there was a novel, *Chokher Bali* ('The Mote in the Eye', 1903), the first attempt of Tagore to break away from the Bankim Chandra Chatterjee tradition of romance and to get real. Thus these were amazingly prolific years.

According to one of his closest friends, Charles Freer Andrews, Tagore spoke of certain distinct turning points in his life. One such turning point was getting to know villagers when he was assigned the task of supervising the estates of the family. According to Andrews, 'Rabindranath's soul caught the flame of patriotism, not in Calcutta but among the villagers'.[14] That may indeed partly account for the differences one can see between his approach and the conventional nationalist thought current from Surendranath Banerjea to Aurobindo Ghosh and Chittaranjan Das's times. Tagore's approach stemmed from his understanding of the nature of Bengal's society, the problems facing the peasantry, the need to develop *atma-sakti* or inner capability of the people as he perceived it. The conventional position of the urban middle-class leaders, with Calcutta as the focal point of their activities, emphasized other things such as the governance by the colonial state, the aspirations of the Bengali middle classes, the constitutional structure, and politics of agitation. As a member of the landed class Tagore was not in the best position to identify himself with the rural poor and he remained an observer outside of Bengal rural society. But a mechanical interpretation of an intellectual's class position leaves out the possibilities of an imaginative mind's ability to build bridgeheads of sympathetic understanding into social terrains which are far from one's class position, inherited or earned. This might have been Tagore's chief achievement in his attempts to understand the social and political milieu in Bengal in his times. This is reflected in his creative work such as the short stories Tagore wrote while touring rural Bengal, as well as in the programme of rural reconstruction he conceived of at Sriniketan and in his political and social essays. Andrews has a point when he surmises that 'it is not wonderful, therefore, that Bengal, from whose soil he seems to draw his deepest inspiration, should have been inspired by his music and song with a high consciousness of its own destiny'.[15]

'The Sage of Santiniketan':1909-1919

Around 1908–1909 Tagore arrived at a crossroad. He seemed to retreat from the position he held in the public domain. Although he was one of the progenitors of the nationalism associated with the anti-partition movement, he became increasingly critical of narrow nationalism and the contemporary state of nationalist politics. He withdrew himself into life centred on his school in Santiniketan. This is the focus of chapter four.

Consider some of the events paving the way to Tagore's retreat from political life in 1908–1909. He was sorely disappointed with the split in the Indian National Congress after the Surat session and he condemned the partisan spirit driving both the Moderate and Extremist factions. His presidential address at the Bengal Provincial Conference (later the Bengal Provincial Congress Committee) in February 1908 was his last political engagement for several years. His speech condemning both the factions in the Congress did not endear him to either of those groups. Moreover, the political assassinations which occurred from 1908 raised doubts in his mind about the efficacy of the tactics of violence of the revolutionary nationalists. His recommendation of an alternative path, rural reconstruction for nation building, found no takers. In October 1908 Tagore surprised many people by his silence when a number of political leaders in Bengal were incarcerated by the government. Tagore's withdrawal was complete when in 1908 he wrote essays which pointed to the futility of terrorism as well as its long-term implications. In one such essay entitled 'Ends and Means' (*Path o Patheya*) he summed it up: For the time being, he said, many Bengalis were happy that militant actions and assassinations provided proof that they were not cowards, but whatever the provocation due to an alien government's actions 'to commit suicide is not the way to set things right'; excited as they are, people must be told that the path is 'through the open highway, no shortcut to attain the aim is possible.' It was an advice which Tagore surmises will be rejected by those who believe that 'secret action alone is the true method'.[16] Tagore developed and refined this argument years later in his novel *Char Adhyay* ('Four Episodes'), written in 1934. Evidently this was a problem festering in his mind for years. And he showed the courage of his conviction in refusing to endorse acts of terrorism.

The other issue engaging his mind at this time was the conflict between tradition and modernity, between blind religiosity and rationalism, between 'Hindu nationalism' and humanist values. This intellectual conflict emerges loud and clear in *Gora* (1910), a novel exploring ideas. Here there is a discernible antithesis between Hindutva-centred nationalist consciousness and that motivated by human values. The personal location of the main protagonist, Gora, in an ambiguous position between Europe and India, imparts another dimension to the basic ideological conflict. Perhaps more than any other novel *Gora* can be viewed as the clearest exposition of Tagore's position between the civilizations of the West and East. In a different form, shorn of the historical specificities, we have a contraposition of status quo versus change, in the play *Achalayatan* ('The Changeless Regime', 1912). And the other major fictional work of this period *Ghare Baire* ('Home and the World', 1916) addresses, inter alia, the question of ends and means, the conflict between human values and the agenda of nationalist politicians. It is deeply disturbing not only because of the focus on that issue, but also because the choice of protagonists in the novel brings to the centre stage the question of women's agency, their emancipation in social circumstances like that of the Tagore family. *Ghare Baire* does not have the epic proportions of *Gora*, but it is a tension-laden portrayal of a home that is torn between two kinds of world outlook: on one hand, that of nationalist idealism, and on the other, that of pragmatist politics. On the way to the denouement, exposing the hollowness of ideas and practices of the pragmatist protagonist, Tagore also makes a searching analysis of the limits of middle-class politics, isolated from the life and mind of the common people. If the task of nation building was a battle for the mind of the nation, both the novels were virtually manifestoes stating

Tagore's own approach to the issues which the Indian nationalists were grappling with. That is not to say that the message was all that mattered, because it was the art in it which possibly mattered more to the creator. Tagore often said so in some rare self-reflective critiques of his own work.

For the common man, the decade 1909–19 was, of course, chiefly remarkable because of the celebrated event, the award of the Nobel Prize in 1913. At this time Tagore was just harvesting the fruits of his work earlier and getting them translated for a foreign readership. In terms of his intellectual life, it is doubtful if this episode was significant. However, these English translations, sometimes edited by his intellectual associates in England, were significant in representing Tagore as the 'spiritual' poet of the East: *Gitanjali* (1912), *The Gardener* (1913), *The Crescent Moon* (1913), *Fruit Gathering* (1916), and a few more, all published in England and the United States. Tagore's withdrawal from the public and political domain to the 'spiritual' domain was a disappointment to many of his followers, but it went into the making of a new icon, 'the sage of Santiniketan'. More about that will follow later in these pages.

New Directions: 1919–1929

The year 1919 marks a turning point because Tagore was drawn out of his retreat once again into the public domain. It occurred at a dark moment in national history, the Jallianwala Bagh massacre that led to the renunciation of the knighthood by Tagore. The following decade, the subject of chapter five, was significant on account of the renewal of Tagore's renewed engagement with nationalist politics as well as his ideological differences and debates with Gandhi. The decade also saw some path-breaking creations like the plays *Mukta-Dhara* ('Free Current', 1922) and *Rakta-Karabi* ('Red Oleander', 1926), allegorically addressing basic issues of freedom and domination, the liberating spirit of man and the exploitative system of Mammon. Apart from stylistic innovations in the 'prose-poems' he wrote at this time, a break with the past was signalized by a novel, *Yogayog* ('Relationships', 1929), he wrote at the end of this decade; Tagore had already broken away from the romantic tradition of Bankim Chandra Chatterjee, but now his dissection of gender relationships with a cruel scalpel was far in advance of the muted and mealy mouthed treatment convention required in Bengali fiction till the nineteen twenties.

The return to engagement in national politics was a notable departure from the preceding phase and it began as an act of individual resistance in response to a series of historic events: a repressive piece of legislation known as the Rowlatt Act, the beginning of popular movements in several parts of India against the Act in response to Gandhi's call, the firing on an unarmed political gathering at Jallianwala in Punjab, and severe and vengeful repressive measures in Punjab under Martial Law. Tagore made one abortive attempt to gather public support for a protest meeting and then he resolved to lodge an individual protest. He wrote in a justly famous letter to the Viceroy against 'the enormity of the measures taken by the Government in the Punjab', which were 'without parallel in the history of civilized governments.' And Tagore went on to say: 'The very least I can do for my country is to take all consequences upon myself in giving voice to the protest of the millions of my countrymen . . . I for my part wish to stand, shorn of all special distinction, by the side of my countrymen.'[17] Soon after this act of individual defiance, Tagore lent support to the movement led by Gandhi. In the long run, it was the advent of Mahatma Gandhi and the beginning of a mass movement under his leadership which brought about a renewal of Tagore's commitment to the nationalist movement. At the same time, he had major differences with Gandhi on several issues, such as (a) the adequacy of the *Khadi* programme as an alternative path to development, (b) the negative approach in Gandhi towards the knowledge system and technology of the West; and (c) the regimentation which Tagore perceived in the Gandhian fold contrary to Tagore's ideal, 'swaraj of the mind'.[18] On the other hand, while the two thought leaders debated those issues in the public, their personal friendship was enriched by mutual appreciation in these years.

In his creative life, perhaps, more important were the two plays he wrote in this decade, putting in dramatic form the contraposition between freedom and necessity, between the individual's emancipation and the constraints of the system they were located in, between humanistic values and reasons of state. In *Mukta-Dhara* the contraposition is between the reasons of state articulated by the king and his henchmen and, on the other hand, the assertion of human rights, represented by the oppressed peasantry of a colonized land led by a saintly mendicant. In *Rakta-Karabi* the dialectics are equally clear—it is the conflict between the oppressed workers of *Yakshapuri* ('Mammon's Land' would be a rough translation.) and the minions of a mysterious ruler who remains hidden from view. In both the plays the contraposition of ideas is clear, but in neither the resolution of the contradictions is convincing. There is a fixed idea in many of Tagore's works, including these two, about the 'conversion' of the ruler, or someone like that, at the apex. It may well be interpreted as the liberal faith, typical of late enlightenment, in the power of ideas in the battle with interests. Be that as it may, these two plays were remarkably in advance of their times. Today *Mukta-Dhara* finds relevance in environmentalists' thinking, while *Rakta-Karabi* continues to evoke egalitarian sympathies.

The new directions in which Tagore ventured forward in this period brought him to the frontier of 'modernism' in literature—a territory on which a new generation of writers who looked upon themselves as 'post-Tagore' had staked their claim. As we shall see later, Tagore almost reinvented his style in the prose-poems in *Lipika* ('Letters') and in *Purabi* ('Eastern') and *Mohua* by the end of the nineteen twenties. The book that imprinted itself on the mind of the next generation of Bengali writers was a *tour de force*, a brilliant novelette *Sesher Kabita* ('The Farewell Song') published in 1929. Buddhadeb Bose, a leader among the modernist writers of his generation wrote: 'It seemed the book was addressed to us, new writers, as an indirect admonition from Gurudev, intended to teach us a lesson'.[19] We shall keep the details of Tagore's encounter and experiments with modernism for the relevant chapter.

Finally, what surprised the world was that towards the end of the 1920s Tagore revealed himself as a painter. The first exhibition of his paintings was organized in Paris in 1930 and that met with much critical acclaim. Exhibitions in seven major cities in Europe and North America established him as an artist. Appreciation was noticeably more limited in his own country than abroad. Tagore was somewhat tentative in courting this new Muse of art. As regards his paintings, he wrote: 'An apology is due from me for my intrusion into the world of pictures. . . My pictures are my versification, in lines. If by chance they are entitled to claim recognition, it must be primarily for some rhythmic significance of form. . .'[20] We shall see later that it was his untrained and therefore unspoilt vision in his art which attracted art critics like Ananda Coomaraswamy who saw in Tagore's paintings 'modern primitive art', 'truly innocent, like the creation of the universe'.[21] Tagore developed a strong critique of 'Oriental Art' which the majority of the artists in those times idealized, and that was specially true of the Bengal School.[22] That did not help to make him popular as an artist among the artists.

Towards the Religion of Man: 1930–1941

In the last decade of his life, discussed in the sixth chapter, Tagore's literary output was particularly prolific and variegated. It almost seems that, conscious of the approaching end, his creativity bursts forth in philosophical writings, experiments in new literary forms, his venture into the world of graphic arts. He continued to be in demand as an influential public spokesman and thus he was busy sending 'messages' and delivering addresses. But the political public appears to occupy less space in his mind than it did earlier. Engagement with the idea of the 'religion of man' provides an overarching unity to the writings of this period.

It has been argued in this chapter that a kind of humanist universalism formed the core of Tagore's philosophy of life and this finds its ultimate expression in the concept of 'Religion of Man'. This was the title of his Hibbert Lectures in Oxford (1930) as well as his Professorial Lecture at Calcutta University (1933). The idea was also touched upon in *Bharat Pathik Rammohun* ('Rammohan, the Pilgrim of India', 1933) and the lecture on Buddha at Mahabodhi Society (1935). The elaboration of this idea may be seen in various creative works such as the drama *Chandalika* ('The Untouchable Girl', 1933) and the novel *Char Adhyay* ('Four Episodes', 1934) which are about casteist exclusion and sectarian politics of violence, confronted with humanist values. Finally, in the shadow cast on the world by World War II, Tagore delivered his last testament on the theme of humamist values at the core of human civilization, shortly before his death, *The Crisis in Civilization* (1941). It is no exaggeration to say that this theme was so much in his thoughts that it ceased to be a matter for philosophical exposition, it became a part of his personal outlook on life and that finds expression in most of his poetry in these last years of his life.

An innovation in form introduced by Tagore in this period was the 'prose-poem', after a half-hearted attempt in *Lipika* ('Letters') earlier. *Punascha* ('Post-script', 1932) was the first experiment in this form and there followed *Shesh Saptak* ('The Last Chords', 1935), *Patraput* ('Platter of Leaves', 1936), and *Shyamali* ('Dark Maiden', 1936). Tagore looked upon the experiment as a liberation of poetry from metrical discipline, but he faced a good deal of criticism for having made it 'easy' for all and sundry to become poets! Around this time Tagore began to engage in debates on modernism in poetry. In an essay on 'Modernism in Literature'[23] he argued that on the one hand the 'bold creativity' of young Bengali writers was most welcome, but on the other hand the tendency to be imitative, to mimic the modernist Western style of the day, was unfortunate. In 'Modernism in Poetry'[24] Tagore discussed some works of T.S. Eliot, Ezra Pound, Amy Lowell, et al. From the late 1920s Tagore's correspondence with modern poets (e.g. Buddhadeb Bose, Jibanananda Das, Sudhindranath Datta and Samar Sen) also throws light on Tagore's encounter with modernism in these years.[25]

Innovations by Tagore in literary forms and his venture into painting in old age surprised many of his contemporaries. He offered a historical explication: Tagore believed that his sensibilities were shaped by 'three movements, all of which were revolutionary'—those associated with Rammohan Roy who opened up the mind to new ideas, Bankim Chandra Chatterjee who 'aroused our literature from her age-long sleep', and the National spirit which taught people to assert their own cultural personality. At this confluence of three movements, Tagore says, he sought 'guidance for my own self-expression in my own inner standard of judgement'.[26] It is interesting to observe that in his self-portrayal Tagore presents himself as well as the three movements he mentions as 'revolutionary', or at least heterodox. He was, he says, a 'literary outlaw' who 'never had complete acceptance from my own people, and that too has been a blessing, for nothing is as demoralizing as unqualified success'.[27]

Finally, a characteristic of the last decade of Tagore's life was the recurrent motif of death. In his last years he lost many of his companions in his creative life, Dinendranath Tagore (1935), Jagadish Chandra Bose (1937), Charles Freer Andrews (1940), and Surendranath Tagore (1940). Tagore's poems are full of the imageries of the impending end and that thought occurs in the book-titles: *Shesh Saptak* ('The Last Chords', 1935), *Prantik* ('Terminal', 1938), *Senjuti* ('The Evening Lamp', 1938), *Rogsajya* ('Sick Bed', 1940). And yet Tagore's spirit renewed itself to explore new forms, new arts, and new ideas. He wrote and translated into English a poem on the intimations of mortality:

The bell tolls the last hour at Your porch,
And my heart responds to the creaking of the opening gates of farewell.
In this deepening gloom of the twilight,
I will gather what flickering flames remain to light my consciousness . . .[28]

The Inner Life

The biography of a poet, arguably, is insignificant because he should be known through his poetry. The great poets of India, Tagore wrote in 1901 while reviewing a biography of the poet Tennyson, have no biography.[1] Little is known about the life of Valmiki or Kalidasa. And that is as it should be, he said, for the details of the poet's life more often than not, are trivial. Tennyson's biography by his son, Tagore observed, abounded in such trivialities; the poetic life of Tennyson was something apart, the story of his outer life was irrelevant. At the same time, Tagore conceded, there were creative writers like Dante who were different, because their genius would be manifested not only in their life but also their life's work as one seamless whole. In such instances, life history and the corpus of writings illuminate each other, Tagore surmised. It is an inspiring thought. But to look at the interrelationship of the inner and outer life of Rabindranath Tagore is not easy for a biographer.

In many statements about his intellectual evolution, Tagore spoke of his 'inner life'. In 1904, in one such statement, he underlined the importance of the 'inner consciousness'.[2] In 1917 he distinguished between the 'subconscious' (*upachetana*) and conscious level in his mind, to point to the emergence of thoughts from below.[3] In 1940 he reflected on 'the mystery of vitality working in me'.[4] While he highlighted the inner life in such statements, he did not ignore the outer life that resides in history. In his last statement about his own intellectual evolution he wrote:

> I do not know whether I shall have another opportunity, and that is why at the age of eighty I want to make known the truths I saw in my life time . . . Thus I have to look at the evolution of my inner life and also my engagement with the outer world.[5]

As we have seen in the introduction, Tagore wrote several times about his life as an author: the first time when he was forty-three years of age and later at age fifty-one, fifty-six, seventy, seventy-eight and eighty. These were not so much reminiscences, more like statements of his credo. What is interesting is how he looked back upon his creative life at different points in his literary career. On one point, however, he remained consistent and constant: that there was a continuity in his literary creations, a continuity in his inner life. That, he said, is what he perceived with hindsight. He had, he said, never consciously guided himself along that trajectory. When he was forty-three, called upon to write about his literary life, he affirmed that there was a creative power which imparted to his writings a unity and continuity of evolution: 'Without knowing what it added up to, I had written poem after poem—and now in the light of the total corpus, it is revealed to me that beyond the fragments of meaning I saw in them at that time, there was a continuous signification flowing through all the writings.'[6] He surmised that the cunning of creation is that each act of it seems complete by itself; the author is unaware of the direction of the series of acts of creation. Tagore said, addressing his Muse:

> You speak through my words
> The tune is yours.
> . . . I do not know whose message I carry
> And for whom I sing.

The idea of a unity and a continuity of discourse evolving by itself, unknown to the author, is not uncommon. But Tagore went beyond it in postulating that there was a link between this creative power within and the eternal and the universal in the world without. And further, he believed that there was somewhere a creator who was the author of his life, 'someone who imparts to the fragments of joys and sorrows, the good and the bad things in life, an abiding significance'. Thus emerges the Tagorean concept of *'Jiban-devata'*, which can be roughly translated as 'the Maker of Life'.

In 1917, at the age of fifty-six, Tagore looked back again at his past creations in an essay on his philosophy of life entitled 'My Religion'.[7] What is religion, he says, but that which 'dwells in our mind and creates it'? A new note is struck by Tagore when he says that once he was in the stage of communing with nature but there came a time when his poetry 'ascends from the step of Nature on to the step of Humanity'. Communing with Nature finds fulfilment in efforts to establish communication with Humanity.[8] 'I do not yet know what my religion is . . . But I am certain that it is not in the quiet of inactivity nor in just the pleasures of an aesthete.'[9] At one stage of his life, he turned towards his responsibility to Humanity, and that is the message in the verses in, *Naibedya*, and *Chitra*; that was the message from 'He who guides human history in this world . . . From now onwards the spell of uninterrupted peace was over.' The poet had been 'like a truant boy' playing upon his flute the livelong day, but now:

I appeal to thee, Muse, full of wiles
call me back to the world's firm shore.
Gather yourself, O Poet, and arise
If you have courage bring it as your gift.
There is so much sorrow and pain,
A world of suffering lies ahead.

Thus the poet comes out of 'the cool shade of my heart' and stands 'on the wide dusty highway amidst the crowd'.[10]

In another statement about his literary life in 1912, Tagore made an interesting observation. 'I know of the profusion of my writings, and that a good portion of that will fail', i.e. fail the test of time to be of lasting value; producing too much does not ensure immortality and, regardless, he wrote on. But, Tagore added, in his own defence:

> The only thing I must say for my part is this: I have given to the world of literature what I thought was worthwhile without trying to supply what is in demand. My object has not been merely to please the readers, it has been to present what I think is worthy of the world of letters . . . But this approach does not yield uninterrupted praise for beginning to end—and I have not received such praise.[11]

Tagore went on to say a few things which were evidently about his social and political writings:

> The fact that self-empowerment [or development of one's own capabilities] alone can bring to man genuine advancement . . . is an old truth which I have never been able to state without getting roundly abused. But I have never short-changed readers to gain popularity in the market . . . This has often caused severe differences between me and my audience, my readers . . . I have not avoided such distressing experience by resorting to strategies.[12]

This was written soon after Tagore faced a lot of criticism because of his open differences with nationalist leaders during the anti-partition agitations from 1905, and later Tagore's critique of the methods such as political assassination and secret society activities of the militant nationalists from about 1908. The statement on his political differences with the political leadership in Bengal is also significant as an indicator of the importance Tagore attached to his political writings, actuated by his intense sense of patriotic responsibility.

When Tagore spoke of his literary life at his seventieth birthday celebration in 1931, he was a little sceptical of the variety of roles he had played as an institution-builder, as a political and social thinker, as an opinion-leader.

> As I reach the end of the long cycle of my life when I see the whole course of it, I realize that I have only one identity and that

is that I am only a poet . . . I am not a theorist nor a scholar nor a Guru nor a leader.[13]

This is an anxiety, a desire for withdrawal from the roles Tagore had entered in the middle period of his life; the roles he had taken on as the founder and Gurudev at Santiniketan, as a political commentator though not actively in politics, as a spokesman of Indian civilization addressing the world at large. Tagore tried slowly to cast aside these roles in the last years of his life, but without success, for the world around him would have none of that.

In June 1939 Tagore wrote a prefatory note to the new collected edition of all his works to be published by Visva-Bharati.[14] 'My writings have taken twists and turns and various forms due to changing environment and state of things around me, some signature of unity [despite change over time] marks them as writings related to one another. But the author remains unaware of it.' Tagore also reflects upon the fact that history may value writings which are not necessarily great creations from the literary point of view. 'These writings are products of diverse times and mental environments.' Over time his mind evolved and the surrounding world also evolved and the course of history changed: 'Literature is like a boat floating down the river of history . . . History remembers everything, literature forgets a good deal.' Tagore surmised that he saw on many of his writings 'the mark of oblivion' awaiting them in the future; nevertheless, those might find a place in his collected works. Much that is produced as literature may be forgettable, but all that is also part of history, part of the process of evolution.

In an essay he wrote in 1940, around the time of his eightieth birthday, he returns to his view that essentially he was a poet and that he owed to 'some unseen power intellectual at the centre of my evolution in life' the unity in his intellectual evolution through his life experiences.[15] Since many commentators have offered 'spiritual' explanations of this persistent belief in the continuity and unity in his creative life, an important question is whether Tagore claims a divine intervention in his life, or a god-given destiny. Tagore's language may occasionally tend to suggest that, but it is vitally important to note that he denied this in the following manner in a short piece he published in 1905, soon after the first of the series of essays we have reviewed here. In 1905 he felt compelled to make two points. First, what he presents as a power outside his own mind and guiding his evolution is not exclusively his alone; that power guides all humanity. 'To perceive a universal power working in one's own life and writings is not self-pride . . . That power is not any particular person's property, it works through everyone.'[16] Secondly, he points out that the unity in his creative life could be something other than divine dispensation. 'The *idea* which was not within our consciousness in the beginning "makes us say and do things" and the force of idea works through the unconscious. This realization was somehow expressed by me . . . Whether that statement is true or false is another matter, but this is not a matter of pride, because it is not one individual's property. However, if in one's own life evolution an idea is clearly perceptible then it is impossible to ignore it as something too common or well known.'

In this statement of 1905 he repeatedly used the notion of an *idea*, devoid of any religious or spiritual association. Thus it is possible to look upon Tagore's statements about some unknown power guiding his life and work without ascribing to him the absurd and egoistic belief in his destiny being divinely ordained. There might have been a spiritual aspect as well, but we need not interpret things exclusively in that light, the force working towards the unity he saw in his life's work.

Jiban Smriti ('Memoirs') covers only the first twenty-four years of Tagore's life. Apart from pen-pictures of the early years of his life, which appear in a kind of golden glow burnished by fond memories, the reflections in this book on his own writings are of great value. Although it breaks off at age twenty-four, the series of letters he wrote and published (*Chhinna Patra*, 1912) throw a lot of light on his intellectual interests in the following period, 1887 to 1896. Those letters form almost a diary. Moreover, there are about 2500 letters which he wrote to a vast range of correspondents and these provide a window into his mind in a manner. In particular the letters Tagore wrote to Charles Freer Andrews are of special value since Tagore confided in him thoughts which he did not wish to put in any publicly available form. We have depended a great deal on these letters of Tagore.

A Loneliness: His Destiny

The loneliness of being Rabindranath Tagore in late nineteenth century India is an important element in his mental environment that we should try and understand. Tagore believed that solitude was his lot. 'All through life,' he writes to Andrews on 18 April 1921, 'I have ever worked alone; for my life and work have been one. I am like the tree, which builds up its timber by its own living process . . .'[17] Later he also told Andrews of his terribly lonely childhood: 'I was very lonely—that was the chief feature of my childhood—I was very lonely. I saw my father seldom: he was away a great deal . . . I was kept in the charge of servants of the household after my mother died . . .'[18] Very similar is Tagore's description of his lonely childhood in his memoirs, *Jiban Smriti* and *Chhele Bela*. Likewise, as a young man, he spent a great deal of his life in solitude. He had to supervise the Tagore family estates in North Bengal, and stay on his boat on the river by the sand-flats for months together with no other companion than servants and boatmen. 'Sometimes I would pass many months absolutely alone without speaking, till my own voice grew thin and weak through lack of use.'[19]

Such solitude may have formed his personality. He wrote to Andrews:

I have a strong human sympathy, yet I can never enter into such relations with others as may impede the current of my life, which flows through the darkness of my solitude beyond my ken . . . I have a force acting in me jealous of all attachments, a force that tries to win me for itself, for its own hidden purpose . . . This loneliness often becomes hard for me to bear . . .[20]

Tagore attributed his restlessness, his passion for travel to a positive desire for solitude, though loneliness was irksome: 'Now I understand at last that the restlessness that has been so persistent with me is of this nature—I must come out from the life of habit, the life of compromise . . . I think the first step towards it is going to be solitude.'[21] Solitude, retreat from his busy life, supplied his 'mind with its natural food' while the crowded life in the work-a-day world his mind lived 'on half-rations'.[22] What he does not say is that he had few peers in his life, persons he could share his thoughts with. Charles Andrews and Mahatma Gandhi were the only companions of that kind in his mature life; when he was young he had a few persons close to him in Calcutta such as Loken Palit, Priyanath Sen and above all his brother Satyendranath Tagore, but they passed away in 1915, 1916 and 1923. Judging by the masses of letters he left behind there were very few persons of that kind around him in the last decades of his life. In Santiniketan there were distinguished scholars like Kshitimohan Sen and Bidhu Sekhar Bhattacharya, but in an institutional set up intimacy did not grow. Moreover, the reverence habitually accorded to 'Gurudev' Tagore by people around him from the middle of his life created an inseparable distance and hence his isolation.

Tagore recurrently speaks of his 'inner life'. He does it at moments of crisis, such as what he called the periods of mental 'depression'. He also speaks of it in moments of new spurts of creativity. For instance, on 30 June 1915, in a letter to Andrews, he confides:

> Possibly my life is on the eve of another bursting of its pods and scattering of its seeds; there is that continual urgency in my blood, the purpose for which is hidden. The conclusion is being forced upon me that poets should never bind themselves to any particular work; for they are instruments of the world's mood. And after years of building up all kinds of benevolent schemes, my life is emerging once again upon the open heath of irresponsibility, where the sun rises and sets, where there are wild flowers, but no committee meetings.[23]

Tagore began writing the famous *Balaka* series of poems shortly before this. After a bout of depression in May 1914, Tagore resolved the problem in this manner: he continued to feel the burden on his conscience that he was unable completely to perform his duties as he perceived them to his school, his family, his country and in general, he wrote to his son, 'in this life I have been unable to realize my ideal . . . such an intense darkness enveloped my mind'.[24] However, he resolved to limit his efforts to what was possible for him without departing from his vocation in the domain of creativity, and not try all the time to 'take up the role of a beneficent angel'.[25] He wrote later, not entirely in jest:

> I am afraid the present time is a tremendously difficult one in India for the . . . poet. It is no use protesting that he is lacking in understanding . . . No, he must attend meetings or write editorials; or accept some responsibility of grave and national importance, in order to make a fool of himself.[26]

Absence of a Public

In 1894 Tagore arrived at an important theoretical formulation which was neglected by his contemporaries but now, in the light of the recent scholarly interest in the 'public sphere', we can appreciate the point he made. He spoke of the absence of a public sphere. He pointed out that in India the distinction between the 'public' and the 'private' was unknown, and in fact the word 'public' did not exist, if one considered its European usage. How did Tagore come upon this realization? Bankim Chandra Chatterjee passed away in 1894 and Tagore, among others, proposed a public meeting to pay tribute to his memory. An old and eminent poet was requested to preside over the meeting but he declined to do so on the ground that such a meeting would be inconsistent with Indian tradition, to mourn in a meeting in public was unknown in Indian culture.[27] Tagore wrote an essay on the need to introduce the concept of a public sphere in India. He argued that Indian society, traditionally centred upon family and kinship relationships, was just beginning to see the growth of 'the Public . . . This is a new phenomenon;

the word is also new to us. It is impossible to translate it into Bengali . . . In Europe the manner in which associative patterns developed make prominent personalities visible . . . They are in the foreground of public attention . . . Our Public is yet an adolescent'. In India 'the lack of density' in public sphere activities at that time, Tagore surmised, failed to draw people out of familial and kinship roles into a broader sphere which is created by a consciousness of the duties which devolve upon the 'public'.[28]

In his reminiscences of his visit to England published in 1912, Tagore writes about 'the thinkers in England'.[29] The thinkers he talks about are Bertrand Russell, H.G. Wells, and G. Lowes Dickinson whom he met in London and Cambridge; but the focus is on the intellectual community which they represented. Tagore surmised that the community of intellectuals or thinkers in England was hard put to meet the demands of their society since,

. . . behind each individual's mind there is an alive mind of their country; waves of thought, the confluence of discourse, always impact their minds. That cannot but keep the intellect awake and vocal . . . When thought currents have a velocity, the pleasure [of pursuing thoughts] is evident. That pleasure is an integral part of the social make-up of the intellectuals here.

Apart from the absence of a sufficiently large and active intellectual community in India (in the early years of the twentieth century), Tagore felt another constraint on intellectual life in India: the educated community was isolated and fragmented.

When I am out of my country I forget that in our country there is much less awareness of the wide world and its people . . . When I return I look around and ask myself, where is the consciousness of that larger perspective, who is aware of our existence in the wider arena.[30]

He perceived in India not only a lack of awareness of that wider world and India's role in it, he also saw, the inner mind 'imprisoned in numberless divisions and conflicts' which 'we hide in verbiage spewed from political forums' though the conflicts remain very real in everyday life, in inter-provincial jealousy and animosity.[31] Tagore detested that kind of parochialism. He held up as the ideal Rammohan Roy and Dara Shikoh who acquired deep knowledge of 'the Other', the religious community to which they did not belong. Then, he said regretfully, at some point of time in India's history a night of ignorance descended on the Indian mind. Few Hindus understand what Islam means, the way Rammohan Roy perceived it; few Muslims know Hinduism the way Dara Shikoh understood it deeply. It is ignorance which separates people, knowledge would have united them, but that consciousness—which alone can be the true basis of nationhood—was absent in the India of his times.[32]

In particular, Tagore felt the absence of sympathy in Bengal for his mission: the unification of India in the cultural domain and the universalization of India's role in the global human civilization. In several of his sermons at Santiniketan in 1926, he spoke of this experience. For example: 'For a long time I have brought up sons of Bengal in my ashram, but I have had no support from Bengal. That is the divine dispensation . . . From outside of Bengal I received support, that is a blessing.' Tagore said that it was that support from other parts of India for Visva-Bharati which would advance his effort beyond the limits of Bengal; that is why one had to discard 'pride in belonging to Bengal', a greater entity claims the role of nurturing Tagore's ashram or the Visva-Bharati.[33] Tagore recalls, in another speech in 1933, that he had little support from Bengal in his struggle to build his school in Santiniketan. When his endeavour began, he says, 'I received no help from my own people; their opposition and animosity without reason, impeded this school, but I ignored that and carried on my effort regardless.'[34] Tagore could recall only two persons from Bengal who donated towards the development of his school in Santiniketan till 1933. He surmised that,

. . . regrettably the Bengali mind is infertile, it cannot sustain institution building. The animosity which feeds on unreasonable malice destroys what has been built, destroys the resolve that builds, and cannot accept anything with the respect due to it. That this endeavour [Tagore's school] has survived is in the teeth of this kind of antagonism.[35]

At the end of this speech of 1933 Tagore said:

I have endeavoured all by myself, I gave up all hopes of cooperation. There was little prospect of much cooperation . . . I cannot deceive myself that the Visva-Bharati as an institution will survive meaningfully for ages. I only pray that I should continue to serve it without such delusions.[36]

Whatever the reason, Tagore seems to have felt that his was an almost lone endeavour. The year before he died, his speech at Santiniketan was a farewell statement:

Again I remember the long and arduous path that led to this *ashram*. No one will ever know the intolerably woeful history of that struggle against unrelenting adversity . . . In the present times, please do not deny that devoted endeavour its due, please accord it recognition. History has witnessed many reversals, great achievements of civilization have met with dissolution epoch after epoch, and yet the potentials of the human race have not been exhausted . . . That is the path towards hope . . . [37]

In all these statements made over a long period, one thing is recurrently notable: Tagore's disappointment with the support he received from his people, especially the Bengali people, a sense of loneliness in his life as an institution builder in a society, and a mindset that was hostile, or at best apathetic. It is possible that Tagore's stern judgement was directed mainly against the middle classes. What of the rural folk?

It is probable that his enforced exile from Calcutta, his engagement in the work of overseeing the Tagore estates in the distant rural hinterland, was a liberating education to young Tagore. He wrote about fifteen years later to Charles Andrews:

It was a great event of my life when I first dwelt among my own people here [he was writing the letter at Sheleida in present-day

Bangladesh] for thus I came into contact with the reality of life. For in them you feel the barest touch of humanity.

. . . One is apt to forget them, just as one does not think of the earth on which one walks. But these men compose the great mass of life, which sustains all civilizations . . .[38]

Further, in Tagore's writings about rural people and their problems, Tagore showed a loving sympathy which no one can miss. His mind was engaged sometimes with the question of supply of potable water (it was scarce in and around Santiniketan), sometimes the prevention of malaria (common in east Bengal), sometimes with the problems of indebtedness and high interest rate on the loans peasants were compelled to take (Tagore put a good part of his Nobel Prize money in a rural cooperative credit society), and almost always in the task of providing education in rural Bengal (hence his school for the rural poor in Sriniketan). Tagore also found in rural folk literature and songs of village *Bauls* mental pabulum which he missed in the Babu culture of Calcutta. It seems that Tagore's sense of alienation or lack of contact was chiefly with the urbanized middle classes, and yet they were his chief audience. They were the people who had access to his writings. Should we dismiss Tagore as a poseur who anticipates many other intellectuals in Bengal who professed antipathy to their own class, and highlighted their sympathy with the 'common people'? That appears to be an inadequate explanation, for such attitudinizing was not yet fashionable in Tagore's times. Perhaps we should allow Tagore the space to be different from the common run of intellectuals. It is possible that he indeed meant what he said. Or else he would not have given a good part of his life to address the problems facing the people of rural Bengal.

Tagore's Universalism

Tagore was evidently keenly aware of the limits of an exclusive nationalist identity, and more so of the limits of the parochialism inherent in a regional identity—given the identity defined by the articulate middle-class intelligentsia of his times, the *bhadraloks*. We have also seen that from around 1917 Tagore postulated that his inner life had ascended to a consciousness of Humanity, a step higher than his poetic communion with Nature. Indeed, his concept of a *Jiban-devata* guiding his creative life, one constant idea that recurs in his own statements about his 'inner life' which we have cited, could be derived only from a universalist notion of the purpose that guides humanity. In the idea of a humanist universalism Tagore found a resolution for many of the conflicts within his mind.

Tagore's notion of universalism was historically situated at a critical moment in (a) the negotiation between Indian civilization with the dominant Western civilization, (b) the conflict between rising Asian nationalism and the imperialist countries of the West. Of these, the second conjuncture and his critique of nationalism have received more attention than the first. As we shall see later in these pages, Tagore departed from the general tendency of Indian intellectuals in the late nineteenth and early twentieth century towards nationalist chauvinism in the discourse of civilization. This chauvinism was the natural product of the particular historical situation in those times. The disparagement of India's civilization by the colonial observers in the nineteenth century from James Mill onwards, the European assumption that the only trajectory of civilizational development was that charted by the West, the failure of India's civilization to develop in the manner Europe had developed—these were the ideas which the Indian intelligentsia strongly contested in Tagore's times. The discourse thus developed included vainglorious depiction of ancient 'Hindu civilization', as well as perfectly valid criticism of the infirmities in the European approach to the issue of civilization. This discourse of civilization from the Indian point of view was not only a response to the European lack of esteem for Indian civilization, but also in part an anticipation of nationalist consciousness, though nationhood was as yet in an incipient stage.[39] A distinctly different position was adopted by Tagore in arguing that the impact of Western civilization had positive potentials and that India's fight against European imperialism did not necessarily involve rejection of everything that Europe contributed to world civilization. We shall examine Tagore's views in detail later, but the core idea is clear—the universality of human civilization and the need to look at Indian civilization in that global perspective.

Secondly, Tagore's universalism was also based upon a critique of what he perceived as a narrow-minded nationalism that had originated in early modern Europe. He contrasted the syncretic civilization of India and India's openness to diverse ethnic groups and cultures and religious beliefs, with the aggrandizing nation states of Europe which gained power and prosperity through the subjugation of alien elements inside and colonized peoples outside. He traced the origins of the imperialist urge in the Western powers to their aggressive nationalism. As we shall see later, Tagore's critique of nationalism, roughly from around 1917, when he wrote a book on the subject, made him thoroughly unpopular in the West as well as in India. After the end of World War I and the Versailles Peace Conference, for a while, 'internationalism' was in fashion. However, that resembled Tagore's idea only superficially. 'Internationalism' would imply a relationship among units which are nation states while Tagore was opposed to 'nationalism' of the kind that forms the basis of such a state system. The post-war internationalism had a political, state-centred approach alien to Tagore's conception. The distinctive feature of Tagore's universalist approach was that it was wholly cultural, to the exclusion of political means. He wanted the world to look beyond national boundaries to the unity of mankind. We may also consider the term 'Humanism' to describe Tagore's vision, but Tagore's ideas in this regard clearly exceeded the boundaries of just passive devotion to human interests to include an active internationalism in the domain of culture and civilization. Hence we use the term 'Humanist Universalism'.

Tagore's ideas of a universalist kind became known to the world only in the decade following the award of the Nobel Prize in 1913. But the roots of it can be traced to earlier times. A notion of universalism was inherent in the philosophy in Tagore's poetic writings as well as his interpretations of the Upanishads, a text that the Brahma Samaj focused upon since the days of Rammohan Roy. When he was in his early forties, Tagore wrote that his Maker (*Jiban-devata*) had attuned his creative powers to the music of the entire universe.[40] Tagore's critics saw in this arrogance and self-praise; we have discussed elsewhere what Tagore said in clarification, but the point is the presence of the universal in Tagore's conception of the self and the world from early days. In 1913 in his lecture at Harvard University and elsewhere in the United States, later published as *Sadhana: The Realization of Life*, Tagore elaborated on the idea 'relation of the individual to the universe'. He pointed to the ancient Indian conception of a fundamental unity of all creation and the reverence for the divine permeating the world.[41] In the text of his lecture in Madras in 1919, *The Centre of Indian Culture*, and in the essay 'East and West' in *Creative Unity* in 1922, Tagore reverted to this theme.

I have no distrust of any culture because of its foreign character. On the contrary, I believe that the shock of such forces is necessary for the vitality of one's intellectual nature . . . what I object to is the artificial arrangement by which this foreign education tends to occupy all the space of our national mind and then kills or hampers the great opportunity for the creation of new thought-power by a new combination of truths. It is this which makes me urge that all the elements in our culture have to be strengthened, not to reject the Western culture, but only to accept and assimilate it . . .[42]

Thus, speaking in Adyar, Madras, Tagore spelt out the future agenda of his Visva-Bharati university.

Our mind has faculties which are universal, but its habits are insular . . . The modern age has brought the geography of the earth near to us, but made it difficult for us to come into touch with Man . . . The most significant fact of modern days is that the West has met the East. Such a momentous meeting of humanity, in order to be fruitful, must have in its heart some emotional idea, generous and creative.[43]

That was Tagore writing in the United States in 1920–21. But Tagore did not take his message only to America. During his visit to China and Japan in 1924 he made the same effort to cross cultural boundaries. When Liang Chi Chao, President of the Association of Chinese Universities recalled India–China cultural exchange, that for '700 or 800 years we lived like affectionate brothers' from the Tang Dynasty onwards, Tagore replied: 'My friends I have come to ask you to reopen the channel of communion which I hope is still there; for, though overgrown with wounds of oblivion, its lines can still be traced . . . for no political or commercial purpose, but for disinterested human love and for nothing else'.[44] Thus Tagore hoped to make this ideal of the universality of human civilization a reality. In the meanwhile the effort of Visva-Bharati was defined by Tagore at the first meeting of the Executive Council: 'Though this Visva-Bharati is India's own, it must become the site of the entire world's endeavour' to not only disseminate but generate knowledge; when the 'entire world is developing a universal consciousness', will India be left behind?[45] Universalism in Tagore's thoughts had three elements in it: (a) a poetic transcendentalism in his outlook on the world of Nature, (b) a cultural outlook representing the human civilization as a unity in the midst of cultural diversities, (c) an agenda of bringing about commingling of the civilizations of the West and the East through education and generation of knowledge leading to mutual appreciation. The first of these elements can be seen in his writings at an early stage and, indeed, it might have been a part of the Upanishadic philosophy he imbibed from his childhood. The second element emerged in his writings from his fifties and found expression particularly in his public pronouncements during his numerous trips abroad. The third component of Tagore's universalism became part of his public activities in the last twenty years of his life, roughly since the foundation of Visva-Bharati Society; however, the ideas at the root of that action agenda can be seen in his writings much earlier.

Tagore believed that his ideas were founded in history. He saw in the impact of Christianity in Europe the impact of the East on

Western civilization. He saw in the Christianization of Europe the entry of 'foreign thought-power with all its Oriental forms and feelings'. He argued that this was one of the earliest instances of the commingling of two cultures, for 'much of the spirit of Christianity runs counter, not only to the classical culture of Europe, but to the European temperament altogether' and yet it enriched Europe's civilization.[46] Tagore looks upon Rammohan Roy as one of the creators of cultural universalism, for 'he was the first great man in our age who had the profound faith and large vision to feel in his heart the unity of soul between the East and the West. I follow him, though he is practically rejected by my countrymen'.[47] Roy could play such a role because he 'was never a schoolboy of the West, and therefore he had the dignity to be a friend of the West'; 'his education was perfectly Eastern—he had the full inheritance of the Indian wisdom'.[48]

Why did India turn its back on the West—if indeed it did, which is debatable? Tagore's answer was twofold. It was, he surmised, in part in retaliation. 'Stung by the insult of cruel injustice, we try to repudiate Europe, but by doing so we insult ourselves. Let us have the dignity not to quarrel or retaliate . . .'[49] Secondly, the turn politics had taken in the 1920s, Tagore complained, diverted India from her true path. Even those who are aware of the unwisdom of being indiscriminately opponents of Western culture and civilization believe 'that India requires to be strong and rich before she can raise her voice for the sake of the whole world. But I refuse to believe it'.[50] And the others, the majority, have a tendency to blindly reject the West due to a political reason. Writing on board the ship which he took to return to India in July 1921, when the Non-Cooperation movement was on, Tagore wrote despondently: 'The India about which I have been dreaming belongs to the world. The India that I shall reach shortly belongs tremendously to itself. But which of this must I serve?'[51]

This dilemma was all the more poignant because Mahatma Gandhi was commonly perceived as 'anti-Western'. Was it not Gandhi's message in *Hind Swaraj* in 1909? 'I believe that the civilization India has evolved is not to be beaten in the world. Nothing can equal the seeds sown by our ancestors . . . India remains immovable and that is her glory . . . India has nothing to learn from anybody else and that is as it should be.'[52] And what was Tagore's dream? 'The moment we take part in the building of civilization we are instantly released from our own self-seclusion . . .'[53]

He added:

> When we have intellectual capital of our own, the commerce of thought with the outer world becomes natural and fully profitable. But to say that such commerce is inherently wrong is to encourage the worst form of provincialism, productive of nothing but intellectual indigence . . . We know that the East also has her lessons to give, and she has her own responsibility of not allowing her light to be extinguished.[54]

The inevitable conflict between these two points of view worked itself out in the debates between Gandhi and Tagore in the early nineteen twenties. We have addressed that theme later. But it is important to bear in mind one outcome of that. Mahatma Gandhi possibly qualified his position a little when he wrote in 1921 those memorable words in his reply to Tagore's critique: 'I do not want my house to be walled in all sides and my windows to be stuffed. I want the culture of all the lands to be blown about my house as freely as possible. But I refuse to be blown off my feet by any.'[55] Tagore himself might have written these great words of the Mahatma.

From the point of view of Tagorean universalism the fundamental difference with Nationalist enthusiasts was deeper. They failed to understand Tagore moving away from the espousal of nationalism in the Swadeshi agitation against the Partition of Bengal of 1905. Parallel with the concept of universalism there developed in Tagore's writings a strident critique of nationalism. The lectures he gave in Japan and the United States in 1916–17 were published from New York under the title *Nationalism* (1917) and the work is well known, because it caused a storm of criticism and denunciation of the author in both those countries. It was very courageous but impolitic on the part of Tagore to speak up against nationalism while World War I raised popular nationalist passion. Since this work written in English is very well known—recently a new edition has come out, edited by the historian E.P. Thompson—and often quoted, let us look at another contemporary source on his ideas on the subject, his private letters to his friend Charles Andrews. In these letters Tagore is even more forthright than in the book on nationalism. 'I love India, but my India is an idea and not a geographical expression. Therefore I am not a patriot—I shall ever seek my compatriots all over the world.'[56] He points to the fact that patriotism, ideologized as nationalism, was 'a comparatively later growth in European history' and it became a form of 'national egoism'. The Pathans and the Mughals were free of that incubus and thus they 'contributed to the richness and strength of Indian civilization'. An interesting point he makes incidentally is that

Christ gave no expression to his patriotism, which was so intense in the Jewish people. It was because the great truth of man, which he realized, through His love of God, would only be swamped and crushed within that enclosure. I have a great deal of the patriot and politician in me, and therefore I am frightened of them; and I have an inner struggle against submitting to their authority.[57]

Basically Tagore believed, by the time he reached his fiftieth year, that there was a conflict between the spirit of the usually accepted notion of nationalism and the humanist universalism he preached. He writes in his private letters in January 1921 that he was at one time touched by the 'heat and the movement' of the Swadeshi era, but

After a certain point is reached, I find myself obliged to separate myself from my own people with whom I have been working, and my soul cries out: The complete man must not be sacrificed to the patriotic man, or even to the merely moral man. To me humanity is rich and large and many-sided.

Therefore he reacted against it when he saw 'the repression and curtailment of humanity . . . often advocated in our country under the name of patriotism'.[58] In these observations, arising from his innermost thoughts expressed in private letters, Tagore flags the 'inner conflict' he speaks of time and again, and the basic contradiction between his loyalty to his people and his dedication to the idea of universalism. It is astonishing to see how the term *Visva-kabi* is vulgarized in literary discourse today without paying any attention to Tagore's long and painful search for a resolution of his inner conflicts in the concept of humanist universalism.

The Life of the Mind in India

Tagore found the intellectual environment in India in his times wanting in some respects. First, there were the limitations of the education that was imparted to Indians under the colonial regime. 'In the West the mind of man is in full activity. It is vigorously thinking and working . . . But in our Indian universities we simply have the results of this energy, not the living velocity itself. So our mind is burdened and not quickened by our education.'[59] Second, he pointed to the limitedness of the average Indian individual's life, i.e. life beyond the home.

> It is difficult to achieve greatness of mind and character where our responsibility is diminutive and fragmentary, where our whole life occupies and affects an extremely limited area . . . We, in India, live in a narrow cage of petty interests; we do not believe that we have wings, for we have lost our sky; we chatter and hop and peck at one another, within the small range of our obstructed opportunities.[60]

'In India the range of our life is narrow and discontinuous. This is the reason why our minds are often beset with provincialism.'[61]

Third, Tagore was of the view that in India the mental climate—he was writing in the 1920s—was not ready for the vigorous pursuit of new ideas. 'In India, in our modern schools, we merely receive our ideas from textbooks, for the purpose of passing examinations.' Nor do ideas generate the kind of enthusiasm which goes into the pursuit of ideas in Europe. 'Our principal object and occupation are going to be the dissipation of politics, whose goal is success, whose path is the zigzag of compromises . . .'[62] Tagore sensed a kind of moral failure in the lack of engagement with ideas, except in politics; 'we do not possess genuine enthusiasm, which is a gift of the soul'. And finally, Tagore was disappointed that many of his compatriots had developed a mindset against responding to ideas coming from the West. 'Whatever we understand and enjoy in human products instantly becomes ours, wherever they might have their origin . . . Therefore it hurts me deeply when the cry of rejection rings loud and clear in my country.'[63]

These are the reasons why the life of the mind, Tagore thought, was underdeveloped in India but he was optimistic about the future. On the one hand, 'the difficult problem is how to gain our freedom of soul in spite of the cramped condition of our outward circumstances; how to ignore the perpetual insult of our destiny, so as to be able to uphold the dignity of man.' India's mind was sending out 'our starved branches to the sunlight and air, and the roots of our life must pierce the upper strata of the soil of desert sands till they reach down to the spring of water which is exhaustless'.[64] In other words, Tagore was hopeful that India's mind would one day get reinvigorated from the springs of her undying civilization. The overriding idea in Tagore's statements about the life of the mind is that 'the ultimate reality for man's life is his life in the world of ideas, where he is emancipated from the gravitational pull of the dust and he realizes that he is spirit'.[65]

As early as 1893, when Tagore was thirty-one years of age, in an essay on the 'Bengali writers' Tagore expounded the idea that a characteristic of the literature in Bengal was a lack of faith in the importance of ideas; the readers remain unaffected by the writings they read in Bengali, and the writers have 'no sense of responsibility' about the ideas they expound.[66] Thus there is a hiatus between the readers and writers, in the absence of serious criticism as well as the application of ideas in real-life situations. What did Tagore mean? Decades before he wrote thus, many social reformers' writings had impacted society and two decades after he wrote thus the nationalist ideologues equally impacted their readers. Perhaps what Tagore meant was that in his Bengal he missed the intensity and density of intellectual and creative work, the continual interaction between that and an enlightened public, which characterized nineteenth century Europe, as Tagore perceived it. This view of 1893 remained substantially the same twenty years later when Tagore had had a closer acquaintance with top-flight intellectuals in Europe.

After Tagore was awarded the Nobel Prize his response to a felicitation to him by prominent citizens of Calcutta who visited Santiniketan (23 November 1913) was somewhat rudely sincere. He chose to recall on this happy occasion unhappy memories of 'the insult and disparagement it has been my fate to receive from my countrymen'. If the Nobel Prize had any value that was in the appreciation by the intellectuals in Europe; but the resultant felicitation in his own country, Tagore suggested, was a 'momentary excitement' which would soon disappear because only a few among the celebrants truly appreciated Tagore's writings. Thus Tagore did not feel that he could accept the honour and felicitations which came his way in his own land just because of recognition abroad and the Nobel award.[67] He probably continued to sense the lack of a sympathetic chord in his immediate surroundings. For instance he confided in Jagadish Chandra Bose, one of his few close friends in 1925: 'At last I have returned home. But the vortex of loathsome pettiness oppresses the soul. The sudden transit from one perspective to another almost reduces in size my own self.'[68] And at the same time when he was abroad, he pined for his country; that is abundantly clear from his letters from abroad.

Tagore might have been reflecting on the recent past. There were moments when his feeling of alienation from the middle classes in Calcutta was intense. For instance, when the biggest leader of Bengal, Chittaranjan Das attacked him in his presidential address to the Bengal Provincial Conference, a Congress organ, in 1919, Tagore was deeply mortified and felt that he was alone and supportless in Bengal. He said so in some of his letters at that time.[69] Nor did he find much solace in the fact that some of his supporters defended him against his detractors with the feeble weapons of ill-educated minds.[70] Prominent critics over many years were Bipin Chandra Pal, Chittaranjan Das, Suresh Chandra Samajpati, Dwijendra Lal Roy, and generally the anti-Brahma Samaj segment of the Hindu intellectuals in Bengal; however, many of them also joined the chorus of praise for Tagore on some occasions. A lot of the criticism and counter-criticism of those times appear to be, from all contemporary accounts, emanating from personal motivations situated in patron–client networks, and factional struggle within a small circle of middle-class persons with literary ambitions unequal to their capability. A similar sense of alienation is evident in an incident chronicled by a witness, Prabhat Kumar Mukherjee: when the Bengal Literary Academy (Sahitya Parishad) planned to felicitate Tagore on his fiftieth birthday in 1911, there was a storm of opposition and Tagore forbade such an event: 'I realize that in my 50th year my luck is the same as it was till now. On the completion of my fiftieth year I have received another birthday gift, the charge that I am hungry for adulation—I, therefore, relieve the Parishad of this obligation to felicitate me.'[71]

In his early writings Tagore chiefly speaks of Bengal which he knew well. In 1880 Tagore wrote about the state of poetry in Bengal. This essay, combatively entitled 'Why Bengalis Are Not Poets', was later excluded by Tagore from reprint or inclusion in his 'Collected Works'.[72] In Europe, he surmised, the mental environment was vastly different for it engendered activity and pursuits which exercised the mind; the mental environment which produced a Shakespeare also produced a Newton and both excelled in the exercise of imagination in different ways. In contrast, people in Bengal were lethargic and inert by habit. 'There is habitual lethargy, habitual inertness, apathy towards all things; that is why the Bengali is not a whole man . . . We see everything with half-closed eyes. We are lacking in curiosity.' And that was so because life in Bengal, Tagore felt, was crippled in many ways. When society advances creativity finds expression in science, philosophy, poetry; that environment was missing in Bengal in his times Tagore said in 1880. At the same time he warned over and again against imitation of the literature of the West for that would be untrue to the soul of this country. He recalled that at one time India was like Europe in his times, productive in different domains in which the life of the mind flowed and fertilized. But in modern times the picture is different. 'We know that our ancestors,' he said, 'fought battles and ruled over large kingdoms and created works of art and traded with distant countries, and they also created poesy; but we are distant from those times. We live as if among the ruins of a palace where we cannot replace even a single piece of stone, we can only spread cow dung over the ruins of what there had been.' This was Tagore's scathing evaluation of the creative capacity of the worn-out remnants of a people who had lost their heritage.[73] At the same time Tagore had hopes of a literary regeneration; we shall return to that theme later in these pages.

In 1901 Tagore wrote a scathing comment on Bengal's parochialism. 'The Bengali people, petty-minded by nature, are neglectful towards people of other regions. Unfortunately the few Bengalis who have recently done well in their sphere of activity are mainly in politics. Thus politics has become an ideal area of activity for the new educated community.' He went on to say that vanity born of that success in politics has given Bengal an illusory sense of superiority. 'This limitation of this outlook needs to be attacked and destroyed now. Our petty self-pride is misleading us every day.'[74] He goes on to say that Bengal must recognize and pay respect to outstanding thought leaders like Mahadev Govind Ranade; he compared Ranade with Rammohan Roy and said such are the people outside of Bengal to whom Bengalis must pay their obeisance. The occasion of this writing was unimportant: the review of Ranade's life and work by Sakharam Ganesh Deuskar in Bengali. The point was to expose the narrow provincialism prevailing in Bengal.

The chief weakness of the people of Bengal is self-pride, which is why they are unhappy if they do not hear all the time words of praise . . . This vanity, hunger for flattery, obscures their vision and they do not perceive others clearly. We deprive ourselves on account of this blindness. ·

That was Tagore's observation, against the grain of the statements by others in a Bengali literary conference in Banaras in 1923.[75] He pointed out that Bengalis living outside of their province do not normally make any effort to study and internalize the culture of their place of residence, the language and literature of the people of the regions where they live. 'The mind which is truly alive has a curiosity perennially alive. The mind that is dead is incurious about what it can see, it is unwilling to see. Whatever is different from it, due to weakness of the faculty of sympathy, would be ignored.' And therefore Tagore called for an endeavour of the Bengali mind, wherever it was located beyond the borders of Bengal, to appreciate and internalize the culture of the people of the region. In other words, he wanted Bengal to overcome narrow provincialism. At the same time Tagore believed that each province or linguistic region was destined to attain its true place in the ongoing construction of the Indian nation through the development of its own language and literature. Likewise the Bengali people can be part of the nation-building endeavour only through the medium of the language that reaches to every man and woman in Bengal. 'Through the development of Bengali literature, as the mind of Bengal matures, the unification of Bengal with all others in India will be facilitated.'[76] This was the Poet's agenda from the middle period of his literary career. This was also his agenda for the creation of a public for literature in modern India.

A Multitude of Roles and Conflict Within

If the public sphere was underdeveloped and there were few public spokesmen, if the life of the mind was constrained by the colonial environment, the intellectuals had to play a multidimensional role. Tagore played a variety of roles. He was a poet, a preacher, a teacher, and a patriot, and, indeed, to some of his admirers almost a prophet. In an amusing letter to Andrews in 1921 he writes of the inner conflicts as a result of this multiplicity of roles.

> Sometimes it amuses me to see the struggle for supremacy that is going on between different persons within me . . . When the call comes to me to take some part, in some manner or other, in some political affair, the Poet at once feels nervous, thinking that his claims are likely to be ignored, simply because he is the most useless member in the confederacy of my personality . . . I sit dumb and muse and sigh, when sheaves of newspaper cuttings are poured upon my table, and a leer is spread upon the face of the Practical man; he winks at the Patriotic man sitting solemnly by his side; and the man who is Good, thinks it is his painful duty to oppose the Poet, whom he is ready to treat with some indulgence within proper limits . . . I jump up from my judgement-seat and holding the Poet by hand, dance a jig and sing, 'I shall join you, comrade, and be drunk and gloriously useless.'[77]

In the letter that followed Tagore added that 'I have a great deal of the patriot and politician in me, and therefore I am frightened of them; and I have an inner struggle against submitting myself to their sway'.[78] And again:

> when the touch of spring is in the air, I suddenly wake up from my nightmare of giving 'messages' and remember that I belong to the eternal band of good-for-nothings; I hasten to join their vagabond chorus . . . Is it not good for the world that a poet should forget all about resolutions carried in monster meetings.[79]

And again: 'Why should I be anything else but a poet? Was I not born a music-maker?'[80]

The responsibility of being on a 'mission' was particularly irksome to Tagore when he took to lecturing, collecting funds for his school, meeting the media, etc. 'I wish that I could be released from this mission. For such missions are like a mist that envelops our soul . . .'[81] He wrote this from America in 1921, one of his most successful trips. And laughing at himself he added: 'I rouse myself, strain my mind, raise my voice for prophetic utterances . . . and to my utter dismay, discover I am not a leader, not a teacher, and farthest of all from being a prophet.' Tagore perceived 'conflicts within my nature.' Among other causes the conflict between 'absolute poetdom' and doing-good-to-others was a major cause of internal conflict.[82] The basic problem was that, 'Poesy creates its own solitude', whereas doing-good takes one into the crowd and dependence on organization and 'means and materials that are outside me'. Hence a role conflict.

The second problem was the quest for popularity. That is because 'when a person has some mission of doing some kind of public good, his popularity becomes the best asset for him.' Hence there develops a craving for popularity and for public honours. 'The man who constantly receives honour from admiring crowds has the grave danger of developing a habit of mental parasitism upon such honour . . . I become frightened of such a possibility in me, for it is vulgar.'[83] On the other hand, the poet 'is appointed to the perpetual comradeship of man—not as a guide, but as companion', therefore the poet has no need for a following, a crowd of people. Therefore, Tagore felt that since his only true place in the world was that of the poet, 'One day I shall have to fight my way out of my own reputation.'[84]

There was a third source of internal conflict as Tagore perceived it. 'Ever since the scheme of the international university [i.e., Visva-Bharati at Santiniketan] has been made public, the conflict in my mind has been unceasing—the conflict between the vision of the ideal and the vision of success.'[85] There was, he felt, always the danger that the Truth or the values at the core of the ideal might be compromised for the sake of success in that endeavour. He was aware that 'all over the world the prudent and the wise are in the habit of making a pact with Mephistopheles', and thus to put in danger the real god. In a letter to Charles Andrews, Tagore writes in the middle of 1921: what 'creates conflict within my nature' is the fact that 'I have to deal with and make use of men who have more faith in the material part [of setting up an institution] than in the creative ideal. My work is not for the success of the work itself, but for the realization of the ideal.'[86] The men whom he needed for building and running an institution were 'ready for all kinds of compromise' and 'when you say that the result is not greater than the idea itself, then they laugh at you.'

Of all the three sources of 'inner conflict' Tagore mentions, the most recurrent one, mentioned most often is the conflict between his poetic self and other selves. Sometimes he felt that a via media was possible; for example, when he wrote to W.W. Pearson in 1918: 'It is not by meticulous care in avoiding all contaminations that we can keep our spirit clean and give it grace, but by urging it to give vigorous expression to its inner life in the midst of all the dust and heat' of life in the outer world.[87] But probably Tagore found this difficult in course of time as the demands on him from the outer world multiplied. His private letters reveal that most of the time Tagore was torn between his loyalty to his Muse and his sense of responsibility to society.

> My heart . . . is like a leaky boat, full of water, that can just keep itself afloat, but the least burden of responsibility becomes too much for it . . . I want to say 'No' emphatically to all the importunities of the world, to all the social and moral obligations.[88]

The result of this conflict was that he felt 'oppressed with a burden whose nature we hardly know.'

Beyond the conflicts between the different roles Tagore perceived at different times, there was one constancy: Tagore thought of himself essentially as a poet. He writes to Charles Andrews from Chicago in 1921: 'Why should I be anything else but a poet?'[89] And again:

> When I came to this world I had nothing but a reed given to me, which was to find its only value in producing music . . . But now came the schoolmaster in the midst of my dream-world . . . I left aside my reed . . . In a moment I became old and carried the burden of wisdom on my back, hawking truths from door to

door. Why have I been made to carry this burden, I ask myself over and again, shouting myself hoarse in this noisy world where everybody is crying up his own wares? Pushing the wheelbarrow of propaganda from continent to continent—is this going to be the climax of the poet's life? It seems to me like an evil dream, from which I occasionally wake up at the dead of night and grope about in the bed asking myself in consternation: 'Where is my music?' It is lost . . . You know that I have said somewhere that 'God praises me when I do good, but God loves me when I sing.' . . . How I wish I could find my reed again . . . When I know for certain that I shall never be able to go back to that sweet obscurity which is the birthplace of flowers and songs, I feel homesick.[90]

Spells of Depression

It is necessary to touch upon a part of his life rarely examined by Tagore scholars: the spells of 'depression' he underwent. He acknowledged it as a fact a number of times. In January 1915 he writes to Charles Andrews of one such spell: 'I feel that I am on the brink of a breakdown. Therefore I must take flight to the solitude of the Padma.'[91] He surmised that man's 'subconscious nature' needs attention in times of 'depression', and in February he writes that 'I had been suffering from a time of depression'.[92] From the solitariness on the banks of the Padma he writes on 3 February 1915: 'Directly I reached here I came to myself, and am healed. The cure for all the illness of life is stored in the inner depth of life itself, the access to which is possible when one is alone.'[93] Another such bout of depression is recorded in Tagore's letters in October 1914. He escaped from Santiniketan to Surul and felt that he was 'coming out of the mist once more'. As usual it was Andrews to whom he confided about this depression. A few days later on 7 October 1914 he writes, 'My period of darkness is over. It has been a time of very great trial to me', and he attributes it to 'loneliness' and 'the cry of the old life', presumably meaning certain memories.[94] Earlier to that, in May 1914, he had had one of his worst spells of depression.

I am struggling on my way through the wilderness. The light from across the summit is clear; but the shadows are slanting and deep on the slope of the dark valley. My feet are bleeding and I am toiling with panting breath. Wearied, I lie down upon the dust and cry and call upon His name I know I must pass through death. God knows, it is the death pang that is tearing open my heart. It is hard to part with one's old self. One does not know, until the time comes, how far it had spread its roots and into what unexpected, unconscious depths it had sent its thirsty fibres draining out the precious juice of life.[95]

In another letter next day he speaks of the

. . . intense glow of suffering. Sometimes Death brings the torch to light it, and sometimes a messenger whose face is hidden from us . . . I ask him questions. He answers not. But the fire is burning fiercely, exposing the hidden corners of my being with all their unsuspected accumulation of untruth and self-deception . . . Let nothing be spared that awaits destruction.[96]

About this time in an undated letter to his son Tagore wrote in less sibylline and symbolic terms about the same crisis:

When I was in Ramgarh my conscience tortured me terribly that I had failed to perform my duties to the School, the Estate, the Family, the Country . . . The thought came to my mind over and again that since I was unable to realize in this life my ideal, I should rather end that life and begin a new life with a new dedication. Such an immense darkness enveloped my mind . . .[97]

He writes to his son Rathindranath in the autumn of 1914:

Night and day I think of death and hanker for death. I feel that I have achieved nothing and will achieve nothing, that my life has been a big failure from beginning to end; I look upon everyone else with distrust and disappointment . . . When I am in this distorted frame of mind I feel without reason and evidence that whenever I have failed, there must be an enemy [to blame] . . . I have always believed in allowing everyone to decide on his own path according to his inclination, but nowadays I have a peculiar obsession driving me to impose an ideal on you.[98]

On 23 May 1914 Tagore senses that he was out of the woods. 'Now I feel that I am emerging once again into the air and light and am breathing freely. It is an unspeakable relief to come out into the open and normal, to regain the balance of life once more.'[99]

The comments of Charles Andrews on these episodes of 1914, in Tagore's mental life, are revealing:

Some explanation must be given concerning the special series of letters which the Poet sent me each day from Ramgarh near Nainital, in the latter part of May 1914. He had gone in good health to the hills . . . but he told me afterwards that the mental pain he experienced soon after his arrival was almost equivalent to death agony. He had hardly expected to survive it . . . This suffering which is referred to in the letter on May, entirely passed away [in June] . . . But early in July the darkness again came down upon his life and seemed once more to overwhelm him. It appeared to have no external source, either in bad health or bad climate, and the school work was progressing wonderfully. But he spoke to me constantly of the mysterious and unbearable weight of mental oppression which drove him into solitude . . . For three months this depression continued. There are hardly any letters during this period [because both Andrews and Tagore lived in Santiniketan or Surul]; but I have the most vivid and painful recollections of his suffering.[100]

The period from October 1914, 'the next few months was one of increased tension, followed later by a gradual recovery from the mental strain that had been oppressing the poet so long'.[101]

In January 1915 Tagore again speaks of a 'breakdown', 'deep depression', but in February he claimed to have been 'healed' in the solitude of the boat he inhabited on the banks of the Padma in north Bengal.[102] Six years later Tagore again suffered from a spell of depression, Andrews writes, this time due to illness in Andrews' opinion, during his visit to America. 'The letters which he wrote to me during those months were often full of gloom.'[103] In this period when Andrews perceived in Tagore 'depression of mind', Tagore does talk of his 'depression of spirit' in America in December 1920. But the causes he attributes to it are more material than they apparently were in 1914–15.[104] He is keenly aware of his 'heavy load of helplessness' in dealing with the business of collecting money for his school, he is aware of being 'awkwardly cumbersome in my inaptitude'. And what was the reason? 'During the greater part of my life,' he writes to Andrews from New York in December 1921, 'my mind has been made accustomed to travel the inner paths of dreams, till it has lost all confidence in its power to thread its way through the zigzags of the outer world. In fact, its attention has never been trained to accept the miscellaneous responsibilities of the clamorous surface of society . . .'[105]

The spells of 'depression' which Tagore himself mentions fairly often in his letters were not connected with the 'nervous disorder' he supposedly suffered from at the age of sixteen. His biographer Pal, on the basis of his scrutiny of the accounts books of the Tagore family, surmised: In the cash expenditure accounts there is evidence that in 1876 a good deal of expenditure on record is on account of payment of fees to *Kaviraj* (indigenous medicine) practitioners, purchase of crates of beer, medicines etc.

> A lot of beer was purchased. . . presumably this was bought not as an intoxicant, but as medicine . . . An informant in [the] medical profession has informed me that in those days beer was used in the treatment of nervous disorders, *Kaviraji* medicine and ghee could have been used for the same purpose. This possibility alerted us. Rabindranath's uncle, Brajendranath Ray, was insane, his [Rabindranath's] brothers Birendranath and Somendranath also suffered from insanity, his nephew Ksitindra Nath had been a victim of insanity temporarily. There is little difference between genius and insanity.[106]

There is indeed evidence that Rabindranath's brother, Birendranath—the fourth son of the family—suffered from insanity about 1868, soon after his marriage.[107] Likewise there is evidence that Rabindranath's brother, Somendra Nath, the seventh son, was certified insane by a doctor in 1879 and this was put on record at the High Court.[108] However, these cases as well as the medical treatment recounted by Prasanta Kumar Pal appear to be quite irrelevant to the bouts of depression Rabindranath suffered from about 1914. His was perhaps a problem of an overactive conscience and a life overextended into too many spheres of activity. To those who have witnessed a close relative falling a victim to insanity the maddening thought of losing one's mind may occur; but there is absolutely no evidence of that kind as far as Rabindranath Tagore is concerned.

Inner and Outer Life

The 'depression' that Tagore spoke of a number of times in his life seemed to be critical moments in a consistently conflict-ridden mind. The spells of depression are significant chiefly because they cast light on the tensions and conflicts which were probably quotidian in his life. Delving into what Tagore called his inner life—which he said, was the key to the significance of his writings—one realizes how complex it was and how changeful his inclinations. He himself commented on it in one of his letters in 1890:

> The variousness of the human mind, the way it leans this way and then the other way. . . that is the sign of life, that is its humanness, that is its reaction against becoming a lifeless object. Our impulses . . . impart dynamism to our life . . . We go through doubts [indecisions] each day, we do not know the end of our journey . . . The man who has no impulses, the life-force, the man whose mind is not evolving through mysterious divergences, he may be happy, he may be a saint, and his narrow and strait path may be lauded by many as a sign of a sturdy mind, but in life eternal he will be found wanting.[109]

We have tried to understand Tagore's 'inner life' by drawing upon his own thoughts, his words, and his statements about his own self. Many of the issues he wrote about—the low state of development of a public sphere, limitedness of the urban middle-class public he addressed, the multidimensional roles he had to play like other members of a small elite in India, the difficult negotiation between the urge for modernity (commonly represented as Western civilization) and the assertion of an Indian identity (inevitably shaped by indigenous tradition), and above all his solitude—formed a part of the existential condition for a man like Tagore. Tagore's 'outer life' was thus historically determined. But did that make Tagore entirely a creature of history? He rebelled at that thought. He did not, as far as one can make out, put it in terms of the oft-used binary, Freedom and Necessity. But that is what his rebellion was about. He wrote most clearly about this a few months before his death. Rabindranath (he writes of himself in the third person) 'in his sphere of creativity stands alone, history has not bound him in generality'. He makes an incontestable point that he felt that in his inner life he had freedom, and that he was not 'just a British subject in the domain of general history'. That is where his inner life was different from his outer life. On the debate about historical determination he wrote that his answer 'comes from within where I am nothing but a poet. There I am the creator, there I am by myself, I am free'.[110] He concedes that history brings into being the constituent elements which the creative writer works upon, and some of those elements are generated by the social environment, but the creator is not thereby created. The creator uses those elements and thus reveals his creativity. Tagore argues, or rather declares, that the essential act of creation is explicable in terms of 'the opaque history of inner self', not in terms of external history. Thus Tagore reconciles Freedom and Necessity, demarcating freedom of the inner life from the historically determined outer life.

CHAPTER TWO

The Enchanted Garden
1861–1890

There was a garden in our house which did not deserve to be called a garden . . . Only those flowers which survive gross neglect would try their best to do their duty . . . Nonetheless, I could not believe that the Garden of Eden was any better than our garden. To me that garden inside our house was a veritable paradise . . . When I look back at my childhood the thought that oftenest crosses my mind is that at that time, my life and the whole planet were enchanted or mysterious.

Rabindranath Tagore wrote thus in 1912 in his reminiscences and he recalled the same enchanted garden in 1940 shortly before his death.[1] That mysterious and familiar garden, that enchanted space in his life, is a recurring theme in Tagore's writings. The theme of the present chapter is how he grew into manhood in that enchanted garden and how he grew out of it. That enchanted garden is almost a metaphor for Rabindranath Tagore's life in the Tagore house, the family residence.

Rabindranath Tagore highlights in his memoirs that house and his family background. The family's wealth and culture, in particular, demand our attention. In Rabindranath Tagore's times, his was one of the wealthy families of Calcutta, but they were relatively poor among the very rich. They were among the very rich in his grandfather Dwarakanath Tagore's (1794–1846) times but after his death they went through hard times, eventually to regain moderate wealth, mainly in the form of landed property, due to the business acumen of his son Debendranath Tagore (1817–1905). Dwarakanath Tagore flourished in business at a time when India was in a transition: the East India Company's monopoly business in India was being whittled down on the one hand by the incursion of English private entrepreneurs, the 'Free Merchants', and on the other by the authorities in England who were increasingly under the influence of the Free Trade ideology. In this transition period there were opportunities for Indian business, both in Bombay and Calcutta, to collaborate with British Free Merchants and make a fortune. Dwarakanath Tagore, schooled in childhood in institutions then run by Englishmen in Calcutta, did exceedingly well as a functionary in the East India Company's commercial operations in the 1820s, beginning a small private business, on the side so to speak. He entered big business in 1829 when he appears as one of the founders of the Union Bank and soon after in insurance business. From 1834, when he resigned his job with the East India Company, his enterprise Carr, Tagore and Company diversified into export of silk and indigo as well as coal mining, an inland steam shipping company, sugar manufactures, etc. The windows of opportunity for native Indian businessmen began to close in course of the 1840s, as British capital, mainly in the hands of agency houses or managing agencies, began to strengthen its hold over Indian business, excluding natives from big finance, export business, steam shipping and indigo and silk manufactures. Native businessmen of Bombay were less unlucky in that both in opium and raw cotton business, their opportunities were less affected. Thus Dwarakanath's huge business success was doomed to failure. The great crisis of 1847 which Karl Marx, among others, talks about in his *Capital* caused a business collapse in Calcutta. Dwarakanath died in 1846 and his bank died next year. Debendra fought his way out of near bankruptcy and meticulously repaid numerous debts, a story he recounts in his autobiography. He gave up the extravagant lifestyle which his father had introduced in the family; from the Tagore estates account books which have been preserved carefully, it is clear that he was a cautious spender and a careful landlord.

The financial status of the Tagore family calls for comment here. There is an impression abroad that Rabindranath Tagore was a very wealthy man. This was not quite true, particularly in the early part of his life. The ancestral home in Jorasanko, in the northern part of Calcutta, had a number of impressive edifices built by Dwarakanath. A large number of dependent relatives and a retinue of servants lived in the lesser nooks and corners of the sprawling house, while lavishly constructed and furnished rooms were set apart for the head of the Tagore family and the adult males and their families. The property law in Bengal was different from that of other parts of India: the law of *Dayabhaga* gave the head of the family (the *Karta*) the ownership rights in Bengal, while in north India under the *Mitakshara* law, the male offsprings of the family acquired joint ownership rights upon birth. From the Tagore estates account books it seems that Rabindranath Tagore and all the other sons of Debendranath used to get on a monthly basis an amount fixed by the *Karta-babu, the pater familias*, Debendranath, for their personal expenses. Additional expenses for special reasons or occasions were met by the *Karta* from out of the Tagore estates income. For example, Debendranath paid for Rabindranath's two trips to England when he was in his teens, as well as the large dowries paid on the occasion of Rabindranath's daughters' marriages. The monthly allowance paid to Rabindranath was never enough because he spent a lot of money travelling, on buying books, and from 1901 on his school in Santiniketan. Numerous letters to his close friends requesting small loans every now and then bear witness to his perpetual need for money and indebtedness when he was a young man. As a child, he says, he was given an austere upbringing:

In our childhood there was scarcely even a touch of luxury. In general the style of life then was simpler than now [he writes in 1905] . . . Our clothes were so simple and few that a list will look shamefully inadequate to young people today. Till I was ten I never wore socks. In winter a white shirt on top of another was enough.[2]

Incidentally, it is possible that the austerity thus described was a slight exaggeration; the family account books, it has been shown, record the considerable expense that was incurred in the 1860s for young Rabi's shirts, socks, shoes, etc.[3] It is difficult to say whether indeed these articles were actually used by Rabi or purloined by the servants, or whether forty years later his memory failed him. But the general point he makes appears to be that luxuries were unknown to children of his age in the Tagore family. When he was a child his father tried to instil in him the habit of accounting carefully for money and when he was thirty he was given training in the management of the estates (*zamindari*) and the task of supervising the estates in north Bengal and Orissa. Tagore's life was far from being that of the idle rich. However, his engagement in the supervision of family estates was seasonal and there were intervals when he had the leisure to engage in writing. As regards the family as a whole, the situation varied—e.g. his brother Satyendranath of the ICS lived in great style—but on the whole the family learned to do without luxuries. He writes in his memoirs, 'We were getting accustomed to gracefully accept decline from the grand style of life of olden times.'[4]

Though the Tagores were a rich family in a state of decline, their salience in the cultural world of Bengal remained unaffected. Dwarakanath was one of the most Westernized Bengalis in the early nineteenth century—a collaborator and business rival to English merchants, a friend and associate of Raja Rammohan Roy, a benefactor to colonially sponsored charitable societies and newspapers like the *Englishman* and School Book Society, and a dignitary who was granted audience in the Vatican and in the royal courts of Louis Philippe and Queen Victoria. He declined to perform the Hindu ritual of penance for the sin of having visited Europe and this marked his separation as an outcast from the womenfolk of his family and some conservative kinsmen. His biographer Krishna Kripalani and historian Blair B. Kling have suggested that this thoroughly Westernized Tagore alienated not only his wife and son Debendranath, but also his grandson Rabindranath.[5] Kling has cited a letter in the Tagore family papers which mentions a bonfire in Jorasanko in which Rabindranath Tagore burnt his grandfather's papers after Debendranath's death in 1905.[6] We have no conclusive proof that there was indeed such a bonfire, but there is no doubt that Rabindranath Tagore took pains to distance himself from Dwarakanath, as did Debendranath.

Dwarakanath was a man of the world and often shared with his European guests the pleasures the urban rich were accustomed to; Debendranath was a moralist who rejected that way of life except for a short period of indulgence around 1831–35. Dwarakanath was an entrepreneur to the core; Debendranath prioritized his spiritual life over business and all else, it is commonly believed. Dwarakanath was Anglicized and that facilitated his collaborationist role in business with Englishmen; Debendranath felt so estranged from that culture that he promoted Bengali exclusively in his associational activities, in journalism, and within his own family with great deliberation. Rightly or wrongly, Rabindranath Tagore was persuaded that the ideals Debendranath held up were the right ones in that clash of cultures between his grandfather and his father.

Debendranath was a contemporary of the Derozian radicals but was not part of that group. He joined Hindu College after the influential teacher H.L.V. Derozio was forced to resign by the conservative Hindu patrons of the college. While he was in Hindu College, approximately from the middle of 1831 to the end of 1834, Debendranath was a founder member of a society called Sarva-tatva-dipika which resolved to exclude English language from its deliberations. This was a striking contrast to the Derozians' generation and foreshadows the strong indigenist and Bengali-centred cultural agenda of Debendranath.[7] In 1839 he was again a founder member of the Tattva-bodhini sabha which, *inter alia,* aimed to prevent 'unfortunate developments like the acceptance of English language as if it was the mother-tongue' as well as the spread of Christianity.[8]

In 1842, while Dwarakanath was away in England, Debendranath took over the leadership of the Brahma Samaj, started the *Tattva-bodhini Patrika* (1843) and he formally converted to the Brahma faith (December 1843). This was the outcome of a long process he describes in his autobiography beginning with his first encounter with death, the demise of his grandmother in 1835. He chalked out for himself a vision of Brahmaism that was all his own. On the one hand, he was radical in refusing to perform the last rites of his father through orthodox Hindu rituals, at the Brahma-style marriages he declined to perform the rituals which involved idol worship, and he was an active proselytizer of the Brahma faith contra the Hindu majority in the society around him. On the other hand, he appeared to be a conservative in retaining rituals of the Brahmin caste (son Rabindranath Tagore was given the sacred thread in a 'vedic' *upanayana* ceremony), and he retained the custom from Rammohan Roy's times that only Brahmins could lead Brahma Samaj prayers from the podium. Moreover, he was probably the chief sponsor of the marriage of Rabindranath's daughters at an unconscionably early age. He disagreed with Keshub Chandra Sen in respect of certain reform proposals leading to a split and the formation of a new sect within Brahma Samaj, and he virtually insulated his family and a few followers into a sect called 'Adi Brahma Samaj' which was almost indistinguishable from the 'Hindu' society. On the one hand he was hailed by Brahma Samajists as a 'Maharshi' (great sage), and on the other the leading Hindu conservative leader Radhakanta Deb awarded him the title 'Protector of National Religion' for his valiant battle against the influence of Christianity. His attitude to the womenfolk of the family was conservative and backward-looking. Significantly, his wife Sarada Devi was a shadowy figure in the remote recesses of the 'inner quarters'. Born in a conservative Hindu family, she was far from being a Brahma Samaj enthusiast like her husband. She gave birth to not less than fifteen children. Understandably, the children were left to the care of servants, and she scarcely appears in the reminiscences of Rabindranath. But there is one touching poem Rabindranath wrote in memory of his mother. This is the translation made by the poet himself:

> I cannot remember my mother.
> Only when I send my eyes into the blue of the distant sky,
> I feel the stillness of my mother's gaze on my face
> Has spread all over the sky.[9]

Rabindranath was his father's obedient son. However, he did not personally agree with some of Debendranath's positions; for example, why should not non-Brahmins be allowed to read prayers as priests in the Brahma Samaj? It seems that Rabindranath Tagore tried to introduce that small change and he failed. He says he failed to get men to fill up the position of *Acharya* and then he realized that Debendranath had foreseen that practical problem and therefore retained the old convention.[10] On the whole, there is no denying that Rabindranath Tagore did not have the commitment to Adi Brahma Samaj which his father had to the end of his life. But Rabindranath Tagore's poetic vision of the world was, it seems, coloured by the philosophy at the core of the Upanishadic beliefs of Debendranath Tagore.

The Family: Freedoms and Constraints

Rabindranath Tagore seems to have believed that the greatest gift he had from his father and his family was intellectual freedom.

> The role of my family in the evolution of my life has to be studied. When I was born our home was not walled in by the outmoded past and the social conventions born of meaningless habit. The temple established by forefathers was empty; its rituals were never known to me. All the false customs and prescriptions which hamper man's mind . . . did not leave a trace in our home, in the inner quarters or elsewhere. That means that from when I was born the way my life has evolved was not overshadowed by the outworn *shastras* of another age.

Rabindranath Tagore looked back and wrote thus shortly before his death, in 1940.[11] In the middle of his life he held the same view and he attributed the freedom from the constraints of tradition to Debendranath: 'He gave us the freedom to decide our own path. He was not anxious that we might make mistakes . . . He put before us certain ideals that should guide life but he never raised the rod of authority.'[12] However, we must remember that face-to-face contact between father and son was very limited, in fact almost none, until Rabindranath Tagore was twelve years of age when his father took him on a trip to the foothills of the Himalayas. Rabindranath has said in many reminiscences, his father was inaccessible and his childhood was spent under the rule of servants of the Tagore family. His was thus a lonesome childhood and he was left to his own devices—free to run out into the garden or sneak into his father's untenanted rooms and library. That too was a kind of freedom: 'Paying too much attention to children was not customary' in that household and 'inattention is liberating—it gave to our mind freedom.'[13]

Is it possible that these golden memories of childhood are slightly gilded? For one thing, the story in the inner quarters of the women was a bit different. The women were given what was called in those days *zenana* education. That is to say they were taught at home: for instance the family account books mention one Miss W. Robson who was paid Rs 30 per month for 'teaching in the inner quarters' in 1867–68; primers were brought for Kadambari Devi, wife of Rabi's elder brother Jyotirindranath in 1869; one of Rabi's sisters attended classes in the residence along with her brother in 1869; and the writer amongst the senior Tagore women, Swarna Kumari Devi writes that '*antahpur shiksha*' was on the agenda of the Tagore family and Rabindranath Tagore's mother was also a beneficiary.[14] Finally we also know from the family account books that Rabindranth's wife, Mrinalini, was given 'private tuition' in 1884–85. That occasion was exceptional enough for Debendranath to write to Rabi: 'Send your wife to Loreto House to educate her. It is a good arrangement that she will be taught separately, not with other students in the class. The expense of Rs 15 per month for school dress and tuition will be paid out of general [i.e. the Tagore estates expense account] fund.'[15] In the long run, some daughters of the Tagore family did have the privilege of going properly to school and attending classes, but that was a bit later. On the whole, private and *zenana* education dispensed by female visiting teachers was the dispensation decided upon by the family authorities in Rabi's childhood and youth. As a result, with some exceptions, the women of the Tagore family remained in an enclave of home-education with no contact with the external world and the institutions of formal education. This backwardness of the female quarters was compounded by the fact that the dependent relatives who found shelter in the Tagore residence were without any education at all. Rabindranath said in 1940: 'I have seen in my childhood so many charity-dependent women in our house . . . They were, like the other women in our country, in a state of ignorance and darkness . . . The household was full of their mutual quarrels and disputes . . . This poisoned the atmosphere of the household.'[16] It has been said, perhaps correctly, that not only did Satyendranath, engaged in the ICS, feel it necessary to keep his wife and daughter away from that fetid atmosphere but Rabindranath himself tried time and again to take his wife and children away; he succeeded in doing this when he set up an establishment in Santiniketan but his wife could spend less than a year there before she passed away.[17]

Another unlovely aspect of family life to which young Rabi drew attention was what he called 'domestic dominance', i.e. the grossly asymmetrical relationship between the elders and the young. When he was in England as a mere teenaged visitor he wrote a series of essays of which one was on this subject. On issues raised by young Rabi on certain subjects his elder brother Dwijendranath, as the editor of the journal where the essays were being published, wrote rejoinders in refutation of Rabi's views. The particular essay in question on 'domestic dominance' was excluded from the collection called 'Letters of an Exile in Europe' (*Europe Pravasir Patra*) but it was published in the journal *Bharati*. Rabindranath writes in this essay in 1880:

Recently the word 'independence' has entered the portals of Bengali literature . . . When shall we understand that unless we expel the spirit of dependence in our bone and marrow, in our heart, until the thirst for independence flows in our veins to our heart, we shall remain dependent. We are creating in every family a band of slaves. We teach our children and our younger brothers slavery, twenty-four hours a day.[18]

There is good internal evidence in the essay that its attribution to Rabindranath is correct, but whether the general observation about the unequal relationship between the elder and the young people in the family apply to the Tagore family is, of course, indeterminable. Whether indeed Rabindranath found his father to be 'austere and domineering', as Krishna Kripalani puts it, is likewise difficult to determine with any sense of finality.[19] All that one knows is, on the evidence of family records up to the death of Debendranath, it was the *Karta-babu*, the *pater familias*, who made all the important decisions. And, if he was unable to intervene in decision making, his displeasure would be made known. Thus the wife of Satyendranath of the ICS was made to feel that she was being a little too forward, attending parties at the Bengal Governor's Palace or riding on the open fields next to the Fort on the Ganges. Satyendranath's letters show how he was made aware of his father's displeasure.[20] All that notwithstanding, it must be conceded that on the whole Rabindranath was right in pointing to the contrast between the prevalent conservative cast of mind in Bengali society at that time and the liberal outlook which marked out the Tagores as an exceptional family and that is what gave birth to creativity in music, literature, fine arts and intellection in general. It will be silly to look only at the few instances of a conservative outlook of the elders in conflict with the ideas and style of living of the younger generations. The confluence between the two produced a complex discourse of modernity within indigenous parameters and that is what produced a Rabindranath Tagore.

First Assertion of Freedom

The freedom of the mind which Rabindranath spoke of as the greatest gift he had from his family—obviously he meant the elders of the family who were in a position to control freedoms in a traditional undivided family—no doubt mattered. But it is possible that young Rabi created a domain of freedom for himself. His first act in that direction was his rebellion against the system of schooling. His childhood seems to be in retrospect a steady campaign of non-cooperation with the efforts of the family to make him conform to the regime of school education. The social norms of middle-class Bengal since the early nineteenth century 'Renaissance' required that the young should receive 'English education'. Young Rabi resisted all attempts to educate him in a proper school and to introduce him to English, the language which was expected of a proper Bengali *bhadralok* in the colonial metropolis Calcutta.

Rabindranath has written a good deal about this, his first rebellion against prevailing norms. At the age of three years and ten months he was enrolled in a school which he calls Oriental Seminary in his memoirs; from the family account books it now appears that the school was called Oriental Training Academy.[21] The disciplinarians among the teachers there put off Rabi's initial enthusiasm for going to a school like everyone else. He moved to the Normal School a few months later, in November 1865 when he was four and a half years old. This school was officially known as the Calcutta Government Pathshala.[22] He recalled in his memoirs later, the caricature of a song in English the students had to memorize and the low cultural level of his classmates as well as teachers at this school.[23] The family moved him next to an 'Anglo-Indian' school run by one Mr D'Cruz, the Bengal Academy, in 1872. The memoirs record this shift as an entry into a 'feranghi' school and the family account books record considerable expenditure to dress the boy appropriately.[24] But this school too was an object of hatred to young Rabi: 'By many subterfuges I began to avoid attending school in Bengal Academy. I was then enrolled in St Xavier's school. That step was also not successful.'[25] This fourth school where Rabi enrolled, St Xavier's on Park Street in Calcutta, is recalled by him gratefully on account of a Jesuit teacher of Spanish origin: he 'seemed to carry within his silent and lonely self a spirit of dedication to divinity' and he spoke kindly to young Tagore.[26] However, Rabi appears to have been unhappy and in March 1876, when he was about fifteen years of age, he was allowed by the family elders to drop out—two of his cousin brothers stayed on and obtained their school-leaving certificates—and Rabi was then allowed freedom from formal schooling. He was to be educated at home.[27] This long rebellion against formal schooling for 'English education' which Bengali bhadraloks were expected to undergo, disappointed his family. He records in his autobiography the family's disappointment with the rebel, the non-conformist:

My elder brothers tried now and then [to bring Rabi into disciplined school education] and gave up all hopes in me. They even gave up rebuking me. My eldest sister said once: 'We all hoped that Rabi would someday become a man but our expectations have remained unfulfilled'. I was quite aware that my market price in the world of the bhadraloks [or genteel society] was diminishing, but I was unable to subject myself to the daily horror of those schools which were like prisons or hospitals, far away from the life and the beauty of the world around me.[28]

What then educated Rabindranath Tagore, how did his intellectual capital accumulate in his childhood? It is clear from his memoirs and contemporary accounts that he was self-educated, and the basic means of doing so was provided by a system of home education. He seems to have drawn upon the 'literary climate' of the Tagore family, and the tuition he received from the teachers employed, a substitute for institutional schooling which he rejected. As regards the regime of home education by tutors we have a lot of details in the poet's memoirs which we might omit. The spirit of this education offers a great contrast to that of the schools in colonial India. The emphasis was on Bengali and Sanskrit languages and

some classical works when he was in his teens. As a child the regime
of home education was as follows:

> What we were taught at home was much more than the school
> syllabus. I had to rise from bed before sunrise to wear a wrestling
> costume and wrestle with a professional. Then I put on my body
> smeared with earth [from the wrestling arena] a dress and took
> lessons in Physics, the *Meghnad-badh Kavya* [a Bengali classic by
> Michael Madhusudan Dutt], Geometry, Arithmetic, History and
> Geography. After we returned from school the teachers of drawing and
> gymnastics would take us over. In the evening lessons in English . . .
> On Sunday mornings I had to take music lessons . . .

There were also lessons in basic Sanskrit grammar, and occasionally
there were also laboratory demonstrations illustrating principles of
natural science and anatomy.[29] It is not on record how long this
regime of education continued but it is likely that it was not as
demanding as the schools with their systems of punishment and
examination. Rabi's extremely irregular attendance in school is on
record and in the last school when he was enrolled in 1875, St
Xavier's School, he was on the rolls for less than three months; he
was not promoted to the higher class, whether for having failed in
the examinations or for not having appeared in the examination is
not recorded in the school register.[30] By that time Rabi's interest
had shifted totally from what the school taught to what he learned
by himself or occasionally from a few tutors at home.

Young Rabi writes how he was moved by the 'thunder-laden
rhythm' of *Meghadutam* by Kalidasa, although he did not know
Sanskrit well enough fully to understand the text.[31] Likewise as a
child, he discovered among his father's books an old Fort William
College edition of old Bengali Vaishnava lyrics, not perhaps suitable
for his age even though he was a precocious child. He recalls that
he translated *Macbeth* into Bengali—adding that a great disservice
to Shakespeare had fortunately been lost and forgotten.[32] Compelled
to read Michael Madhusudan Dutt's *Meghnad-badh Kavya*, he
detested it and one of his earliest literary essays was a stern and

rather unwarranted critique of that work. On the other hand, he enjoyed reading the archaic Maithili poems of Vidyapati which he copied with his own notes on obscure words and usages.[33] Above all, he imbibed from the 'literary climate' in the family an appreciation of literature, though he denied himself formal training in the languages. Many elders of the family were actively engaged in writing and composing music and young Rabi looked to them as a source of inspiration. He also points to something unusual in that family. There were many Bengali upper-class families which had literary interests but the Tagores had musical talent. 'In our family from childhood there was cultivation of music around us. This was a boon to me because I internalized music very naturally. It was a disadvantage too. Since I did not learn and practise music formally, my training was incomplete. I never acquired command over that art.'[34] Tagore also makes an interesting social observation. Not only his family but many others in the social circle at the Tagore family seat shared in the joys of a cultured way of life, because there was an old tradition of meeting all and sundry in a *majlis*. Rabi saw the last remnants of that way of life and in his old age he mourned the loss of the Majlisi spirit which created the ambience he was brought up in.[35]

Finally, the accident of birth in a family like the Tagores allowed Rabindranath access to a wider world outside Calcutta society from the age of sixteen. His brother Satyendranath, the first Indian officer in the Indian Civil Service (ICS), opened up many learning opportunities to him. He spent eighteen months as a ward of his brother first in Ahmedabad and later in Bombay. While he was a guest of the Tarkhads, one of the elite families of Bombay, he formed a friendship with Annapurna Tarkhad, perhaps a potentially romantic relationship that was interrupted by his father's orders to young Rabi to proceed to England. His education at a school in Brighton and then at London University College was by no means a cause of satisfaction to the family elders, but the opportunity to get into London's social and cultural life was evidently a great experience to the youth. The family elders had nursed the hope that Rabindranath would become, like his brother Satyendranath, an officer in the ICS. There was some such plan no doubt because we have in the West Bengal State Archives a letter to the Secretary, Government of Bengal, signed by Rabindranath on 12 March 1878 requesting an age certificate since the applicant 'intended to proceed to England for the purpose of competing in the Indian Civil Services Examination.'[36] Young Rabi, then under seventeen years of age, was persuaded to sign such a letter, but his course of life and activities in England destroyed all hopes of the family elders. That was signalized by Debendranath's decision to summon him back to India early in 1880.

The exposure to English society—more than to English education—did not, however, turn Rabindranath into a brown sahib. In fact his cruellest sarcasm in the letters he wrote from England was reserved for such sahibs. That was possibly because of an aspect of the culture he imbibed as a child. This was, as he perceived later, strong patriotic sentiments. A patriotic cast of mind, he wrote, was kept alive by his father despite the incursion of some elements of Western culture and behaviour patterns. One manifestation of this was the emphasis on Bengali language, which is evident in young Rabi's home education plan. The other form in which it found expression in the family was participation in proto-political associations. One such association was a caricature of a secret society and called Sanjivani Sabha. A more serious attempt was the Hindu Mela—in the usage of the 1860s the term 'Hindu' was synonymous with 'Indian' and the object was to promote the love of the motherland. A third form was to finance cottage industry. For instance the Tagore brothers supported an enterprise to produce matchsticks. Tagore comments that to make a few boxes cost almost as much as the total fuel expenditure of a village for the year; lighting the sticks was not easy because their 'burning spirit of patriotism' was not enough to make the matchsticks more flammable! Thus Tagore presented humorously the upper-class flirtation with impractical and ineffective patriotic activities.[37] But at the core of that spirit of patriotism was an element that evidently shaped his mind at a time when men of his class were given to imitating the West in all manner of ways. Above all it kindled in him a love for the Bengali language.

A Tragic Episode

'It is not meaningful to pile up all one's memories [in one's memoirs]. That is why in my memoirs I have arranged my memories according to an organizing principle. That organizing principle is the key to my life, that is to say the evolution of my literary life.' Rabindranath wrote thus in the unpublished manuscript of his *Jiban Smriti* or 'Memoirs of My Life'.[38] We have tried in these pages to highlight those parts of his early life which appear to be relevant to the evolution of Rabindranath's literary life. Among the many personalities Rabindranath recalled in his memoirs, one was unique in importance. This was Kadambari Devi, wife of Rabi's elder brother Jyotirindranath. This is how Rabindranath recalled his relationship with Kadambari Devi: When he was about seven years of age, 'a new bride, bedecked with jewellery, entered the inner quarters of our home and that added to my curiosity . . . I was keen to get acquainted', but she was inaccessible in the women's quarters.[39] That was in 1868, when Jyotirindranath married Kadambari who was nine years of age. Rabi's mother Sarada Devi died in March 1875 and Kadambari Devi 'began to take care of the motherless child. It was she who tried day and night to draw us near, to feed and clothe us, and to take our mind away from the loss we had suffered'.[40] The following years, he said, were filled with the 'affection and endearments' ('sneha o adar') from the youngest bride of the family, Kadambari Devi.[41]

But there came a time when death entered his life again, Kadambari took her own life on 19 April 1884.

> When I was twenty-four my acquaintance with death was more lasting in effect . . . When you are a child life easily bypasses death—but

in later age you cannot escape death so easily. That is why the
intolerable shock stayed in my breast. Till then life as I knew it
had no vacuity . . . I saw nothing beyond it and accepted that as
eternal. Suddenly death entered and created a vacuum in a moment
in one part of life . . . The person near me whom I knew so well,
disappeared in a moment like a dream, and I looked at the world
and thought, what is the meaning of this strange annihilation! . . .
The bottomless dark that was revealed through the fissure in life
occupied my mind day and night.[42]

From Tagore's memoirs, written in 1912, about twenty-eight
years after Kadambari's death, it almost seems that Kadambari dead
had a greater impact upon him than Kadambari alive. Actually
there is plenty of evidence that there was a relationship of deep
affection between the two. In 1885 he published a tribute to her
memory which is worth reading for more reasons than one. It is
important because it was written right after Kadambari's death. It
is also important to note that it was not included in his standard
collections of writings. In that tribute young Rabi writes:

The 'companion of my childhood' has departed, she has parted from
me in tears—she has left her love (*bhalobasa*) for me . . . She had so
much affection (*sneha*) for me, how often she played with me, she
was an immediate witness to hundreds of things that happened in
my life. Those seventeen years of playing together, those seventeen
years of sorrow and happiness, those seventeen seasons of rains and
spring-time were shared with her. When she used to talk to me all
of those seventeen years of my brief life would awaken to her call.
No one knew me, and knew me the way she did.[43]

We shall later see a number of poems Tagore wrote in memory
of Kadambari. The shock of her suicide found expression in the
tribute of 1885 in this manner:

Those who are good, those who offer love, those who have a heart,
they get no happiness in this world. Like a *veena*, their sensitive
soul responds to the world every moment . . . The heartless
inhuman people . . . do not know that such a *veena* is the blessing

of God—they think of themselves as the Masters—they know no
better than to laugh and to pay no attention to it, and they spurn
the sweetness and the purity of that divine gift—thus the music
dies for ever.[44]

Whether these words apply to Kadambari's husband Jyotirindranath,
we do not know. He has often been seen as a rather negligent
husband; it is also true that he spent the later part of his life
almost as a penitent seeking forgiveness in exile on top of a hill
in Ranchi. That is not of much importance. The question that has
engaged various Tagore 'specialists' is how we interpret Tagore's own
words about his relationship with Kadambari Devi. There are some
commentators who just stop short of suggesting an illicit relationship
between the two. This seems to be in the same class as gossip in
the servants' quarters about what happens in the families of their
employers. There is no evidence to support the view that there was
illicit love. Tagore was quite open about it. Kadambari was the first
woman in the family with whom he shared his inner life, showed
her his writings, drew upon her affectionate companionship, and
he was moved to the depth of his heart when she chose to end her
life. He was not alone, he says in feeling blessed, in the presence
of that kind and pure soul in that family. 'You are no more there
in festive times, nor in times of stress, nor are you there with the
ailing. You are no longer there to welcome, with the affection of
the pure in spirit, those who visit your rooms. Who will gladly
receive the little girl whom you loved?' This is probably a reference
to Rabi's wife, then eleven years of age. And finally: 'That stream
of affection and caring tenderness and solace which poured on the
family has now run dry—only a scattering of hard rocks, masses
of self-centred isolates, remain to mark the path of the stream that
there was.'[45] These are not confessions of illicit love as some would
have us believe, these are confessions of a lonely heart which had
found resonance in another.

The sordid details of Kadambari Devi's death are not of
great significance. It is commonly believed that one cause of her
unhappiness was that she was childless; the other cause was that

her husband Jyotirindranath took her for granted so to speak and the day she committed suicide he had neglected to keep a promise to take her on a steam boat trip down the river. A third reason that has been mentioned is that she discovered that her husband was on intimate terms with another woman, perhaps an actress. Biographers of Tagore have speculated on the reasons. Krishna Kripalani who married Rabindranath's granddaughter may have said the last word on the question, why she secretly bought opium and committed suicide. 'No one knows why. If the secret was known to any members of the family it has passed away with them. In the absence of any authentic evidence, any surmise or guess would be not only profitless but disrespectful to the memory of one of the finest specimens of Indian womanhood.'[46] Thus ended a companionship between young Rabi and Kadambari, a companionship which began when he was seven and she was nine years of age. Tagore, looked back upon those times, over and again. While she was alive he dedicated two of his books of poems to her and after her death two more, including the famous *Bhanu Singher Padabali*.[47]

In Rabi's world Kadambari Devi occupied much more space at the time of her death than his wife, Mrinalini. Rabi seems to have been hustled into marriage by his sister-in-law Jnanada Nandini, wife of Satyendranath. She took it upon herself to find a bride. The bride-hunting party included Kadambari Devi and a match was arranged in somewhat unexpected quarters: the proposed bride was Bhabatarini, daughter of a humble clerk in the Tagore estates office. She was under ten years of age; in the 1860s that was the preferred age for the daughter of a good family to be given away in marriage. The bride had spent all of her ten years in a village in Jessore. It is possible that the first reaction of Tagore to the proposal of marriage with a child-bride was resistance. The reason to think so is that we suddenly find his father summoning him to his hill-residence in Mussoorie. Rabi was instructed: 'Come here and see me immediately . . . From the Estates fund take money for your travel costs. Buy second class return ticket.'[48] Rabi dutifully proceeded to meet his father and it is likely that he gave his consent to marriage because immediately after that we find expenses of his impending marriage being itemized in the family account books.[49] In December 1884 the marriage took place. It was not a spectacular event, nor was much money spent on it. The event took place in the Tagore residence, not in the residence of the bride's father; that was a consequence of the social disparity between the Tagores and the bride's father, their own employee. It seems that the Tagores felt that the bride needed to be 'polished': her name was changed to Mrinalini, she became a ward of the wives of two elder brothers, and Rabi was instructed by his father to arrange her education in the Loreto House. The family account books mention expenses of tuition, textbooks, school uniform, music class, etc. paid to Loreto House, a Christian missionary school patronized by upper-class citizens of Calcutta.[50] However, it was felt that a daughter-in-law of the Tagore family should not sit in the class like other girls, and separate classes were arranged for her as desired by Debendranath. An interesting if trivial fact is that the bride did not stay in the Tagore residence for some months after marriage, she stayed at her sister-in-law's house, the residence of Satyendranath Tagore, who as an ICS officer was obliged or preferred to maintain an establishment separate from the Tagore family seat. Mrinalini did not live in the Tagore residence till after the death of Kadambari.[51] That, incidentally, kills a lot of idle speculation about jealousy between those two ladies of the family. The point of giving attention to Mrinalini Devi's induction into the Tagore family is to illustrate a certain insensitivity to the identity of the daughter-in-law being 'remodelled' and also a snobbishness that was acceptable in only a highly hierarchized society that there was in those times.

Tagore's Family

What do we know of Tagore's conjugal life? Pitiably little. In a poem he wrote addressing his wife Mrinalini in 1902, the year he lost his wife, he writes these rather touching words: 'You stole from all-conquering time a few trifles—who will give shelter to these things now?'[52] Tagore found a few old letters after his wife's death, letters written by him to her between 1890 and 1902, chiefly during those days when he was away from his home in Calcutta on tour in the Tagore family estates in north Bengal. In most of these letters he addresses her as 'chhoto-Bou' or 'Chhuti' and signs as 'Rabi'. He often writes in a bantering tone and he talks mainly of those little things of everyday life which make a home: he has given up eating rice and lives on *roti*, to the surprise of all Bengali acquaintances;[53] he saves a bottle of wine for celebrating his birthday;[54] he dreams one night that he is being scolded by his wife,[55] he wishes to be reunited with his wife and children[56] and so forth. But in his letters to his wife there is none of that intellectual and poetic talk which characterizes Tagore's letters to his niece, daughter of Satyendranath, Indira Devi, published by Tagore, *Chhinna Patra*. Letters to Mrinalini are about everyday life and he sends to his wife and children kisses marked with a cross quite often.[57]

What does this correspondence tell us about Mrinalini's life in the Tagore family residence? Once again, precious little. There is only one surviving letter from the wife to the husband. However, there are passages in the husband's letters to his wife which throw some light on Mrinalini's life in Calcutta. 'Do not entertain in your mind discontentment', he writes in 1892, 'for everything in the household is not within our control; try to accept things in a calm spirit'; and in 1901: 'I thought to myself yesterday: in this terrace you have spent so many evenings and nights of soul-killing sorrow.'[58] The fact seems to be that Tagore was often away from home in the years between 1891 and Mrinalini's death in 1902, and living cooped up in the rooms allotted, and proximity to domineering family elders—specially the females of the species—was not always very enjoyable in that great institution known as the Hindu Undivided Family. Only the last few days of her life Mrinalini, having moved to Santiniketan, escaped from this situation.

There are some revealing figures in the account books of the Tagore family of 1902. Debendranath, the head of the family, spent

Rs 3749 in May 1902 on his 86th birthday.[59] The total expenditure at the funeral ceremonies of Rabindranath's wife Mrinalini Devi was less than Rs 213 in November 1902.[60] Debendranath earmarked in his will Rs 10,000 for the funerary ceremonies to be held after his own death, which occurred in January 1905.[61]

The skewed distribution of expenditure perhaps reflects the status of different family members, specially of women. It is also relevant to note that upon his wife's death Rabindranath wrote a letter begging for contributions to a fund in memory of his wife. He asked acquaintances and friends to contribute to the cost of the boarding and lodging of residents at his ashram in Santiniketan: 'I have connected this begging mission with the memory of my wife who has departed.'[62] It is not known how much money was received in memory of the wife of the most distinguished son of Debendranath Tagore who earmarked ten thousand for his own funeral ceremony.

To Tagore the important element in his family background was not so much its socio-economic status as the mental climate that prevailed. 'In shaping my life the role of my family needs to be understood . . . From my birth the life that was shaped remained untouched by the *shastric* injunctions of old times.'[63] Those centuries-old beliefs and practices which imprison the human mind in India 'had no place in the outer or inner quarters of our household'. Tagore greatly valued this gift of freedom from his family. This is what he idealized reminiscing on his eightieth birthday in 1940, at the end of his life. However, when one examines the details of life in that household, the rituals observed, the social practices of Debendranath Tagore's Adi Brahma Samaj, the observance of caste rules, the persistence of child marriage up to his times, the conclusion is unavoidable that there is an element of idealization in his depiction of his family background. The freedom Tagore speaks of was only a relative freedom in the prevailing historical milieu. He evolved by himself towards a degree of freedom from the debris of the past; the extended family he belonged to was a complex patchwork of different shades of traditionalism qualified by the ideas of reason and tolerance which came to Bengal with Raja Rammohan Roy.

Morning Songs

Young Rabi had the misfortune to have a great number of his juvenile verses published with the greatest of ease. His own family published several literary journals, his elder brothers were generous patrons of the young poet; as a blue-eyed boy of that family he gave command performances of recitation or songs at elite gatherings, and his undoubted talent was recognized very early by family acquaintances, among them Ishwarchandra Vidyasagar and Bankim Chandra Chatterjee. Given this combination of circumstances, it was easy for Rabi to publish seven books of verse before he reached adulthood: (*Kabi-Kahini*, 1878; *Banaphul*, 1880; *Valmiki Pratibha*, 1881, a musical drama; *Bhagna-hriday*, 1881 and *Rudrachanda*, 1881, both verse dramas; *Sandhya Sangit*, 1882; *Kal-Mrigaya*, 1882, musical drama). When he reached manhood there came in a rush five other books of verse in 1883–84: (*Prabhat Sangit*, 1883; *Chhabi o Gan*, 1884; *Prakritir Pratishodh*, verse drama; *Saisab Sangit*, 1884; *Bhanu Singher Padabali*, 1884).

A general characteristic of the works written in his adolescence was that they were surcharged with emotion, and brimming with a tragic sense of life! Often, in the verse dramas, the main protagonist is a poet. A number of his books were dedicated to the person who appreciated his poems the most—Kadambari Devi. Almost all the musical and verse dramas were written, in a manner of speaking, for Rabi's family members; as soon as they were written, they were performed in the Tagore family residence, with his brothers, sisters-in-law and cousins, he himself, and on at least one occasion, his own wife acting in them. Sometimes his elder brother, Kadambari's husband, took part in composing the music. It is also evident from Rabindranath's reminiscences that his first audience was within the family. And yet a lot of poems written when he was in his teens are indeed very precocious in speaking of love and the pangs of separation and a broken heart, etc. It is tempting to surmise that young Rabi's literary effusions were indulgently accepted as the idiom of poetic creation; perhaps he was lisping in a language that was not his own but that of romantic poets conventionally admired in those times. Like all young minds he also learned through imitation. There is a telling story in his reminiscences. His father happened to be present at a time when Rabi was reciting a poem which was all about the sorrows man suffers in this life and the saving grace of God; his father laughed uproariously to learn that the child author was already suffering the sorrows men are destined for![64]

The literary creations of Rabindranath in the period we are looking at were not of momentous importance. In fact, when he was seventy, in 1931, he looked back on those days and wrote: Only in *Manasi*, a collection of poems published in 1890, 'in terms of my norms', the verses have crossed the border distinguishing them from poems.[65] We may thus regard 1890 as the end of an era, as well as marking the beginning of his maturity as a poet. On the previous productions the mature Tagore passed severe judgements. Of *Bhagna Hriday* ('The Broken Heart', 1881), a drama in verse he said: 'When I started writing I was eighteen years of age. I was no longer a boy nor yet a young man. It was a juncture when the perception of reality was unclear. There were glimpses of it, but in a shadowy way.' He goes on to say that from age fifteen or sixteen till he was twenty-two or twenty-three years of age there was a time when 'in the indistinct light dawning on an immature mind, emotions assumed disproportionate and weird shapes and seemed to lose their way in a nameless, pathless, endless dark forest'.[66]

Of *Sandhya Sangit* ('Evening Songs', 1882): About this time there was an impression abroad that his poems were 'obscure, unclear', all mist and shadows. 'Though I did not like it, this was not baseless.' Those writings were by a youth who knew little of the real world.[67] He considered those writings 'quite raw, considered as poetry. The language, ideas, and theatrical forms had not developed clearly'.[68] Of *Chhabi o Gan* ('Images and Songs', 1884): 'What one writes at the moment when the mind is brimming with emotions is not necessarily the best writings . . . Not only in poetry but in all artistic work, the creator must create a distance', i.e. distance from the emotional state to allow imagination to distil emotion into art.[69] Of *Bhanu Singher Padabali* (1884): 'The poems could be detected as artificial if you put them to test', for they did not ring true, they produced the tintinnabulation of a cheap musical instrument.[70]

On the whole, in this self-criticism by Tagore when he looked back upon those years, the essence of his critique was lack of maturity in his early writings. Tagore thought later that his early writings were marred by an excess of emotionalism. He attributed this to the tendency in Bengal literary circles in those times to look to their models in English literature. 'What moved us in their [English] writings was the impetus of emotions.' Tagore surmised that due to the timid and 'tedious and circumscribed' existence condition in Bengal in those times the Bengali writers were attracted to the extravagant emotions which they found in, for example, Byron. Tagore realized later in life how different the historical contexts of Europe and Bengal were. From the beginning of the Renaissance in Europe there was an exciting re-assertion of individuality and human emotions, and that found expression in European literature. Unfortunately, nothing comparable to that happened in India. 'In Europe there was truly a thunderstorm and the reverberations of that were heard in literature. In our society there was only a little breeze that raised a murmur—but we were not happy with that, and we resorted to exaggeration, an artificial thunderstorm.' That imitation of the rebellion of the Romantics in Europe was quite irrelevant to the reality in India.[71] Thus Tagore, upon mature reflection, saw through the emotional extravagance of his juvenile romanticism, a fashion of those times in Bengali literary circles. On the whole he looked upon his juvenile writings as immature in form and content and refused to include most of them in his 'Collected Works'.

An incidental point in this context is that Tagore also confesses to being influenced by the wave of atheism in the West in his young days. 'In the beginning of my youth an impudence turned me towards that [atheist] offensive. The religious faith practised in our family was irrelevant to me—I did not accept it.' He mentions Jeremy Bentham, John Stuart Mill and Auguste Comte and says their ideas were 'discussed by our youth . . . Atheism was an intoxicating thing for us'.[72] But he points out that those ideas which came from the West came 'accidentally to hand to us'. They were not the natural outcome of historical evolution, quite unlike the situation in Europe. That point is, of course, valid and it possibly forms the basis of Tagore's frequent critique of imitations of the West. But the most remarkable thing about this statement in his autobiography is that young Tagore did not accept his family's religious beliefs. He made a similar statement in his Hibbert Lectures at Cambridge. It seems to have been a closely guarded secret in his young days, while his father was alive.

Whether we look at his flirtation with atheism or a fancy for romantic rebelliousness, the root seems to be in a deep dissatisfaction. He was unable to define it to express with the clarity that he usually attained later in life. 'A depression envelops man's life when he is deprived of fullness, when he is unable fully to realize his own self, when in lethargic inactivity one dozes at noon time. How to get out of that lethargic depression has always been my anguish.'[73] Where was the 'life of freedom', where was 'the immense life-force', where was 'the realization of the greater life of humanity in one's own life'? The life he saw around himself, he thought, was in his society 'fragmented and circumscribed'; it was like a village pond. Basically Tagore, reflecting upon his life in his first thirty years, felt that his had been an existence in a society that was stagnant, never stirred by a current or a movement towards some end with a purpose.[74] This is how Tagore perceived his early years in his reminiscences in 1912.

Anticipations of Maturity

From 1882–83 one can perhaps notice a transition from the juvenile and immature phase, as perceived by Tagore, to greater maturity.

This transition can be perhaps dated from around the time when Tagore wrote a poem which he later regarded as a turning point in his literary life. There is more than one account of the ecstatic moment when he wrote the poem 'Nirjharer Swapnabhanga' ('The Awakening of the Stream'). Let us look at his statement to C.F. Andrews on this experience. It happened while he was staying for the time being with brother Jyotirindranath at Sudder Street in Calcutta in 1882:

> One morning standing in the veranda [balcony] . . . suddenly in a moment a veil seemed to be lifted from my eyes. I found the world wrapt in an inexpressible glory with its waves of joy and beauty bursting and breaking on all sides. The thick shroud of sorrow that lay on my heart in many folds was pierced through and through by the light of the world, was everywhere radiant . . . For some days I was in this ecstatic mood.[75]

In the unpublished manuscript of his reminiscences Tagore wrote in 1911–12: 'I wrote the poem "The Awakening of the Stream" in a new and strange spirit of gladness, and unknown to me that poem was the prelude to all my poetry.'[76] This was the beginning of a series of poems which were collected in *Prabhat Sangit* ('Morning Songs', 1883). The poet comes out of his tragic mood, from out of the shadows of the 'forest that the heart is'. 'In the early part of my life I had some day entered in my own interior a cave of undefinable darkness inside myself,' he wrote, 'and now I perceived the reality outside.'[77] To Tagore this was a turning point and there is indeed a buoyant spirit in the writings from 1883–84. Moreover, the new phase also meant a break from the long narratives in verse to the lyrical form which was Tagore's forte. Further, the new phase also meant a departure from the imitations of some contemporary Bengali poets; Tagore himself says that he began to cultivate a style of his own.[78]

There is one curious thing which awaits our attention: this is the fact that on occasions Rabindranath, the analytical thinker in his essays, seems to be a totally different entity from him as the poet. For instance, in 1880 he wrote as essay on 'Angst Without a Cause'.[79] He says sarcastically that there is a 'causeless anguish' or angst displayed by the young poets; ironically about the same time in *Sandhya Sangit* ('Evening Songs') he surrenders to that sentiment. In other essays also Tagore shows a sharp mind, quite unlike a poet of indefinable sorrows like Goethe's Young Werther. In an essay written in 1881 Tagore declares the social norm that marriage is forever cannot be accepted; a man and a woman may find a true companion in each other and that was rarely to be found in the marriage relationship which society endorses and preserves as permanent.[80] One cannot help speculating whether these thoughts arose out of the author's own personal predicament of that moment. The most remarkable essay written at that time was an essay arguing that limitless emotional imagination cannot produce great poetry. Imagination that is at work in science or in philosophy is also the imagination at work in creating great poetry; thus it is idle to expect that Bengal will produce great poetry merely by virtue of excess of emotionalism.[81] Making fun of the 'causeless angst' of would-be Romantics, questioning 'holy matrimony', critique of Bengali poets who were all emotions but without ideas which inspire great poetry—these were signs of a rebellious young mind. But these essays remained, by Tagore's decision later, excluded from his 'Collected Works'. Perhaps the author was not satisfied with these fragmentary writings for there was no disciplined pursuit of ideas in them, which is characteristic of Tagore's mature essays from the 1890s onwards.

When Tagore was about twenty he wrote what is commonly regarded as his first novel, *Bou Thakuranir Hat*, (1883). Readers today would find it disappointing. Conventionally Bankim Chandra Chatterjee's *Durgesh Nandini*, published as a book in 1865 is treated in literary history as the first Bengali novel. Thus the genre was quite new when Tagore entered the field. It was a historical romance based on the life of a semi-legendary late medieval king in east Bengal who had defied the Mughals. Unlike a long story (*Karuna*) he wrote about this time, Tagore admitted this novel into his 'Collected Works'. But he wrote of it critically: 'It is like a picture drawn by an untrained hand, there is no sign of a mature and a disciplined mind.'[82] Its significance, he said, was that it signalized the attempt of a mind hitherto lost in its interior explorations, turning towards the world outside.

A style all his own began to show in his book of verse in 1886 (*Kadi o Komal*). Tagore now veered towards the sonnet form, or variations of that form. That seemed to mark the transition from the emotion-laden early writings to the poems with greater ideational content from now onwards to the later phases (*Naibedya, Gitanjali*). He also began to experiment with metrical innovations. At the same time he retained his command over the old style. In *Mayar Khela* ('Playing with Chimeras', 1888), he reached the zenith of his artistry in the musical drama form, and similarly in *Visarjan* ('Sacrifice', 1890) he produced the most powerful verse drama of his early life. The leitmotif in *Mayar Khela* was that the devotion of true love is different from worldly persons' attraction for one another. But what is much more potent than the message is the quality of the simple lyrics married to music in a gossamer network of a plain story of love returned and love unrequited. *Visarjan* on the other hand is a thunderous storm—the clash between the two protagonists who represent absolute faith in infallible tradition and, in contraposition, the challenge to that infallibility on the issue of violence in the temple ritual of sacrifice. In these works Tagore presented ideas in conflict in a manner he never attempted till now and this characteristic remained a hallmark of his dramatic works in later years.

The same maturity marked the series of poems collected in *Manasi* (1890). Tagore himself looked upon this work as a turning point, for this is when 'an artist appears to join the poet' in him. The art appears in metrical experiments and in details such as 'according full sound value to compound letters to empower rhythm'.[83] As regards the ideational content, Tagore thought that these poems show a spirit of 'resignation'; if so, that was a prelude to the next phase of *Naibedya*, and the spiritual poems series leading to *Gitanjali*.

What was more evident, however, was a new tone in his love poems—they were, if not spiritual, certainly transcending carnal love. Tagore translated into English only about ten poems from *Manasi*. Here is one illustrating the new tone:

> All fruitless is the cry
> All vain this fire of desire.
> . . . I clasp both thine hands in mine,
> And keep thine eyes prisoner with my hungry eyes;
> Seeking and crying, where art thou,
> Where, O, Where!
> Where is the immortal flame hidden in the depth of thee!

The translation is entitled 'Desire for a Human Soul'.[84]
And another:

> I have ever loved thee in a hundred forms and times,
> Age after age, in birth following birth.
> . . . We two have come floating by the twin currents of love
> That well up from the inmost heart of the Beginningless.
> We two have played in the lives of myriad lovers
> In fearful solitude of sorrow,
> In tremulous shyness of sweet union
> In old, old love ever renewing to life.[85]

Perhaps Tagore felt that the love poems in *Manasi* did not lend themselves to easy translation and that is why he translated so few of them. But in Bengali literature the publication of this book secured for him the reputation of an established poet. Tagore's own opinion in 1931 was that the book passed muster as a book of poems, not mere verses.[86] Thus it marked the end of an era in his literary career.

CHAPTER THREE

Into the World
Tagore in the Public Sphere
1891–1908

From the beginning of the 1890s, Tagore entered the public sphere. He became the literary editor of a journal, *Hitabadi*, in 1891. He was also one of the founders (1894) of the first Bengal Literary Academy, later known as Bangiya Sahitya Parishad. He accepted the position of the editor of the journal *Sadhana* in 1894, and later of the journal *Bharati* (1898–99) and *Bangadarshan* (1901–05). These were also the years when he began a series of political writings and also appeared in public forums to express his opinion on political issues for the first time. His poems and songs gave voice to the spirit of the Swadeshi movement, against the partition of Bengal in 1905 by the British government. He was the originator of the idea of *Rakhi-bandhan* as a symbolic means of reasserting Bengal's unity despite the partition made by the government. There was also another kind of public role which he assumed as an ideologist of a national education movement and the builder of his school in Santiniketan. During these years, Tagore burst into the public sphere, a great change from his days as a very private poetic soul till 1890, his enchanted solitariness. This chapter in his life came to an end around 1908 when he withdrew himself from the public political sphere.

The Tides of History

What did the tides of history bring to India in the period we are looking at now, 1891 to 1908? With the death of Ishwarchandra Vidyasagar (1891), Bankim Chandra Chatterjee (1894) and M.G. Ranade (1901) an era came to an end. The beginning of the new one was marked by the acclamation for Swami Vivekananda after the Chicago Parliament of Religions (1893), turbulent events around the sedition trial of Bal Gangadhar Tilak (1897), the partition of Bengal leading to the Swadeshi movement (1905), the split between Moderates and Extremists in the Congress (1907), and the formation of militant nationalist groups by Aurobindo Ghosh among others in Bengal (1906–08). British authorities also struck back, with the arrest of Aurobindo Ghosh for the 'bomb conspiracy', death by hanging suffered by Kshudiram Bose after an attempt to kill a British officer, and the severe sentence of exile for Bal Gangadhar Tilak—all of that in 1908. A new political climate brought home to India the need to think of the efficacy of moderate 'mendicancy', as well as the efficacy of individual acts of violence.

The global scene was also becoming turbulent, perhaps explosive. The birth of a new Asia was prefigured in the Boxer Rebellion in China (1900), the emergence of a united Saudi Arabia under Ibn Saud (from 1902), Japan's victory in the Russo-Japanese War (1905) which impacted India as the first defeat of an European power in Asia, the declaration of a plan for a republican regime by Sun Yat-sen (1907). In the meanwhile, more immediately relevant to Indians was the foundation of the Congress in Natal by M.K. Gandhi (1894), followed by an anti-apartheid movement against the racist regime in South Africa (1907–08). And anticipations of a revolutionary future were to be seen in the foundation of the Bolshevik Party by V.I. Lenin (1903) and the uprising against Tsarist rule (1905). To the perceptive mind of those times these events in India and abroad could not have been irrelevant or distant. Rabindranath Tagore's imagination and consciousness was, as we shall see, not untouched by the tides of history. In the 1890s he abandoned his enchanted solitude and entered public life.

Tagore's Personal Predicament

We do not know very much about Tagore's family life—not as much as one would like to know, except the story we can piece together from the letters which have survived. Tagore writes in his autobiographical accounts a great deal about the elders of the family in the ancestral home when he was a child, but he is reticent about his wife and his own immediate family. The letters are also somewhat reticent. We have already seen that the letters to his wife bear witness to a loving relationship, but Rabindranath was away from home a good deal since he had to supervise the Tagore family estates. We have also seen that his first child, a daughter named Madhurilata, nicknamed Bela, was born in 1886 and the second child, Rathindranath, in 1888. Three other children were born to Rabindranath and Mrinalini: daughter Renuka (1891), the third daughter Mira (1894) and the youngest son Samindranath (1896). Although in his twenties Rabindranath had written eloquently against child marriage, he arranged the marriage of his daughters at a very early age: the two elder daughters were married off in 1901 and the third in 1907. The only explanation for these shocking decisions can be the pressure of the elders of the family, the fact that the Tagores found it difficult to find suitable matches for their daughters, and the custom of paying dowry at a daughter's marriage. Tagore's father possibly played an important role: it was he who paid in 1901 substantial sums as dowry. The difficulty in getting a suitable match was due to the status of the Tagores as 'Pirali' Brahmins who had been downgraded in the Hindu caste hierarchy on account of their ancestors having associated with Muslims many generations ago. The sordid details of that degradation by a retrograde society and the consequent price to be paid in the form of high dowry need not detain us. Nor should we go into the question of how suitable the matches were or whether the daughters did have a happy married life, which is generally acknowledged to be in question. The outstanding fact is that in this regard Rabindranath was a victim of the social constraints of the Hindu community of his times. It is very likely that his writings, especially from his middle age, condemning the subordination of women in patriarchal Hindu society, were in part an expression of the anguish he suffered in early life having observed the fate of his own daughters.

Perhaps we should also bear in mind the fact that Rabindranath and his wife and children were financially dependent on the Tagore family estates. His own personal income was small till his father passed away in 1905 at the age of eighty-eight. According to his close associate and neighbour in Santiniketan, Prabhat Kumar Mukherjee, Tagore's income was about Rs 250 per month in the 1890s.[1] Only at the age of forty-four did Rabindranath come into money. Prior to that, under the Dayabhaga property law governing succession in the Hindu Undivided Family, the *Karta* and sole proprietor was his father and all the sons drew income from his estates as decided by the father. That Rabindranath's personal financial situation was insecure is clear from the numerous letters we have from him requesting friends for small loans; more generally known is the fact that he had to sell off his wife's ornaments from time to time to meet the expenses of his prime mission in life, to run the school he had set up in Santiniketan. After he made a name for himself he also sold off the copyright of most of his works to publishers to make both ends meet in his personal finances. Finally, occasionally ineptitude in handling money matters was also a problem. Particularly disastrous was a misadventure he entered into in 1895 when he became involved in a commercial enterprise, Tagore and Company, together with his favourite nephew Surendranath, son of his mentor and elder brother Satyendranath. That enterprise, managed chiefly by Surendranath, drained his resources and eventually in 1900 Rabindranath borrowed a large sum of money from a family friend, Sir T.N. Palit, to meet the liabilities of Tagore and Company. Rabindranath had to repay in instalments this debt for eighteen long years, from 1900 to 1918. And yet when he received the Nobel Prize he put the major part of the prize money at the disposal of a rural cooperative bank, for the benefit of farmers in the Tagore estates. On the whole the poet was perpetually in strained circumstances financially for the greater part of his life. Contrary to a commonly held impression, he and his family did not lead a life of opulence.

Rabindranath went through hard times particularly in his forties. The death of his wife Mrinalini (1902), his second daughter Renuka (1903) of tuberculosis, his father Debendranath (1905) and his youngest son Samindra (1907) left him a lonely man. And he sent off his eldest son Rathindra to Illinois, USA, to study agricultural science in 1906 and married off his youngest daughter Mira in 1907. In these five years, between age forty-one and forty-six, the family life he had known till then came to an end. It must have needed enormous mental resources to withstand these deaths and the dispersal of the family, and to continue with his creative writings. A good many of Tagore's devotional and spiritually oriented poems and songs were written about this time. Poetry of the timbre that one sees in *Gitanjali* grew out of his thoughts in those days.

It seems that in two ways Tagore sought an escape from his personal existential predicaments. One was his mission of building his school in Santiniketan, the other was his creative work, his literary life. He personally organized the foundation of the Mandir or Prayer Hall in Santiniketan in 1891, an anticipation of his future role in that place. To this day one can see the inscription of dedication, opening the temple 'to all individuals of every class and community irrespective of religion or status for the purpose of meditation of the *brahma*'. In 1901 he started his school with five students, including his son Rathindra. In 1902 the Tagores sold some of Mrinalini's ornaments to meet the expenses of the school. He held the Spring Festival in Santiniketan in 1907, the first of a series of festivals to match the seasons—the spring, the monsoon, the harvest season, etc.—designed by him; these replaced religious festivals which were not observed in his Santiniketan. At this stage Santiniketan was only a school for young children and the great scholars who adorned the faculty came much later. The school was at this time distinguished from the other ones in Bengal by its emphasis on teaching in the mother tongue, inculcation of moral precepts of *brahmacharya*, simple and austere living for the resident students, and inclusion of cultural activities in which the poet himself took a lead.

The school seems to have been a solace to its creator. The other solace was his literary life. Some of his greatest poems were written in the 1890s. And the fact that he was in need of solace and also perhaps his sense of solitariness in his inner life are revealed in many of his poems at this time.

> What though the day's end creeps up slow and weary,
> And at a command all birds cease to sing,
> What though there is none else in the sky,
> And weariness numbs each wing.
> A magic spell a Great Dread seems to moan,
> Earth's face is hidden in a veil of dark,
> Yet, and yet, O my bird,
> My bird in the dark, yet fly on.

And then the uplifting last lines:

> Fear not, nor look to ties of love,
> Hope not, for Hope is full of guile,
> Mere talk is vain, and vain it is to mourn,
> Homeless you are, and no posies for this while.
> Yours are the wings, yours the immense firmament
> Dark and not a hope of dawn,
> Yet, and yet, O my bird,
> My bird in the dark, yet fly on.

This poem 'Bad Times'[2] was written in 1897; my translation is vastly unequal to the original, needless to say, but the poet offers no complete a translation. There is a new spirit of exalted dedication to a mission, a resoluteness that strikes a new note in these poems of the 1890s. Another is equally famous, 'Now Call Me Back'[3] written in 1894:

> While the world is busy with a hundred chores,
> You played, O Poet, upon your flute the livelong day,

Like a truant boy who has fled from home . . .
Shake off your sleep and rise.
There is fire around . . .
Bloated insolence with million snouts
Sucks the heart-blood of the weak.
Proud injustice mocks at pain . . .
We must bring speech to these dumb lips.
We must light with hope these weary empty hearts,
We must call to them and say:
'Hold your heads high and together stand' . . .
Gather yourself, O Poet, and arise.
If you have courage, bring it as your gift.

Then Tagore goes on to say that his escapism from the real world must end. He appeals to his Muse: Do not 'keep me in restful idleness in the cool shade of my heart'. The poet will now come out and stand 'on the wide dusty highway amidst the crowd'. The task is to fight the good fight, 'unscarred by fear and unmarked with slavery's badge'. This translation by Humayun Kabir is close to the original text.

The spirit of such writings is reflected in the enormous output of political and social essays by Tagore in the years between 1891 and 1908. Purely in terms of volume, these writings exceeded his poetic creations in those years.

Tagore's Political Writings

In 1890 Tagore wrote his first political pamphlet. He practically disowned it later and never allowed its inclusion in his 'Collected Works'. Indeed, his second political essay, in 1893, was diametrically opposite in tone. The tract of 1890 was the text of his first public speech on a political issue delivered at a meeting of the Landholders' Association of Bengal. It was a meeting to submit to the government the plea that more native Indians, enjoying the confidence of their countrymen, should be included in the higher decision-making positions in the government. Tagore says in his speech repeatedly, 'I have no right to talk politics, it has been outside of my mental habit, pursuits and taste.' Nevertheless, with considerable panache he adopts the Indian National Congress's position: the British Government was well-intentioned, there were some policy errors, and the Congress would try and correct such errors. Tagore recalled the services rendered by Allan Octavian Hume, George Yule and William Wedderburn to the Congress; he conceded that the political leaders in India accepted the idea that British administration brought about better governance, and went on to argue that if the well-being of the Indian subjects was the aim of governance, then the subjects should be allowed to take part in policy-making.[4] Later, Tagore deprecated the tone of that essay of 1890: 'We were only flapping our wings within the cage', without challenging that cage itself.

By the standards of the day the demand for Indian participation in policy-making levels of government was regarded as a bold political statement. Can the statements favourable to the good intentions of the British government be read as ironical rhetoric? That is doubtful, for the general tone of his essay of 1890 is by no means anti-British.

However, the Tagorean voice was soon to be heard in 1893 in his second political statement: we deceive ourselves when we think today that our misery will end once we get from the British what we beg of them; let us try by ourselves, as worthy human beings, to stand on our own legs; we should cease to crave to be exceptionally admitted to the favours of Indian rulers when the rest of the countrymen are denied that exceptional status. The most important aspect of this political speech by Tagore in 1893 was the notion of self-development of capability, which he later called *atma-sakti*. Compared to 1890, Tagore's political perception seems to have changed substantially and this essay, 'Rulers and Subjects' was the lead article in a collection of political essays Tagore published under that title *Raja Praja*[5]. Tagore ridicules the 'craving for the sympathy' of the rulers in a section of the Indian public discourse and surmised that 'a reaction of the mind of India' was not far away, for such was the inevitable consequence of the political ideas the British impact implanted in the Indian mind, as well as the conflict with the British authorities in India.

Thus the beginning of the 1890s marked a turning point in Tagore's world-outlook; it marked the beginning of his engagement with the politics of the subject nation negotiating with a new political consciousness. Bankim Chandra Chatterjee presided over the meeting at which Tagore read out his essay of 1893, and that essay bridges the distance between Chatterjee's political vision and the new political consciousness that emerged later in the Swadeshi movement against the partition of Bengal in 1905. Long before that movement began Tagore had burnt his bridges. Not only did he sing the song *Vande mataram* at a reception of the Congress delegates at the Tagore family residence after the Congress session in Calcutta in 1896, but he also attended the Bengal Provincial Conference, an offshoot of the Congress in 1897, and spoke from the podium of a public meeting at the Calcutta Town Hall protesting the Sedition Bill in 1898. The agenda of the political movement of 1905 was anticipated in the social agenda Tagore had framed: he set up a Swadeshi Bhandar in 1897 near his residence in Calcutta to market handicrafts and his speech on 'Swadeshi Samaj' in July 1904 spelt out his programme of 'self-help' which would liberate Bengal from dependence on British commerce and government.

A good number of Tagore's writings in this period were political. Tagore wrote approximately thirty-five major political essays between 1893 and 1908. These were collected together in several volumes. If one translates the titles of his books in these years one can get an idea of the trend and the profusion of the political writings: *Atma-sakti* ('Self-empowerment'), *Swadesh* ('Our Country'), *Bharatvarsha* ('India'), *Raja Praja* ('Rulers and Subjects'), *Samuha* ('The Multitude'), *Swadeshi Samaj* ('Indian Society'), and *Path o Patheya* ('Ends and Means')—all published between 1905 and 1908, putting together the political essays written between 1893 and 1908. Of these thirty-five or so political essays, we can focus only on a few for the present.

Tagore's Changing Political Outlook

Three phases are discernable in Tagore's political writings between 1890 and 1908. The early phase begins with, as we have seen, a new tone in *Raja Praja* ('Rulers and Subjects'): The craving for British sympathy is ridiculed and a new message, the importance of self-development of capabilities of Indian society regardless of government policy, comes to the fore. In the essay 'Englishmen and Indians'[6] he writes: 'Even if I am crying in the wilderness, still I must say . . . to get appreciation from the British is of no consequence', the 'true path to a dignified existence' was not to obtain concessions; every Indian should forget the false prestige of being *almost* an Englishman, his aim should be the dignity of being Indian.[7] This was followed by a strong statement against the Sedition Bill in 1898, entitled '*Kantha-rodh*' ('On Being Throttled', 1898) and '*Atiyukti*' ('Extravagance',1902) in criticism of the contemplated Delhi Durbar. In the latter, Tagore begins with the observation that the Durbar is an Indian institution but, when appropriated by a foreign power for its imperial ends, the institution acquires totally different connotations; then he launches into a critique of European civilization which, unlike Indian civilization, is based upon the principle of self-aggrandizement, the drive to enhance power.

About this time Tagore makes a seminal contribution to Indian nationalist discourse, the conception of a syncretic civilization in India which establishes unity within ethnic, linguistic and religious diversity. This essay of 1902, entitled '*Bharat-Varsher Itihas*' ('History of Bharatvarsha')[8] was in many ways more important politically than many political essays he wrote at this time, for it established a paradigm of historical interpretation which formed a part of the nationalist construction of India's past and the evolution of nationhood, a theme to be taken up by Jawaharlal Nehru and others.

The second phase of Tagore's political thinking may be discerned from about 1903–04 when he wrote against the partition of Bengal '*Banga Bibhag*' ('The partition of Bengal', 1904), and '*University*

Bill, 1904. While these were protests which were by and large in consonance with the nationalist leaders' prevailing attitude at that time, in 1904 he broke away to declare that nationalists needed an agenda other than protest and agitation. This was an essay entitled *'Swadeshi Samaj'* ('National Society').[9] The living spirit of Indian civilization, he said, is in her social organization, in Europe it is in the state; therefore, the construction of independent India must start with our society; and he also said that the fault line within that society along communal lines, the division between Hindu and Muslims, must be addressed and that was possible because of the syncretic nature of ancient Indian civilization. There followed a series of essays which were collected in 1905 to 1908.[10] Through the anti-partition agitation he was with the nationalist leadership, but he continued to assert his own position: he had doubts about the efficacy of the means adopted by the leaders of Bengal, because the boycott of foreign goods was not enough, it was just a negative approach. What was needed was a constructive programme for self-empowerment (*atma-sakti*) which would initiate efforts for village self-government, education on national lines, provision of small irrigation works at the village level, system of rural credit at low interest rates, settlement of disputes without resort to the courts of law, etc. This was the agenda he recommended in his essay *'Abastha o Byabastha'* ('The Situation and the Remedy', 1905).[11] The then national leaders gave scarcely any attention to this agenda of action.

In the years from 1907 onwards we see the third phase in Tagore's political thinking. This was foreshadowed in his writings earlier, but three points now emerged more clearly, each creating a distance between his position and that of various sections of nationalist leadership in Bengal at that time. The first sign of Tagore's turning away was clearest in the essay he wrote *'Byadhi o Pratikar'* ('The Disease and its Remedy') in 1907. Firstly, he drew attention to the assumption behind nationalist agitation against the partition of Bengal that political agitation would be effective, that the rulers would listen to the voices of discontentment.

Tagore pointed to a distinction he had made earlier between the values and practices of the 'small Englishmen' and the 'great Englishmen'. The small Englishmen were those serving the Empire in India, and they were intolerant to native dissidence. The 'great Englishmen' in the higher levels of decision-making in England were more sensitive to certain norms derived from the Western ideology of just and lawful governance. Tagore surmised that in deciding on the government's response to the anti-partition agitation, the 'small Englishmen' predominated. This was not quite the scenario the agitators foresaw. The second point he made was more important: 'today we are all lamenting that the British have secretly encouraged the Muslims against the Hindus. Even if it were true, why should we blame the British?' After centuries of living together the Hindus are unable to accept the Muslims socially, they cannot eat together, they cannot even sit on the same carpet—that was the crucial weakness in Bengal's society and that was naturally exploited by the British. Tagore went on to expose another infirmity in the Swadeshi anti-partition agitation as well as in the nationalist movement in general:

When suddenly the English-educated urbanite goes to the peasant and says 'we are brothers' the peasant does not understand what it means. Those whom we usually call 'that damn peasant', those people whose everyday life is of no concern to us, those people who are no more to us than some statistics in government reports, those whom we do not stand by in their life of misery—those are the people we suddenly call upon as our brothers who must buy [Khadi] cloth at a higher price and face baton charge by the Gurkha [policemen] when we want to fight the government, and that kind of call fails to convince anyone.[12]

Until the leaders of Bengal bridged the distance between them and the common peasant and the Muslim population, Tagore saw no prospect of a genuine, truly national resistance to British rule. Tagore spoke to his own class when he said look within and see how you have failed by the standard of common humanism and hence your political weakness. Tagore's sermon was far from being popular with the nationalist leadership and the next year, in 1908, came a final break when he questioned the path taken by Bengal's militant nationalists, or the *Biplabis* as they were called in Bengal.

In a highly controversial essay '*Path o Patheya*' ('Ends and Means') published in 1908, Tagore criticized the ideas behind the form of political action Bengal began to witness: secret societies, acquisition of bombs and other weapons, induction of very young activists, and political assassination. This path of action created some iconic figures of revolutionary militancy against foreign rule. Tagore did not question their heroism but he questioned the political efficacy of their action. Anguished to see the death of heroic freedom fighters he urged,

> We must not forget ourselves in our excitement, it needs to be explained to those who are excited that . . . whatever the strength of the urge [to resist foreign rule], in action we have to take to the broad highway because a shortcut through a narrow lane will lead us nowhere. Just because we are in our mind impatient, the World does not curtail the length of the road nor does Time curtail itself.

There was no shortcut of the kind militants imagined. Tagore went on, in his own metaphorical language, to point to the limitations of the militants' violence. Anger against repression by government had sparked off violent action. 'But a spark and a flame are two different things. The spark does not dispel the dark in our home', a flame that lasts is needed. 'The flame needs a lamp. And thus long preparation is required to prepare the lamp and its wick and its fuel.'[13] Thus patient preparation in politics was required, not unthinking haste in the path of violence. The preparation would take time if the aim was to build an independent nation; there were many impediments and the existence of British rule was only one and the most obvious impediment. The greater impediment was the inadequate development of a consciousness of unity in a country which was divided by barriers between religious communities, castes, language communities, between people with different social norms and practices. Joint resistance to British rule might be for the time being a unifying factor, but 'the moment the British would leave India the bond of unity thus constructed would snap'. What was the way out? Tagore called upon the nationalist leaders and workers 'to go down to the people, to address every section of them, to bind the land together in a net of constructive programmes in different directions, to expand the scope of your activity to make it open to all and widen the spread in its ambit, so that the elite and the lowly, the Hindu and Muslims and Christians can all be together in an endeavour that unites their hearts'.[14] Till the appearance of Mahatma Gandhi in Indian politics, there was no agenda even remotely like this before the nationalist leadership. Tagore's exhortations only enhanced the distance between him and the then leadership in Bengal. The extremist Bipin Chandra Pal, the future sage of Pondicherry and, in the anti-partition agitation, an ideological leader Aurobindo Ghosh and the 'Hindu Catholic' Brahmo Bandhab Upadhyay, were among the leaders who condemned Tagore's dissent from mainstream nationalism.[15] However, that did not deter Tagore; in his not less than thirty-five political articles, he had thought long and hard over the political issues in question. The communal riots in Bengal in 1907, the self-sacrifice of Kshudiram Bose, a lad in his teens, in an abortive attempt to assassinate a hated government official in 1908, and the general deceleration of the anti-partition and Swadeshi upsurge of 1905—all these produced the critical reactions we have outlined in Tagore's mind in 1906–08. The year 1908 is indeed a turning point and marks the beginning of a new phase when Tagore withdrew from the political domain to his Muse, creative writing.

Fictional Writings

The years 1891–1908 marked probably the most creative phase in Tagore's life. His fictional writings published in these years were the collection of short stories in two volumes (*Galpa-Gucchha*, 2 vols., 1900 and 1901), and the novels *Chokher Bali* ('The Mote in the Eye', 1903), and *Nauka-dubi* ('The Wreck', 1906). *Gora* began to be written in installments in 1907 but the book published in 1910 really belongs to another phase of his life.

The short stories partly reflect his first experience with life in the villages that he visited in remote parts of Bengal to supervise the Tagore estates from 1891 when his father assigned this responsibility to him. As he confided in his letters to Charles Andrews later, this was his first exposure to social reality, a great change from the artificial environment of the life of the landowning classes in the colonial metropolis of Calcutta. These short stories, written in the 1890s, virtually created a new genre of literature in Bengal. It also marked his entry, for the first time, into his contemporaneous society as a keen observer; prior to that his fictional narratives were about an imagined past. This spell of writings was followed by his novels, allowing a more extended and deeper treatment of and reflection on the society around him.

The novel, *Nauka-dubi*, translated into English as *The Wreck* and also into several other languages, is one of Tagore's popular works. It is a readable but trivial story of mistaken identities after a boat wreck on the river. One wonders why Tagore wrote such a story. Perhaps it was written to fill up the pages of the journal he edited at that time. But the novel that preceded it, *Chokher Bali* was of a different order altogether. The novel was remarkable because for the first time Tagore depicted in a narrative not just pallid love, but desire and indeed the urge driven by sexuality. This novel is also remarkable for the ruthless depiction of the suffocating domestic interior of a middle-class Bengali household, the complexity of relationship between women in the inner quarters, the tendency of many men in that environment to be mother-dependent 'like the kangaroo-child' as Tagore puts it, the meaningless fuss about feeding the menfolk of the family, the interplay of suppressed desires and the flexibility of the ethics of the Indian male, and finally the suppression which the widow suffers in such a society. The main protagonist Mahendra—no hero in this novel—and his wife and Binodini, a widow who finds temporary admittance into the family, form the triangle at the core of the novel; but that is situated in a narrative where Mahendra's mother and a friend, Bihari, figure prominently. Tagore commented about forty years later in 1940:

> The story in *Chokher Bali* is driven by the mother's jealousy. That jealousy allowed release to the lust in Mahendra, which otherwise would not have emerged red in tooth and claw the way it did. It was as if the trap-door of a cage at the zoo was opened, unbridled savagery emerges. In modern literature the style dwells not in the chronicle of events, but in the analysis and exposure of the inner things. That was seen in *Chokher Bali*.[16]

Tagore believed that 'the pitiless Divinity which shapes human destiny' had never been depicted in Bengali literature in modern times in the manner he attempted in this novel. Moreover, he also points out that this was his first novel of large proportions. 'Till then I had only indulged in meteoric showers in the form of short stories.' On the whole Tagore's own judgement forty years later was that this novel of 1903 came 'accidentally, in terms of my own inner self as well as Bengali literature of those times. What provoked it is difficult to say'. In any event this novel, like much else in this chapter in his life, marked a turning point. At the same time it will not be unjust to note that the heroic Binodini at the end of the day declares meekly that she was after all a widow, not fit to enter into married life when Bihari proposes to her. Did Tagore's nerves fail? Or was he conceding to the reality of those times? 'Dharma will not tolerate that . . . I am a widow . . . In my next life (*parajanma*) I shall pray to be with you—in this life I have no hopes, no rights. . .' One may suppose that, given the norms prevailing in the beginning of the twentieth century, the fate of a widow could not be otherwise. Tagore probes into his society with a surgeon's scalpel, and the denouement he describes was as real as the rest of the story in his objective vision. There is a passage in *Chokher Bali* where Bankim Chandra Chatterjee's novel *Visha-Vriksha* ('Poison Tree') is talked about. Tagore's novel is a kind of bridge between Bankim Chandra's era in literature and the new age about to dawn. As we shall see in the following chapter, in the novel *Gora* Tagore extended his exploration into the society around him further and his artistic self was by then guided by ideas which he wished to project in his fictional writings.

Other than his short stories and novels, there were two other major literary works he produced in prose in this phase of his life. One was the *Europe Jatrir Diary* ('The Diary of a Sojourn in Europe', 1891) and the other was *Pancha-bhuter Diary,* (later published as *Pancha-bhut,* 1897). The diary of travels in Europe is not so much remarkable for what it recorded, but it was remarkable for its style. Tagore wrote it in Bengali that is spoken, not the chaste and Sanskritized Bengali which was then accepted in literary writing. The other non-fictional prose work was in the style of *belles-letters,* a rich tradition in Bengali literary journals since Bankim Chandra Chatterjee. However, Tagore's *Pancha-bhuter Diary,* consisting of imaginary conversations on grave philosophical questions with a witty lightness of touch, is almost without parallel in Bengali literature to this day. These years 1890–1908 also witnessed a large number of essays on literary criticism by Tagore, collected in books entitled *Prachin Sahitya* ('Ancient Literature'), *Loka-sahitya* ('Folk Literature'), *Sahitya* ('Literature') and *Adhunik Sahitya* ('Modern Literature'), all published in 1907. To this corpus of writings might be added his biographical essays (*Charitra Puja*), also published in 1907.

The Poet Tagore

When one turns to Tagore's poetic creations in this phase, 1891–1908, we find that not less than ten collections of his poems were published in these years: *Sonar Tari,* 1894; *Chitra,* 1896; *Kanika,* 1899; *Katha, Kahini,* 1900; *Kalpana,* 1900; *Kshanika,* 1901; *Naibedya,* 1901; *Smaran,* 1903; *Shishu,* 1903, and *Kheya,* 1906. These were preceded by *Chitrangada,* a novel poetic interpretation of the epic story of Arjuna and the princess he courted. The first version which appeared in 1892 is one of many revised versions of *Chitrangada.* At the root of it, he elaborated later, there is a subtle intellectual question: what if we separate the beauty of a woman from her identity as a woman, is love a biological response to the beauty in a woman or is there love incorporeal? Chitrangada's two forms, beautiful and devoid of beauty, *Surupa* and *Kurupa*, represent that disaggregation of beauty from womanhood. The ideal of love upheld in this narrative poem is this: the woman should neither be a pretty idol to be cherished nor a dependent meekly following the man; she should be the companion by the side of a man in times of stress in life—that companionship reveals the true place and identity of the woman in a man's life. Evidently this basic issue was one of Tagore's deepest and abiding concerns because he returned to this theme, as we shall see later, time and again in re-interpreting *Chitrangada*.

Some of Tagore's best love songs are from this period and we can cite them for he translated them himself. Love will 'dwell in silence in my heart, like the full moon in the summer night'[17] is a poor translation of the original (*tumi rabe nirabe*), but some other translations ring more true.

> I thought I had something to say to her when our eyes met in the road
> . . . it rocks, day and night
> Like an idle boat on every wave of the hours—the thing I had to say to her.[18]

Then:

> You came for a moment to my side and touched me with the great mystery of the woman that there is in the heart of creation.[19]

Then again:

> If by chance you think of me, I shall sing to you . . .
> You will sit alone in the balcony of the south, and I shall sing to you from the darkened room . . .
> When the lighted lamp is brought into the room, I shall go and then, perhaps, you will listen to the night, and hear my song when I am silent.[20]

Further:

Your days will be full of cares, if you must give me your heart
My home by the cross-roads has its doors open and my mind is
absent—for I sing
I will never be made to answer for it, if you must give me your
heart.[21]

Then we have a huge rush of Tagore's so-called 'spiritual' poems.
Earlier, from his early youth, he wrote devotional songs for the
Brahma Samaj, but now his life experiences—the death of his wife
and two of his children—imparted to the poems a new note of a
personally felt, intense spirituality. These again are worth quoting
for he himself translated many of them into English.

'Lord of my being, has your wish been fulfilled in me' (1896).
'They who crowd in my path do not know I am walking alone
with you', (1901) 'Far as I gaze at the depth of thy immensity/
I find no trace there of sorrow or death or separation' (1901), 'I
ask for an audience from you, my King, in your solitary chamber.
/ Call me from the crowd' (1901), 'Light thy signal, Father, for
us who have strayed far away from thee' (1901). 'Through death
and sorrow / There dwells peace / In the heart of the Eternal'
(1903). 'I seek and seek on my heart strings the notes that can
blend with Thine' (1906). Translations of these poems by Tagore
remained unpublished till his death; they evidently form a bridge
to the *Gitanjali* verses which he published in 1912. The point to
note is that the 'spiritual' aspect of Tagore's persona was exclusively
highlighted in the critical acclaim for *Gitanjali* and celebration of
the recognition given to him in the Nobel Prize award of 1913.
His love poems and patriotic songs and many other segments of
his writings were ignored in the construction of his image as the
spiritual poet, 'the sage of the East', in the Western world. *Gitanjali*
included translation from the earlier writings cited above.[22]

There is no doubt that from the mid-1890s along with his
romantic poems there is a flow of spiritual poems, and the personal
tragedies he encountered, the deaths his family suffered, partly

accounts for that spiritual tone and search for solace. However, there were also poems quite different in tone. For instance, the following:

I have felt your muffled steps in my blood
Evermoving Past
Have seen your hushed countenance
In the heart of the garrulous day.

He reflects that the past writes 'in unseen script on the pages of our destiny' and brings 'back to life the unremembered designs for the shaping of new images'.[23]

Smaran (1903) was written as a series of poems immediately after his wife's death. He recalls the vital things and trifles which conjugal life is made of. All the poems are about Mrinalini. He recalls how he found the letters from him to her secreted in her box, 'with timorous heart she tried to steal those trifles from time's turbulent stream', and said 'they are mine only'. Addressing her: 'You came for a moment to my side and touched me with the great mystery of the woman that there is in the heart of creation.' There were such grateful tributes to her memory. And there was also in these poems another note which speaks to us of her love and of hurts he might have caused to her.

The time is past when I could repay for all I received
Her night has found its morning and thou has taken her to thy arms
And to thee I bring my gratitude and my gifts that were for her
For all hurts and offences to her I come to thee for forgiveness.
I offer to thy service those flowers of my love that remained in bud when she waited for them to open.[24]

Do these pain-laden after-thoughts tell us that the poet failed her in some ways?

The poems collected in *Shishu* ('The Child') published in 1903 were written for Tagore's daughter Renuka who was on her deathbed. She died of tuberculosis at the age of thirteen. Many of these poems are not quite the stuff for children because Tagore's spiritual temper intervened. But some poems in that work are indeed common ration in nurseries and schools in Bengal.

Tell me mother
The weekdays come and go fast and thick
Have they a car to reach so quick?
But why does Sunday take so long
Behind the others trudging on?[25]

The writings about children, rather than for children, are accessible in English in Tagore's own translation in *The Crescent Moon.*

I wish I could travel by the road that crosses baby's mind, and out beyond all bounds.
. . . Where Reason makes kites of her laws and flies them
And Truth sets fact free from its fetters.[26]

It is time for me to go, mother; I am going.
When in the paling darkness of the lonely dawn, you stretch out your arms for your baby in the bed,
I shall say 'baby is not there'—mother: I am going.[27]

The thought of death occurs time and again in *Shishu* for the poet was speaking of his dying child.

Translated by Tagore himself, the voice of the child in *The Crescent Moon* in 1913:[28]

Day by day I float my paper boats one by one down the running stream
In big black letters I write my name on them and the name of the village where I live
I hope that someone in some strange land will find them and know who I am . . . When night comes I bury my face in my arms and dream that my paper boats float on under the midnight stars . . .

Unfortunately, Rabindranath Tagore chose to translate in *The Crescent Moon* only some poems, which are actually for adults, addressing the child or about the child, and most poems do not give voice to the child who spoke in the Bengali version, *Shishu*.

Along with the outpouring of spiritual poems, besides ones of loss and regret, the poet wrote an immense number of patriotic songs in the first decade of the twentieth century. There was earlier in Bengal a strong genre of songs and poems in praise of the motherland going back to nineteenth-century folksongs as well as urban 'modern' poets, like Hemchandra Bandyopadhyay (1838–1903) whose *Bharat Sangit* in 1872 inspired Bharatendu Harishchandra of Banaras, the pioneer of modern Hindi literature.[29] But Tagore added a new dimension to that tradition in his poems in terms of ideas as well as style. His idea of patriotism touched and blended with his spiritual philosophy. No one else would have written like this:

> Be not ashamed, my brothers, to stand before the proud and the
> powerful with your white robe of simpleness.
> Let your crown be of humility, your freedom the freedom of the soul.
> Know that what is huge is not great and pride is not everlasting.
>
> (*Naibedya*, 1901)[30]

At the very first protest meeting on 7 August 1905 against the partition of Bengal, held in Calcutta Town Hall some ten days after the government notification, the song that was sung was *Amar Sonar Bangla* ('My Golden Bangla').[31] The tune of this song which was later to be adopted as the national anthem by the government of Bangladesh, was to set a pattern for many of Tagore's patriotic songs; he used folk tunes of Bengal, especially Baul tunes, which, as distinguished from classical ragas, had a specially Bengali flavour.

> Blessed am I that I am born to this land
> . . . The first light revealed to my eyes was from her sky
> And let the same light kiss them before they are closed for ever.
>
> (*Sarthak Janam Amar*, 1905)

'Let the earth and the waters, the air and the fruits of my country be holy' (*Banglar mati, Banglar jal*, 1905). Such songs often focused on Bengal. But the fact that for him Bengal was only a metaphor for the country as a whole is clear from the entire corpus of Tagore's patriotic songs; in fact the first (1905) collection of music score of Tagore's patriotic poems was entitled *Bharat-tirtha*.

Among the many patriotic poems Tagore wrote at this time two particularly stand out since they express especially Tagorean conceptions. Both were translated by Tagore himself into English. The first was '*Chitta jetha bhayshunya uccha jetha shir*'.

> Where the mind is without fear and the head is held high
> Where knowledge is free
> . . . Where the clear stream of reason has not lost its way into the
> dreary desert sands of dead habit
> Where the mind is led forward by thee into over-widening thought
> and action—Into that heaven of freedom, my Father, let my country
> awake.
>
> (*Naibedya*, 1901).[32]

This poem, first published in a journal on 15 May 1901 was written long before the rush of patriotic poems in 1905. Tagore wrote to his friend Jagadish Chandra Bose, the scientist, in March 1901 that he had made it his habit at that time to write 'one poem every day dedicated to Him, who dwells in my mind'.[33] This was one of those poems later collected as *Naibedya* ('Offerings'). To him, it might have been a special one among these daily offerings, for he not only translated it into English but also decorated the manuscript of the poem with a painting when it was published later. It was an expression of one of his recurring themes in his poems and essays, the freedom of the mind.

The second poem that stands in a class apart was to become one of Mahatma Gandhi's favourite songs, *Ekla chalo*:

> If they answer not thy call, walk alone
> . . . Open thy mind and speak out alone
> . . . If they do not hold up the light
> When the night is troubled with storm
> O thou of evil luck,

With the thunder-flame of pain ignite your own heart
And let it burn alone.[34]

This was written in September 1905 at a time when Tagore felt isolated and supportless. His mind was in turmoil caused not only by the partition of Bengal but also by his failure to gain the attention and support of the mainstream nationalist leaders in the anti-partition agitation. The latter's decision to fight British rule with the boycott of British commodities was, in Tagore's opinion, merely negative and inadequate; Tagore advocated a programme of self-empowerment through constructive activities to build a base in popular mind and an alternative to British administration. A few days before he wrote this poem he addressed a meeting in Calcutta Town Hall on 25 August 1905 and read out an essay 'Abastha o Byabastha' ('The Situation and the Remedy').[35] Among his peers who were in the leadership of the anti-partition movement he found no response to his call for his 'constructive' programme. Despite this Tagore did not at that time withdraw himself from the movement. There was, he said, a weakness in the nationalists' mendicancy in the past, but the new agitation to gain the ears of the government was not the path to true national strength for that too was in expectation of a favourable decision from the same government. It will be no exaggeration to say that the then leaders disliked this advice and Tagore was disappointed enough to say that he would walk alone on the path he perceived as right. This is the background to the song Ekla chalo, which demonstrates incidentally, the unity of the whole corpus of Tagore's writings, the inter-connectedness between his socio-political thoughts and his creative writings. Too often these have been separately treated in terms of specializations of literary critics, political historians, biographers, and the like, to the detriment of our appreciation of the evolution of his mind.

CHAPTER FOUR

'The Sage of Santiniketan'
1909–1919

The phase, 1909–1919, in global history was dominated by World War I. Tagore was fortunate that he visited Europe from June to October 1912, well before the outbreak of the World War. Had it been otherwise, the poetry which secured him the Nobel Prize in 1913 would have received little attention. The war of 1914–18 impacted Tagore's mind deeply and in his lecture tours in Japan and the United States in 1916, he began a campaign against the ideology of aggressive nationalism in which he saw the roots of the World War. This did not make him very popular in Japan—she was already an aggressor in Korea which came under her sphere of influence from 1910—or with the United States, where public opinion favoured joining forces with the Allied Powers in the War. That notwithstanding Tagore carried on his campaign and published his critique *Nationalism* (1917).

Tagore's critique of nationalism also alienated many political leaders in India. As we have seen already, he was in particular sceptical of the tactics of individual violence. In 1909 an obscure lawyer, M.K. Gandhi, published a tract entitled *Hind Swaraj*; his position on violent methods, such as the action of Madan Lal Dhingra was similar to, though not the same as, Tagore's. Next year the militant nationalist leader Aurobindo Ghosh sought solace in retreat in Pondicherry. In the following years, Gandhi's passive resistance movement against apartheid in South Africa and the

Champaran Satyagraha (1917) became exemplary instances of non-violent protest movements.

Unlike the anti-partition days, Tagore kept himself aloof from active politics. There is no evidence in his writings that he was jubilant at the revocation of the partition of Bengal by the government; apparently it was a victory of the nationalist agitation, but Tagore had already declared that obtaining a concession from the British government was one thing, and building the nation and working towards self-empowerment was quite another. Tagore did attend Indian National Congress sessions in 1911 (when his song *Jana-gana-mana* was sung) and in 1917. He also wrote against government repression and in defence of Annie Besant and others prosecuted by the government in 1917. But he remained immersed in his literary work, his tasks as the head of the school in Santiniketan, and his numerous lecture engagements at home and abroad.

In the meanwhile another apparent concession from the government was the declaration of a minister in charge of India in England (called the Secretary of State for India) in August 1917: self-governance would be conceded to India in successive stages. That sounded good at that time because in the War the Allies talked a lot about 'self-determination'. Similar noises were heard from a Committee to advise the government on future Indian policy, headed by the Secretary of State for India. The World War ended in November 1918. About three months later a law was made by the British Indian government to enable it to take the strongest possible measures against political agitators and generally to curtail common civil rights. Mahatma Gandhi declared a peaceful agitation against the law (March 1919). To suppress that agitation in Punjab, martial law was declared. Tagore felt compelled to re-enter the political sphere when the government's repression reached an extreme form under the martial law in Punjab.

Tagore tried to mobilize political leaders to protest against the atrocities in Punjab, in particular the Jallianwala Bagh massacre. He failed. He went up to Calcutta from Santiniketan but no support was forthcoming. Then he wrote the justly famous letter to the

Viceroy renouncing his knighthood: 'The time has come, when badges of honour make our shame glaring in their incongruous context of humiliation.'[1] This was a turning point because hereafter Tagore emerged from his self-imposed exile and returned into the public sphere, into national politics. From then Tagore and Gandhi became close friends and adversaries in debate.

Notwithstanding the above developments at the global and national levels, in Tagore's life the decade 1909–19 is important for altogether different reasons. The award of the Nobel Prize in 1913 is commonly held as a central event. But if one considers the role the poet played in various spheres of life and bears in mind the particular conjuncture of events that brought about that award and recalls how many Nobel Prize winners are unremembered in history, it is difficult to deny that that event has been accorded disproportionately high importance. Arguably, in the decade 1909–19, Santiniketan was at the centre of his life. Secondly, in his inner life a totally new phase was signalized by the poems collected in *Gitanjali* (Bengali) and *Balaka*, not to speak of works such as *Gora, Dakghar, Achalayatan* and *Ghare Baire*. Thirdly, the poet known as *Visva-Kabi*, was introduced to the world in reality in this decade through his own translations, imperfect as they are, and his travels through the world. These are the three aspects of his life we should focus upon in this decade.

The Image of Sage

As we have already seen, Santiniketan began as Tagore's school with just five students (1901) and Tagore settled there and brought his wife to her own domain, away from the family seat in Calcutta (1902). He was compelled to sell even his wife's ornaments to pay for the expenses of his school (1902). His service to the National Education movement (from 1905) was only an extension of his own experiments at Santiniketan, like the Vasanta Utsav he instituted there in 1907. This innovation marked the beginnings of a new culture of celebrating the seasons, different from the Hindu cycle of sacred festivals. In the Tagore estates in Patisar he began in 1908 experiments in rural reconstruction which anticipated the future Surul Sriniketan agenda. In 1910 when his son Rathindranath married Pratima Devi, Tagore virtually reconstituted the family he had lost to disease and death. That provided a centre to the Santiniketan community. Incidentally it was the first 'widow marriage' in the Tagore family—perhaps it was possible since Debendranath Tagore was dead. By this time Tagore's ashrams had become a well-known school and his personal charisma began to attract people from afar like William Rothenstein and Ananda Coomaraswamy (visitors in 1911). The Nobel Prize award (1913) turned the trickle of scholarly visitors to Santiniketan into a flood tide. That recognition from abroad induced many in Calcutta to visit the poet in his ashram and this was when at a felicitation meeting he famously spurned praise, because it was from erstwhile detractors (23 November 1913). Tagore as the head of the school at Santiniketan, was awarded a DLitt by the University of Calcutta (December 1913). Perhaps more important from a longer perspective was the visit of M.K. Gandhi and his schoolboys from South Africa in 1914. It was a symbolic assertion of the shared common traits of two great Indian educational thinkers' experiments in schooling. In 1915 Tagore carried his fight for the priority of the mother tongue in education, into enemy territory and spoke to Calcutta citizens of the need to think about the medium of education—it should be Bengali as it was in Santiniketan (December 1915). Yet another front was opened by the sage of Santiniketan when he established a cultural outpost in the Vichitra Club in Calcutta, in his home. In the events at Vichitra, Gandhi, Tilak and Annie Besant were among the spectators—a lesson to parochial Bengalis (September 1917). Santiniketan attracted students from many other parts of the country—for example, Gujarat, Kerala, Punjab, and, of course, the neighbouring provinces—imparting a flavour of the nation as a whole to her culture. In the meanwhile while touring the United States an idea dawned: he wrote to his son from Los Angeles,

Santiniketan must become 'a centre of human studies regardless of nationality' and geography and parochialism.[2] Anyone who has been to Los Angeles or the west coast of the United States would know that the idea was born in an appropriate place. In October 1918 the idea took concrete shape in a conversation with his son Rathindra and friend Charles Andrews: 'Boys from all provinces of India would come together to get an education and culture that is national and at the same time modern . . . Bolpur institution should not be sectarian or Provincial.'[3] In December 1918 the foundation of a building was laid, then named Visva-Bharati Bhavan.[4] At the end of the decade we are looking at, Visva-Bharati university was thus about to be born. The growth of the institution, the evolution of the ashram into Visva-Bharati, is however not central to Tagore's inner life. What he considered central was the idea. The daily life of the community of residents, and above all, the proximity to nature in the life of the ashram mattered deeply to him. This is clear from countless letters of Tagore to his correspondents, specially the teachers of his school.

An important point to bear in mind is that Tagore's image as 'the sage of Santiniketan' was not solely the consequence of his single-minded services to that institution. He was represented in the West as a sage from the East. The translation of his 'spiritual' poems, to the exclusion of his other works and indeed his own choice in translation and self-presentation, constructed an image of a saintly spiritual person who belonged to an ashram, not to the contemporary world.

Several factors went into the making of Tagore's image as a sage, a mystical poet, a man with a spiritual message. One was his withdrawal to Santiniketan from the active public life of Calcutta. Connected with that was the agenda of that ashram and the demands of the role of the head of the institution and a preceptor. (To this day the head of the institution at Santiniketan, now the Vice Chancellor or President, is expected to be a preceptor at certain prayer meetings or assemblies of the university.) Moreover, Tagore's writings in Bengali at this time were heavily redolent of Upanishadic philosophy. His sermons have been collected in not less than seventeen volumes. The poems of *Gitanjali* in Bengali began to be written about this time and, in fact, the sermons from now on often expounded the themes of those verses.

It must be noted here that *Gitanjali* in Bengali is not the same as the more famous English book bearing the same title. About half of the poems in the latter were selected from other books of verse. The predominant note was spiritual, the style that of late medieval mystic poets, and the notion of divinity in the poems was commonly traced to the Upanishads which were a foundational text to the Brahma Samaj. *Gitanjali* in Bengali was published in 1910, to be followed by *Utsarga* ('Dedication'), *Giti-Malya* ('Garland of Songs') and *Gitali* (from gital, i.e. lyrics for song) all published in 1914. All of them formed part of a cycle of lyrics akin to *Gitanjali*. This cycle comes to an end with *Balaka* (1916) which strikes a totally different note, stylistically and thematically. In between 1910 and 1914 Tagore began to translate some of his poems into English; in May 1912 he departed for England, and then the series of events, mentioned earlier, took place, leading to the publication of the translations. Upon the publication of *Gitanjali* in English *The Times Literary Supplement* wrote an ecstatic review: 'As we read his pieces we seem to be reading psalms of a David of our own times'.[5] The rest is history.

Tagore's choice in translating poems with a 'spiritual' message was only one of the reasons for his portrayal as a mystic. There was a natural tendency in the public mind in the West to look for spirituality in the East. It was an old stereotype that many Indians readily accepted. Secondly, the turmoil of World War I from 1914 created a hankering for the peace and calm that mysticism promised. 'The Bengali,' writes Ezra Pound, 'brings to us the pledge of a calm which we need over-much in an age of steel and mechanics. It brings a quiet proclamation of the fellowship between man and the gods, between man and nature.'[6] Moreover, Tagore's first public appearance in the West, in America, focused upon his exposition of religious philosophy. These were his lectures in meetings of the Unitarian Church in Urbana, Illinois, and the Philosophy Club at Harvard University—incidentally the latter performance was witnessed by T.S. Eliot.[7] In the opinion of Krishna Kripalani these first public appearances and the first impression created by *Gitanjali* in English created a lasting impression that Tagore was a religious philosopher. The impression that he was representing Eastern mysticism was precisely the thing his friend Rothenstein feared: 'I was concerned only lest Tagore's saintly looks and the mystical element in his poetry should attract the *schwarmerei* of the sentimentalists who pursue idealists even more hungrily than ideals. Tagore had indeed all the qualities which attract such.' This apprehension recorded by Rothenstein in his memoirs proved to be prophetic.[8] Willy-nilly Tagore became a 'mystic' poet. He became 'an effigy of the sanctimonious moralist' in the West, as Ezra Pound put it in his brutally frank language.[9]

It has been shown convincingly on the basis of research into contemporary journals, newspapers and works of literary criticism that the Western construction of Tagore's works as 'mystical poetry' was tailored to the expectations of his audience there.[10] This was possibly a part of what is now identified, since Edward Said's work on *Orientalism*, as the essentialization of the East in Western perception.[11] Consider, for instance, an American reviewer's impression: 'Of course Tagore is a mystic. He could not be an oriental religious teacher and not be a mystic.'[12] This impression was strengthened by the publication of Kabir in translation by Tagore. This was not unexpected since Tagore's English translation of 1914 carried an 'Introduction' by an English exponent of mysticism, Evelyn Underhill. She suggests that Tagore's mystical genius makes him—as all who read these poems will see—a peculiarly sympathetic interpreter of Kabir's vision.[13] In a review in the *New York Times*, Helen Bullis wrote of 'Tagore as a Mystic' in reviewing this book of translations.[14]

Not all Indians shared this perception of Tagore as 'the mystic'. Lajpat Rai who happened to be in the United States wrote, 'in refutation of More's criticism of Tagore as an effete mystic', in

1917: 'More's condemnation of Tagore's philosophy on the basis of a few lines of verse was unjust.' What is more important, Lajpat Rai argued that what appealed to India was not 'Tagore's mysticism' but his effort to 'show us the way to absorb what is best in the new world without losing what is valuable and priceless in the old.'[15] This is a significant statement from a member of the Indian radical intelligentsia of those times.

It is probable that Tagore, to the extent he wrote in a mystical vein, owed a great deal to Kabir—and this was not unacknowledged by him—but he owed a great deal likewise to many other medieval *sant-kavis*. This included the Sufis, particularly Hafez with whom Rabindranath's father, Debendranath, was quite familiar in the original. Verses by Tulsidas and other *doha* writers were copied by Tagore in his own hand; the manuscript, along with *Gitanjali* poems, was preserved by Tagore and now it is in the Visva-Bharati archives.[16] Tagore had translated a good number of *abhangas* composed by Tukaram in 1877–78, while he was in Ahmedabad and Bombay as a ward of his brother who was in the Bombay Presidency cadre of the ICS. Thus it was a wide spectrum of mystical poetry with which Tagore was acquainted. He evidently drew inspiration from these poets, among them Kabir. In fact, it was not uncommon for poets in earlier times to construct a fictive relationship with a predecessor in a poetic tradition. Imperfect historical awareness of this practice in India has sometimes caused some historians to tie themselves into knots trying to explain anachronisms as a result of a literal interpretation of texts where a 'poet saint' (*sant-kavi*) claims another as a guru. It was, on the part of the poets, an assertion of commonality in ways of thinking, an effort to consciously cultivate commonality with a tradition.

When parallel-hunters point to similarities between Tagore and Kabir or whoever, they sometimes overlook the more important aspect of the matter. Commonalities arise out of the commonly shared cultural archetypes which are part of the common heritage of a people and a civilization. (This would apply on a different scale to the culture of a region and a segment of a language community as well.) In delving into those shared archetypes and symbols, poets remote in not only time and space but also in the domain of sensibilities, create commonalities which we sometimes identify as influence or parallelism. One of Tagore's own statements is quite illuminating, though it was made in a different context, in a letter to an Indian psychoanalyst in 1931:

> If one calls the perceptions of some poets mystical, that is because they have the language to articulate their perceptions—which is what makes them poets. Kabir and other old ascetic poets had this gift of language. But in order fully to understand them, one must to some extent share their feelings. Feeling combined with language creates genius. By language I mean more than words: the language of symbols, of logic, of lines, of gestures, of archetypes, and so on.[17]

While Tagore shared with the medieval mystic poets certain signs and symbols and archetypes, he probably wrote from another domain of literary sensibility, and thus it would be an over-simplification to look for surface likenesses or differences.

Translated into Fame

Tagore appears to be initially rather diffident about publishing in England but after 1913, with the enormous success of *Gitanjali*, he published too much and this required translation into English in a hurry. If one studies his publication history record that impression is unavoidable. Probably he allowed himself to be guided by the business policy of his publishers, Macmillan & Co. of England. His first publication in England was by India Society and it was vetted thoroughly by W.B. Yeats and William Rothenstein. Tagore seems initially to have thought of printing his translation only for private circulation. However, he was encouraged by his friends William Rothenstein, Sturge Moore, and W.B. Yeats to have the manuscript published.

The extent to which Tagore was aided in the task of translation by his English friends is quite a complicated story. It matters because there was a rumour abroad that *Gitanjali* was mainly the work of those friends. Tagore writes to Sturge Moore that at a party at Calcutta Club, Valentine Chirol, an English journalist, told everyone that 'the English *Gitanjali* was practically a production of Yeats'.[18] Tagore was incensed enough to report this rumour to Sir William Rothenstein as well.[19] Rothenstein was of the view that the role of Yeats as editor was valuable but he did not contribute essentially to the text.

> I knew that it was said in India that the success of *Gitanjali* was largely owing to *Yeats' rewriting of Tagore's English. That this is false can easily be proved.* The original MS [manuscript] of *Gitanjali* in English and in Bengali is in my possession. Yeats did here and there suggest slight changes, but the main text was printed as it came from Tagore's hands.[20]

This is an important statement from a direct witness, based on documentary evidence. The rumour, however, persisted.

Yeats believed that Rothenstein 'underestimated the help he and Sturge Moore gave' to Tagore.[21] Tagore became aware of that and wrote to Rothenstein:

> I worked with Yeats and I am sure the magic of his pen helped my English to attain some quality of permanence . . . Please thank Yeats once again on my behalf for the help which he rendered to my poems in their perilous adventure of a foreign reincarnation and assure him that I at least will never underrate the value of his literary comradeship.[22]

This was a generous acknowledgement and it might have satisfied Yeats—who, at any rate, was a great poet himself and editing Tagore's poem was one of the many things he did by the way in his literary career. The two poets appear to be perfectly at peace on this issue. Towards the end of his life Yeats wrote cordially to Tagore that he had no opportunity 'to renew our old friendship' and Tagore equally cordially recalled his 'intense and intimate' acquaintance with Yeats.[23]

Tagore's generous willingness to acknowledge the help he received from Yeats, Rothenstein and Sturge Moore was mainly due to his keen awareness of the fact that his translations left room for improvement. He admitted time and again his inadequacy in terms of contemporary usage in the English language. For instance in 1913 he writes to Ezra Pound: 'I do not know the exact value of your English words. Some of them may have their souls worn out by constant use and some others may not have acquired their souls yet.'[24] Or to Rothenstein: 'Your language is not easy for me to use'; English was, he said, 'a borrowed acquisition, acquired late in my life' and it was 'of an amorphous kind for whose syntax a schoolboy could be reprimanded'.[25] Hence Tagore nursed a diffidence about his translations and several years after the enormous success of *Gitanjali* in English, he wrote to E.J. Thompson who translated some of Tagore's works:

> You know I began to pay court to your language when I was fifty. It was pretty late for me ever to win her heart . . . In my translations I timidly avoid all difficulties, which has the effect of making them smooth and thin. I know I am misrepresenting myself as a poet to the Western readers.[26]

About the same time he writes to poet Sturge Moore: He was unsatisfied with other people's translations, but 'I am convinced that I myself in my translations have done grave injustice to my own work'.[27]

The big question is, if these were Tagore's views about his limitations as a translator, why did he translate his works, especially *Gitanjali*? An easy answer to the question may be that he did it for fame and glory and the Nobel Prize. But that answer is probably wrong. It is a common historical fallacy to attribute motives to results of actions with hindsight. It is impossible that when Tagore began to translate his poems he anticipated the fame and the Nobel Prize that came his way. In fact he says that he gave the translated text to Rothenstein with 'reluctant hesitation' but he was persuaded to publish the text by Rothenstein and Yeats. On second thoughts, he says in 1932, 'I should have felt happy and contented to think that the translations I did were merely for private recreation and never for public display.'[28] In fact there is evidence that he attempted translations well before *Gitanjali*, in early life, and these were discovered and published after his death.[29] He was not unused to writing without any plan to publish.[30]

In any event, Tagore's effort was a cause of some unwelcome experiences. One of them was an incident with Robert Bridges. He seems to be, judging by his letters to Tagore, a person of limited intelligence and unlimited confidence in his superiority. Like many other Poet Laureates of England, he was a second-rate poet who acquired importance by virtue of that position. He writes to Tagore many months after the Nobel award alluding to that: a 'mysterious committee of international judges crowned you with bank notes'; and the letter ends with the warning that Tagore's success should not 'encourage your countrymen inordinately to write their poetry in our foreign language'.[31] In his next letter Bridges refers to the 'silly Komagata Maru affair' in an offensive manner and hoped that Tagore would show his misguided people the truth of British 'principles of liberty'.[32] Soon after he wrote again to request rights to reprint some *Gitanjali* poems for inclusion in an anthology he wished to dedicate to the King. To this letter Tagore responded because Bridges wanted to change the English version by Tagore and Tagore was unwilling. Bridges modestly argued: 'My native Englishing of it [poem] . . . will do great good to your reputation.'[33] But Tagore did not care to better his reputation and remained adamant until Bridges persuaded Yeats to intervene and bring around Tagore and the publisher. The story is instructive from the point of view of the politics of translation as an enterprise and the privileging of native speakers in this process.

That was perhaps one of the reasons why Tagore sometimes regarded his translations as misadventures. He wrote to Rothenstein: 'Sometimes I feel almost ashamed that I should ever go out of my way to court the attention of others', i.e. readers in Europe. After all 'it is never the function of a poet to personally help in the transportation of his poems to an alien form and atmosphere'.[34] As Tagore recalled it, a sequence of events almost accidentally led to the publication of *Gitanjali*. He gave the manuscript to Rothenstein to read. 'The next day you came rushing to me with assurance which I dared not take seriously . . . '[35] Then Rothenstein sent the manuscript to three eminent literary persons, Stopford Brooke, A.C. Bradley and W.B. Yeats. Their highly favourable opinion decided the fate of the manuscript and then Yeats and Tagore worked on it. The other chronicles of events that we have seen are not substantially different.[36]

There is, however, a charge against Tagore, that he 'gave a distorted account of his encounter with Rothenstein in London'; the alleged distortion is in the fact that 'he did downplay his own eagerness for recognition in English'.[37] This is an old problem of historical methodology—attribution of motivation, regardless of the subject's own evidence. Otherwise insignificant, this attribution is an interesting illustration of precisely what Tagore apprehended, that he would be perceived as a man who was trying to 'court the attention of others' abroad. That was a significant phrase about 'the other' of his own civilization. Tagore writes to Rothenstein in 1932, in a rather grand way:

> It was not at all necessary for my own reputation that I should find my place in the history of your literature . . . Latterly I have written and published both prose and poetry in English, mostly translations, unaided by any friendly help, but this again I have done in order to express my ideas, not for gaining any reputation for my mastery in the use of a language which can never be mine.[38]

The question I posed earlier remains: Why did Tagore venture into the exercise of translating his own writings? Arguably, he was lured by an idea, as he often was in his life, which failed to translate into reality as perfectly as he might have wished. This idea was a derivative of his notion of universalism. From the middle of his life that notion became a major component in his philosophy, as we have seen in the first chapter of this book. In relation to the spread of literature across national and cultural boundaries he expounded this idea to the poet Sturge Moore.

> Literature of a country is not chiefly for home consumption. Its value lies in the fact that it is imperatively necessary for the lands where it is foreign. I think it has been good fortune of the West to have the opportunity of absorbing the spirit of the East through the medium of the Bible. It has added to the richness of your life because it is alien to your temperament . . . The Western literature is doing the same with us, bringing into our life elements some of which supplement and some contradict our tendencies. This is what we need.[39]

This was Tagore's theory of universalism applied to literature and hence his inclination towards translation as a means of transmitting elements of culture towards creating a transnational, universal human civilization. He was aware of the fact that translation has its limits and even knowledge of the original language was not enough. 'We cannot but miss a great deal of the purely artistic element in your literature but whatever is broadly human and deeply true can be safely shipped for distant times and remote countries.'[40] This was a part of Tagore's rebellion against nationalist parochialism in literature, his defence of the humanist universalism in literature. On the same lines, Tagore writes to his biographer E.J. Thompson in 1921:

> When a poet's life's works are accepted by his fellow beings it gives him a sense of intellectual companionship with his readers which is precious. But it has a great danger of growing into a temptation—and I believe, consciously and unconsciously, I have been succumbing to it with regard to my Western readers.[41]

To sum up, why Tagore translated so much of his poetry into English is because he valued the intellectual companionship across national boundaries, a part of his universalist philosophy. On the other hand he was aware of the possibility of over-valuing recognition and appreciation in the West. 'What is fatal for our creative workers is to get into the habit of depending upon the approbation of

Western critics . . . The standard of critical judgment must be in the artist's own realizations and in the atmosphere which surrounds them.'[42] Further, there were limits to the art of translation.

As he puts it in a letter to Sturge Moore, translating poems 'is like putting them inside a case which is not their own body'.[43] And again in 1923: 'I know well that poetry in a foreign language never unveils itself to a stranger, their acquaintance must be through a screen.'[44] W.B. Yeats would have endorsed that view because he believed that there was 'entire lack of judgement' on the part of Tagore in publishing too much, too poorly translated.[45] He complained that Tagore 'published intolerable and interminable volumes of mis-translated verse instead of stopping after those first three fine books which Sturge Moore and I corrected.' Tagore did indeed produce a long series of volumes in translation. The first three in English were *Gitanjali* (first published by India Society of London in 1912, and commercially by Macmillan & Co. in 1913), *The Gardener* (1913), and *The Crescent Moon*, London (1913). From 1913 Tagore's books in English were all published by Macmillan of London and the publisher encouraged more works of translation: *Fruit Gathering* (1916), *Lover's Gift and Crossing* (1918), and *Collected Poems and Plays* (1936). All of these were in the nature of anthologies, collecting together poems published in several books of Bengali verse. Apart from these, there were two collections of epigrams and very short verses, possibly inspired by Japanese haiku: *Stray Birds* (1916) and *Fireflies* (1928). While these were all translations, there was one book which contained the only major poem which Tagore wrote in English, entitled *The Child*.[46] Finally, there was one English book which stood in a class of its own: his translation of the medieval mystic saint Kabir's poems.[47] After Tagore's death Krishna Kripalani edited a collection of poems Tagore had translated into English at various times, from the 1890s to the year of his death, left by him unpublished.[48] Tagore's translations from his own works covered a very small fraction of his vast corpus of writings. From the 1920s he ceased to publish such translations.

As we have seen earlier, Tagore faced a dilemma. On the one hand he had doubts about the entire enterprise of translation of creative writings, especially poetry, and also about his own competence as a translator. On the other hand, he nursed a faith in the possibility of creating 'intellectual companionship' across national boundaries, a faith derived from his universalist philosophy. This dilemma remained unresolved. In this day and age of globalization, perhaps the Tagorean dilemma needs to be studied within a broader discourse on the possibilities and limits of cross-cultured communication in the literary idiom.

Ideas in Conflict

The major works in the series of his writings in the decade from 1909 need to be read together for they throw light on one another when considered in juxtaposition. It has been suggested that such juxtaposition enhances our understanding of his works.[49] What are the core ideas which link these works in a web of positions and counter-positions? First, there is the familiar antinomy between modernity and tradition, between India's civilizational identity and challenges to it. That theme dominates *Gora*. It is also in the sub-text of *Ghare Baire*, and it has been suggested by Ashis Nandy that it contains a critique 'by implication, of modernity'.[50] *Achalayatan* is almost didactic in proposing in broader terms a contradiction between forces of change versus the immobility of tradition. In *Visarjan* the same contra-position appears in the ultimate confrontation between the priest who upholds the temple ritual of sacrifice to appease the deity, and the hero who rejects that tradition and pays for his conviction with his life.

Secondly, there is a clash between the Tagorean ideal of humanitarian universalism and the narrow nationalistic focus on the immediate political interests, between the ethical attitude to the issue of ends and means in politics and the 'pragmatic' approach which focuses on the objectives regardless of the means. This is most clearly made visible in *Ghare Baire* in the contrast between Nikhilesh who voices Tagore's anxious critique of nationalist politics of those times—in particular its insensitivity to the Muslim community, the depressed castes like the Namashudras, and the peasant masses— and Sandip who is a very articulate spokesman of militant nationalism rejecting all thoughts of that kind as weakness, impediments to action. In his lectures and essays in *Nationalism* (1917) Tagore fights the same battle and points to the global dimensions of the rise of nationalism, originating in modern Europe's aggrandizing quest for wealth and power, to the detriment of basic human values which lay at the core of human civilization. In *Gora* the focus is on Hindu nationalism and the story is that of the hero's intellectual journey from that point of view to a more inclusive world outlook, looking at humanity beyond the borders of caste, community and race. *Chaturanga* begins with a retrospective vision of the rationalist and humanist values that inspired at one time the Bengal renaissance, in the depiction of the *Jathamosai*, the elderly uncle of the main protagonist in the novel.

The third ideational conflict in the prose narratives by Tagore in this period is that between a 'Hindu' notion of womanhood and the idea of self-empowerment of women in Indian society. It is scarcely there in *Gora* and one has to ferret it out in minor incidents and dialogues. But that is obviously the main theme in *Ghare Baire*. And it is also present in a number of short stories written in the 1910s, particularly 'Strir Patra' ('The Wife's Letter'), published in a literary journal sponsored by Tagore, *Sabuj Patra* ('Green Leaves'). 'The Wife's Letter' is a manifesto of women's fight against a patriarchal society which allows neither agency nor voice to women of the family. In quite a few other stories which came thick and fast in *Sabuj Patra*, there was a female protagonist at the centre of the narrative. One of them refused marriage, another walked out of it, another woman was a heroine in a story of an inter-caste marriage, and there was another story of a husband who has 'sympathy' for his ailing wife but allows her to die of negligence rather than leave the ancestral home to set up a home of their own. It may not be fortuitous that about this time one of Tagore's deepest concerns was the unhappy marriage of his own daughter Mira and his own inability to intervene. He writes to son Rathindra:

> I dealt the first blow in her life—without proper thought and consideration, I arranged her marriage. When I was going through it [i.e. arranging the marriage] I felt a deep anxiety in my mind . . . How can she and her children spend their lives [in her husband's house] amidst insults and antipathy? . . . Her life has already been ruined . . . I am its root cause.[51]

In 1919 the matters came to crisis, Mira left her husband's household, and Tagore advised her not to return there, 'I will not let her burn alive inside a circle of fire.' Whether the marital problems of his daughter, brewing over many years and eventually taken to the court of law in 1928, cast its shadow on Tagore's creative writings is a matter of conjecture, but it is not unlikely. In any event, the conservative critics of Tagore, the defenders of 'Hindu womanhood', provided sufficient provocation to Tagore to think deeply of the gender issue.

These three areas of ideational conflict find reflection in the works we have cited as well as in many others writings. For the present we can look closely at only one or two of his major works to identify the ideas which drove the author's inner life at this time. *Gora* is preeminently one of these major works. It is a novel of epic proportions written over two and a half years and published as a book in 1910. Its moral core is the dilemma of the Indian intelligentsia who were torn between the nationalist aspiration of creating nationhood on the basis of religious revivalism and the more inclusive humanist ideals, between adherence to *shastric* (scriptural) prescriptions and proscriptions on the one hand and freedom from casteist and Brahminic injunctions on the other, between unregenerate Hindu obscurantism and the reformist outlook. The main protagonist Gora, an Irish foundling who was lost in the Mutiny turmoil of 1857, was brought up in an orthodox Hindu family. The irony is that he is quite unaware of his origins and we see him from the beginning of the novel as a stout defender of the Hindu faith, a proponent of all manner of orthodox positions contra Western cultural influence from without as well as reformist urges within his society. The idea of India as a civilization with diverse religions and races and culture within its fold is alien to him. The girl he loves, Sucharita, was brought up as a Brahma and she does not subscribe to his orthodoxy. Gora's relationship with her is therefore clouded by his notion of Hinduism. And Sucharita is constrained by the disapprobation of leaders of Brahma society. A revelation follows: he discovers that he is actually of an alien race and his entire world-outlook collapses like a house of cards. Gora declares at this climacteric moment:

> No, I am not a Hindu . . . From the north to the southern end of India all the temple doors are closed to me . . . I have been liberated today . . . I have become free to reach at a great truth. Today I am an Indian. Within me there is no conflict between the Hindu, Muslim, Christian and such communities. Today I am part of every caste . . . Tell me now how to worship that Maker who is worshipped by Hindus, Muslims, Christians, Brahmos, by all alike—that Maker whose temple door is not closed to any race, any man . . . He who is the maker of India.[52]

Gora and Sucharita thus find a space outside of religious orthodoxy, a space where their lives can unite. Until this resolution is arrived at different ideological positions are articulated and examined. Polemical statements abound but the dramatis personae remain real people. It is a novel about ideas in conflict and often such novels become a collection of stereotypes, of figures that represent ideas. Tagore's art was to write a novel which contained real persons. And yet it was the clearest contraposition of, on the one hand, Hindu religious nationalism and on the other the conceptions of a syncretic Indian civilization and of a 'religion of man' which was higher than all sectarian belief systems. It is true that the resolution of the conflict happens through a kind of deus ex machina, the secret that Gora was an Irish foundling, but that adds to the dramatic impact of the denouement. Thereby hangs a tale. Tagore confided to William Pearson that he spun out the story of Gora to sister Nivedita, viz., Margaret Noble, when she was his guest aboard his boat. Nivedita was of Irish origin. 'She was quite angry at the idea of Gora being rejected even by his disciple Sucharita owing to his foreign origin. You won't find it in *Gora* as it stands now.'[53]

The point Tagore perhaps wanted to make to Nivedita was that the Hindu religion she so enthusiastically espoused did not probably admit her, an alien, with the same enthusiasm. Tagore's target of attack was the failure of a narrowly conceived Hinduism in his times to be inclusive, to be open, and to be true to the spirit of the syncretic Indian civilization.

Unlike the novel *Gora* in *Ghare Baire* ('Home and the World') the message is not near the surface. This is partly because of the style of presentation, a series of first-person narratives by the main protagonists of the novel. Moreover, the fast-moving 'story-line' often serves to take attention away from the inner debate on ideas. In fact Tagore warns us against those who read it for a 'message'. It has been asked, he wrote in 1915, what is the 'purpose of writing the novel *Ghare Baire*. The true answer to that is that the purpose behind writing a novel is to write a novel . . . That is to say, this work is creative, it is not educative'.[54] At the same time, Tagore conceded that 'the author's own times would find expression through the medium of the author. We may not call it purpose, but it can be said that regardless whether the author is conscious of it or not, his times keep working on his mind.' All we can do is to read the signature of the history of those times on Tagore's creative writings, to expect him to give a message is to subordinate the artist in him to the preceptor. That was an adverse commentary from the author himself on the numerous attempts of pundits to 'explicate' *Ghare Baire*.

However, if one were to look beyond the story in this novel towards clues to the signature of the author's times—the historical context—it is possible to identify the clash of ideas which we have noticed in other writings of this phase in Tagore's life. The story revolves around a classic triangle: the introspective idealist Nikhilesh, the unscrupulous pragmatist Sandip who grasps whatever he can, and swaying between these two Bimala who reveres her husband Nikhilesh but willingly surrenders herself into the grasp of Sandip. The historical context, skillfuly woven into the narrative, is part of the story: the militant nationalist drive to acquire funds by all means ranging from blackmail to robbery; the sacrifice of innocent lads misled by the fierce rhetoric of their leaders; the alienation of the Muslim and low-caste peasantry from the cult of nationalism which they perceived as another face of the hegemony of Hindu *bhadralok* who made no effort to reach out to them; the ineffectiveness of an old and effete landlord class in stemming the rot in an exploitative system of which they were a part; the defeat of the high-minded and the well-intentioned in their battle for the mind of the nation. The tragic end of the novel is brought about by several crises which were inevitable in history and in this particular story. Bimala steals a large sum of money from the chest where the family's cash and gold had been safely preserved for generations; she does so to supply funds for a 'national' purpose—or perhaps to satisfy Sandip's greed for money. Sandip makes good his escape when a communal riot breaks out. Nikhilesh goes out, like a knight on the white steed, to quell the communal riot and he is mortally wounded. That is the dramatic end.[55]

What does all this mean? One of several possible answers is that Nikhilesh represented the values Tagore himself upheld, that Sandip stood for the ideas which he battled with from 1908 onwards. Tagore returned to his theme of self-empowerment (*atma-sakti*). The more complex question is the gender issue. *Ghare Baire* was commonly perceived in those times as a critique of the Hindu nationalist conception of femininity, that he had 'insulted Sita' in his depiction of a Hindu wife, Bimala. Tagore's answer to this is worth quoting:

Had it been just a question of aesthetics I would have remained silent, but this is an issue that belongs to the domain of rational discourse. 'If I am asked even though Sandip is a villain, why do you show him insulting Sita [i.e. ideal wife in Hindu imagination]? I will plead the case with reference to Valmiki'. That is to say, literature always depicts the good and the evil.[56]

Tagore added that one could find analogous literary practice from all over the world, but he refrained from doing so because generally it is believed that 'our national literature should be the literature of the frog-in-the-well (*kupa-manduka*).'

These polemics apart, what were the basic ideas at play in this novel? These belonged to two different domains, public and private. In the public domain there was an obvious contraposition of Nikhilesh's conception of patriotism reconcilable with the superior humanist values, as opposed to Sandip's approach which rejects out-of-hand values other than devotion to a most narrowly conceived idea of the nationalist agenda. Thus, for instance, Nikhilesh would abhor infringement on the human rights of his tenants by imposing on them a command to boycott foreign goods, while Sandip would regard that as a sacred duty, an obligation to the mother land. In fact this issue is debated by Nikhilesh with Sandip and he remains unconvinced. The second area where there is a notable difference is the private domain. Nikhilesh believes that his wife has the natural right to be autonomous, to make her own decisions. Sandip believes that it is for him to take over Bimala's mind and she would be his instrument. The interesting outcome of this confrontation between these two conceptions in the public and the private domains is that Nikhilesh fails to win. He is unable to stem the tide of unrest and communal discord among his tenants; he is unable to retain the affection of Bimala which Sandip appears to command with ease. Nikhilesh appears to be so unreal, so bloodless that the bloodshed at the end which leaves him mortally wounded seems to provide evidence one needed that he was really a man of flesh and blood. The detestable Sandip on the other hand wins all the way—including the hand of his 'queen bee' Bimala—until the very end. That leaves us with an interesting puzzle. Did Tagore portray in Nikhilesh his own perception of his failure to convince the public that Tagore's view of politics was the correct one?

Finally, we may turn to some writings in this period of a different order. These are the symbolist plays, *Raja* (1910) or *Arup Ratan* (1920) or *The King of the Dark Chamber* (1914)—several versions of the same theme—and *Achalayatan* (1912) and *Dakghar* (1912). Some of these were staged in England and all of them were staged in Bengal, evoking diverse reactions ranging from derision to intense admiration (for example, the philosopher Ludwig Wittgenstein at Cambridge, wrote his own version of a part of the *King of the Dark Chamber* for the edification of a small group of his followers). *Dakghar*, translated as 'Post Office', was a success when it was staged in the Irish Theatre, the first production of a Tagore play abroad.[57] Perhaps one reason why Tagore focused on this mode of symbolic expression of his ideas was that since his contemporary Maurice Maeterlinck (1862–1949), Nobel Prize winner in 1911, that style was much admired in Europe. And it was indeed a useful artifice to overcome through the use of symbols the linguistic divide to the extent possible. The simplicity of the message of *Dakghar* appealed to all minds regardless of the quality of translation. Among this group of plays *Achalayatan* stands out for its revolutionary message: yield to the urge to evolve, to change, or perish. This play added to the Bengali vocabulary the word *achalayatan*, symbolizing changelessness, an inability to address the demands of the changing spirit of the times. It seems to anticipate the restless spirit of the poem 'Balaka' ('Flying Cranes'); indeed the collection of verses bearing the same title in 1916 is usually regarded as the beginning of a new cycle of poems, different from the 'spiritual' poetry of the sage of Santiniketan. A few lines from the 'Flying Cranes':

Glittering in the evening glow the curving
current of the Jhelum paled in the darkness,
a scimitar, shut in sheath, . . .
On a sudden I heard in the twilight heaven
A flash of sound like lightning
Across the field of space . . . O flying cranes!
Your wings drunk with the wine of the wind,
  leaping high joy's shrill laughter,

awoke waves of wonder in the sky . . .
As this dream of evening dimmed,
there beat aching waves of yearning for the faraway.
O far seeking wings,
a passionate cry broke from all creation's lips,
'Elsewhere, elsewhere, somewhere else.'[58]

That was an ode to the 'faraway', to things beyond the poet's world of the 1910s, a prelude to new directions to which Tagore's mind was destined in the years that followed.

CHAPTER FIVE

New Directions
1919–1929

The decade 1919–29 was marked by two turning points in Tagore's intellectual life: the first was his resigning the knighthood, mentioned in the previous chapter, and the second was the founding of Visva-Bharati. In the history of the freedom struggle the former event marked the point when Tagore burnt his boats—he became a suspect in the eyes of the British police and was under surveillance of informers hereafter; he became quite unwelcome in England, and his publisher Macmillan reports that his book sales there and in North America dropped drastically. In the beginning of the decade the foundation of Visva-Bharati was the fulfilment of Tagore's dream and in the 1920s the institution showed a promise, though the promise remained unfulfilled in later times. The end of the decade was marked by another turning point, the publication of the novel *Sesher Kabita* ('The Farewell Song', 1929), a book of verses, *Mohua* (1929), and a host of poems stylistically novel—all of which were hailed as Tagore's response to new 'modernism'. This decade also saw the publication of three other remarkable works: the plays *Mukta-Dhara* ('Free Current', 1922) and *Rakta-Karabi* ('The Red Oleander', 1926) and the novel *Yogayog* ('Relationships', 1929). In each Tagore explored new directions. In the two plays, the reasons of state and systems of exploitation were counterposed to humanistic values and the emancipation of man from oppression. In the novel *Yogayog* Tagore broke away from the tradition of romantic novel and the mealy-mouthed treatment of gender relationships in Bengali literature since the late nineteenth century. And, finally, in the 1920s, Tagore launched himself into the world of an art new to him and at the age of sixty-nine held the first exhibition of his paintings and sketches in Paris in 1930. On the whole, this decade once again demonstrated Tagore's ability to reinvent his creative self.

The ideal of universalism Tagore had often spoken of earlier would have remained just words if he had not tried the experiment of founding Visva-Bharati (1921). Tagore became a kind of travelling missionary in these years. More than three and half years of this decade were spent travelling abroad—in England, France, the Netherlands, USA, Japan, Sweden, Germany, China, Argentina, Italy, Poland, Greece, Bali and Java. Some of these countries he visited more than once. His object in part was to raise funds for Visva-Bharati and also to mobilize scholars who were willing to support and visit Santiniketan to teach and to make it truly a place where all cultures of the East and West would meet.

Tagore's missions abroad were partly aided by the climate of opinion at this juncture. A spirit of internationalism was abroad since the Versailles Peace Conference (1919) which marked the end of World War I. The newly-founded League of Nations (1919), of which the British Indian government was a member (1920), did not, however, fulfil the expectations created by founders like President Wilson. The positive developments in Asia occurred without its aid, for example, the establishment of the republic in Turkey (1923) by Kamal Ataturk, whom Tagore greatly admired, and the assumption of the leadership of the anti-imperialist struggle in Indonesia by Soekarno (1926). Tagore saw a great deal to be learnt in the development of Russia from the Revolution (1917) to the death of Lenin (1924), but he also nursed a scepticism which was strengthened by his visit to that country in 1930. He was evidently ill-informed about the rise of Mussolini's Fascism in Italy (1922 onwards) and came a cropper in naively showering praise on him during his visit to Italy (May 1926); he recanted after Romain Rolland and others filled him in.

In national politics tumultuous events marked the beginning of this decade. Tagore, for a long time the sage of Santiniketan in his rural retreat, re-entered the national scene after the celebrated renunciation of his knighthood as an act of individual protest against the Jallianwala Bagh massacre (1919). He wrote to the Viceroy a letter which survives as a draft in the Rabindra Bhavan Archives at Santiniketan:

The enormity of the measures taken by the government in Punjab for quelling some local disturbances has, with a rude shock, revealed to our minds the helplessness of our position as British subjects in India . . . [T]he very least I can do for my country is to take all consequences upon myself in giving voice to the protest of the millions of my countrymen, surprised into a dumb anguished terror. The time has come, when badges of honour make our shame glaring in their incongruous context of humiliation, and I for my part wish to stand, shorn of all special distinctions, by the side of my countrymen who, for their so-called insignificance, are liable to suffer a degradation not fit for human beings.[1]

Although Gandhi wrote to some friends that Tagore's renouncing the knighthood was premature, that action drew the two personalities closer to each other. For example, Gandhi obtained Tagore's approval of Hindi being recognized 'as the only possible national language' at the inter-provincial level—provided time was allowed for 'general use as a constant practice', before the adoption of a resolution by the Congress (1921). He obtained Tagore's message on the eve of the launch of the agitation he commanded from April 1919. He did that once again on the occasion of the National Week Conference in Bombay. Andrews was Tagore's emissary at that conference. He invited Tagore to preside over the Gujarat Literary Conference in April 1920.[2] From 1919 to 1922 the Khilafat and Non-cooperation movement brought Gandhi to the forefront of the nationalist struggle and he had the admiration and support of Tagore—indeed the appellation 'Mahatma' was created by Tagore.

The Gandhi–Tagore Debate

Tagore was uncomfortable with some aspects of the movement set in motion by Mahatma Gandhi. First, Tagore felt that an instrumentalist view of satyagraha, the use of it by politicians as a stratagem, a mindless application of it, would reduce it to a mantra—that would only strengthen the existing bigotry and inertia. Secondly, Tagore did not believe that it was right to boycott government schools and colleges until an alternative educational system was available. Tagore had always been the severest critic of the colonial educational system but in the absence of an alternative system open to them, students would eventually return to the colonial institutions. In fact, this did happen, with negligible exceptions where national schools offered an option. Thirdly, Tagore was sceptical of the ritual of burning foreign cloth unless cheaper cloth was made available to the poor; he also questioned the economic rationale of depending on the charkha as the panacea when the issue was to build industry with ability to compete. 'The question of using or refusing cloth of a particular manufacture belongs mainly to economic science', but there was a widespread tendency to use 'the magical formula that foreign cloth is impure' and thus 'economics is bundled out and a fictitious moral doctrine dragged into its place'. Finally, Tagore also raised a question about boycott of foreign goods. How long would it be possible 'to hide ourselves from commerce with the outside world?'[3]

To these questions raised by Tagore in the *Modern Review*, Gandhi's answers, published mainly in *Young India* which he edited, were very confident and precise. In an oft-quoted article he depicted Tagore as 'the Great Sentinel' against bigotry, lethargy, etc. but the poet was ill-informed about the movement Gandhi led, because 'all he knows about the movement is what he has picked up from table talk'. A good deal of what Tagore said, Gandhi believed, was said under 'poetic licence' and not to be taken seriously. Gandhi did not believe that satyagraha had become merely a mantra. He did not believe that students returning to colonial schools proved the incorrectness of this programme. That only proved 'the extent of our degradation'. He also pointed out that he had only recommended spinning for half an hour on the charkha to those who were otherwise employed. And his recommendation of khadi and the charkha was not just an economic message, for 'I do not draw a sharp or any distinction between economics and ethics'. Further, he pointed out that his programme did not stop with charkha, but included a chain of activities for rural reconstruction and cooperation.[4]

Gandhi and Tagore agreed to live with their disagreement on these issues so to speak. Tagore had a deep faith in Gandhi's political sagacity. 'Gandhi's genius is essentially practical, which means his practice is immeasurably superior to his theory,' he said later; as his plans worked out in practice one realized 'the genius of this practical sage whose deeds surpass his words'.[5] Gandhi likewise admired Tagore as a man of ideas. 'The poet lives in a magnificent world of his own creation—his world of ideas.' Gandhi generously allowed for Tagore's individual point of view, for 'our friendship becomes all the richer for our disagreements'.[6]

Despite Gandhi's generosity, Gandhians and nationalist spokesmen in general turned against Tagore and his critique of the Gandhian path in the 1920s. The feeling of revulsion was specially strong in Bengal where Tagore had been, since the Bengal partition, highly regarded for his contribution as a 'swadeshi' poet. For instance, a contemporary Bengali daily in 1928: 'It will not be unjust to say that he is unfit to be a priest in the *yagna* for freedom.' Or in 1925: 'The charkha movement has been revealed to the poet's intelligence as a hoax . . . Only an extraordinary genius can say such an extraordinary thing. The poet's useless labour is sad and pitiful.'[7] Or again a nationalist newspaper in Bombay in 1925: 'The poet is all emotionalism and quite unconvincing to those looking for reasoning.'[8] Some nationalists went so far as to say that Tagore would have been guilty of treason had India been independent.[9]

Arguably, in the 1920s Tagore's attention was focused as much on the Gandhian path as the intractable issue of communalism.

The communal imbroglio became almost an obsession with him from around 1926 when he witnessed a communal riot almost on his doorstep in Calcutta. The failure of an Arya Samaj band to stop playing musical instruments while passing a mosque at the time of prayer on 2 April 1926, led to a riot that caused, according to the Police Commissioner's report, forty-four deaths and injury to 584 people, needing the armed intervention of the Staffordshire Regiment. This was not an isolated event because it was a part of a series of such riots spread over a year at Delhi, Allahabad, Lahore, Panipat, Hyderabad, Bombay, Ahmedabad and some small towns. Tagore wrote a poem burning with anger, condemning 'Dharma moha . . . delusion disguised as faith' and calling for 'the light of knowledge in this benighted land.'[10] And something unthinkable happened when he recommended atheism in his sermon in Santiniketan: 'Straight-forward atheism is preferable to this terrible thing, delusion of religiosity.' This text was never included in his 'Collected Works' by the editors. Whether this was self-censorship or an excess of discretion on the part of his editors is difficult to say.[11]

A Political Suspect

In the documents of the Intelligence Branch of the Government of India in the National Archives at New Delhi there is a report by the director of the Bureau in 1925. Tagore had resigned his knighthood, becoming 'to all intents and purposes a non-cooperator'; not only was he a 'consistent opponent of the government' but his associates like C.F. Andrews, and W.W. Pearson caused suspicion as did some of the nationalist activists employed at Santiniketan. Further cause of the British government's suspicion was the visit of European scholars from Germany and Italy to Santiniketan.[12] Andrews was accused of being 'habitually prone to think poorly of his own countrymen', Pearson had been arrested and deported by the British authorities at Beijing, Rash Behari Bose in Japan was known to be in correspondence with Tagore, Sylvain Levi 'a French Jew of pronounced anarchical leanings', Sten Konow the archaeologist had written 'articles attacking British rule in India', Bhupendra Nath Dutt a visitor to Bolpur, was not only Vivekananda's brother but an associate of Alipore Bomb Case criminals like Barin Ghosh, and so forth. It must be also put on record that to his credit, Lord Lytton, the governor of Bengal from 1922 to 1927, in his comment on the above-mentioned files as the officiating Governor-General of India, said: 'I do not wholly endorse the police opinion of it.' 'Personally acquainted with the institution' at Santiniketan and 'Sir Rabindranath's own influence, aims and ideas', he was wary of basing the government's opinion 'solely upon police reports'. This noting of 18 July 1925 by the officiating Viceroy and, likewise, the favourable report from the director of public instruction, E.F. Oaten (who had been assaulted by Subhas Chandra Bose while he was at Presidency College in 1916), saved Tagore's institution from the government's persecution. But the bottom line for the bureaucracy was that as advised by the police and intelligence department, surveillance and caution in respect of Santiniketan was necessary 'owing to the anti-British views of the professors there'. And Tagore himself was not above suspicion after the renunciation of his knighthood. His letters were opened by the police and an informer was placed among the students to report on him and his institution. The Home Secretary of the Government of India believed that there was 'a possibility of the institution becoming a breeding place of sedition' and therefore patronage and financial donation to it must be discouraged.

This was communicated through the India Office in London to the British officials in New York and that was enough to stop financial aid to Tagore's institution. Thus, the efforts of Tagore to mobilize funds for his Santiniketan in the United States were destined to fail due to these secret reports on him. Recently it has been found that the Department of State in the United States was warned by the British government against Tagore since he was allegedly involved with Indian revolutionaries in the United

States.[13] Tagore eventually got to know of some aspects of the surveillance on him. For instance, he wrote from France to an Indian correspondent Sudhindranath Datta, in England in 1930, in a jocular vein: 'I hope this letter reaches your hands. If it does not, then my message to the person who handles it is that if I have in mind plans of torpedoing the British Empire, I would not be so stupid as to put it down in this letter.'[14]

When Tagore wrote thus there was just a suspicion that the police opened letters coming to Santiniketan. Now we have decisive evidence from the West Bengal State Archives. In exercise of the powers given to the Governor of Bengal under the Post Office Act of 1898, in March 1931 'interception of all foreign postal articles' addressed to 'any inmate of Santiniketan' was legalized; all such articles were to be handed over to the Intelligence Branch, it was officially notified.[15] In the government files we also have translations of Tagore's lectures and even his poems so as to detect any evidence of sedition.[16] The suspicion that the British authorities prevented foreign donors from donating funds to Visva-Bharati has now been confirmed by recently disclosed documents which show that the India Office authorities in London advised their consular establishment to make sure of that.[17]

Tagore's contacts abroad were, of course, carefully scrutinized by the police. An interesting Scotland Yard report dated 17 September 1941 notes the names of those who attended the memorial meeting in London after Tagore's death. Among these 'suspects' were E.M. Forster, E.J. Thompson, V.K. Krishna Menon, K.S. Shelvankar, P.N. Haksar and the Dean of Canterbury.[18] Some European scholars, mainly Jews from Germany, were denied permission to enter India to teach at Santiniketan. A number of Batavian students were denied visas when they wanted to study in Santiniketan in 1933; not only nationalist terrorists but communists were suspected to be in that place.[19] The archival data also throw light on the methods of the police. For instance in 1934 the divisional head of the police department suggests: 'It should be arranged if possible to introduce a lady student and also a boy student to furnish information' about Santiniketan to the police.[20]

Tagore, the Traveller

In the decade beginning 1919 Tagore spent altogether about three and a half years travelling abroad. He travelled a good deal because international peace in the inter-war period made travel possible; the two World Wars stopped travels of the kind Tagore undertook. This travel was in part because his fame after the Nobel Prize brought him numerous invitations. But, above all, it was because of Tagore's restless spirit, a matter of his inner life. He sought refuge in nomadism in 1920–21, 1922, twice in 1924, twice in 1926, and in 1929. In a letter to E.J. Thompson in 1921 he wrote:

All along my literary career I have run against the taste of my countrymen, at least the vocal portion of my province [i.e. Bengal]. It has hardly been pleasant for me, but it has had the effect of making me reconciled to my mental loneliness. In the West—for some little while in England and lately in the continental countries of Europe—the recognition which I met with came to me with a shock of surprise. When a poet's life's works are accepted by his fellow beings it gives him a sense of intellectual companionship with his readers which is precious.[21]

This is partly what drew Tagore to the West, but that was probably not a great reason to him. He adds after those words that appreciation and accolades in the West also constituted

a great danger of growing into a temptation . . . reputation is the greatest bondage for an artist. I want to emancipate my mind from its grasp not only for the sake of my art, but for the higher purposes of life, for the dignity of soul. What an immense amount of unreality there is in literary reputation, and I am longing—even while appreciating like a buffalo the luxury of its mud bath—to come out of it as a *sanyasi*, naked and aloof . . . I am looking back to those days of my youth when I had easy access into the heart of the universe—and I believe shall yet again recover my place there when I am able to sever my mind from the attraction of the literary world which with its offer of rewards tries to standardize creative visions according to criterions [sic] distractingly varied and variable.[22]

This long extract from his letter illustrates vividly the complexity of Tagore's mind—and it also incidentally illuminates his ambiguous relationship with his audience in the West. Tagore sallied forth many times in the 1920s to meet that audience. To chronicle his triumphal march in Europe and America will be pointless and boring. It may be more useful to look at just one series of such visits, those to the United States. Tagore went to the USA thrice about this time: in 1920–21, in 1929, and in 1930.

He had, of course, been there earlier. Rabindranath's first visit to the United States was in November 1912 when he was yet to attain Nobel fame. *Gitanjali* was published on 1 November 1912 in London and appreciation in English intellectual circles was instant. In the United States Ezra Pound introduced Tagore's work to Harriet Monroe who published it in the journal *Poetry* and invited Tagore to lecture in Chicago.[23] There was also an invitation from Professor Woods to lecture at Harvard University in January 1913. The Harvard lectures later formed a part of the book *Sadhana*.[24] On the whole, Tagore's first visit was a quiet affair though he made contacts with intellectual circles. Tagore's second visit from September 1916 to January 1917 was a grand tour since he was already famous as the first Asian recipient of the Nobel Prize. A lecture tour was organized by a professional agent; Tagore spoke in twenty-five major cities, and he visited the west coast for the first time.[25] When he was in California he conceived the idea of a cultural centre in India which would push intellectual and creative work 'beyond the limits of nation.' This statement in a letter to his son Rathindra contained the seed that was later to develop into Visva-Bharati.[26] Reportedly, he was paid high fees for his lectures, but he asked his agent to cancel the last three months of this tour.

Tagore's third visit (November 1920 to March 1921) was not a success since his recent statements condemning nationalism in the West and European hegemony in the world created an adverse reaction in America, which was understandable in the context of the role of United States in the World War which had just ended. Nor did Tagore succeed in raising funds for his university. In 1929 Tagore's brief visit through the west coast of United States was inconsequential. He was in transit from Canada to Japan and nothing of intellectual significance occurred during this trip except for Tagore's critical press statements on the recently published book of Katherine Mayo on the woeful status of women in India.

It was the fifth and last trip made by Tagore in 1930 which was most successful. President Hoover invited him to the White House, popular historian Will Durant introduced Tagore at a Broadway Theatre special performance in his honour, eminent art historian Ananda Coomaraswamy curated an exhibition of Tagore's paintings in New York, he was feted with Franklin Roosevelt and recent Nobel Prize winner Sinclair Lewis among others at celebrity dinners, and so on. His image in the United States was also enhanced by the eminence of his intellectual contacts in Europe, such as Einstein, Bernard Shaw, Romain Rolland, André Gide, et al. On the other hand the fact that Tagore continued to harp on the evils of aggressive nationalism in the West and the subordination of the people in Asia and Africa did not help to endear him to the Western public. There was also a strong reaction among émigrés in America against the approbation Tagore had expressed after his recent visit to the USSR.

On the whole, what was the outcome of these experiences of the poet? It has often been said that Tagore's main objective was to raise funds for his institution. While initially that might have been a factor in his acceptance of invitations to visit, it would be arguably a mistake to look upon that as his main aim. Several times Tagore declined invitations or cancelled lecture tours as, for example, three months of the 1917 tour arranged by his agent. Actually Tagore showed a strong cultural distaste when confronted with the prospect of being, as he put it in a letter to Harriet Monroe, 'a show lion in a circus.'[27] He could not give up his creed, despite its poor reception in the West or in Japan, that aggrandizing nationalism was an evil that brought about the World War and the exploitation of poorer countries by the rich nations. In one of his last lectures in the United States in 1930 he said, addressing his American audience, 'a great portion of the world suffers from your civilization.'[28] At the same time, Tagore was convinced of the need to establish dialogue between civilizations.

A Significant Relationship

Woman, thou hast made my days of exile tender with beauty,
And hast accepted me to thy nearness with a simple grace
that is like the smile with which the unknown star welcomed me
when I stood alone at the balcony and gazed upon the southern
night.[29]

The 'southern night' is the night of the southern hemisphere which Tagore visited in 1924, and the woman thus addressed is Victoria Ocampo, his hostess in Argentina. The verse collection *Purabi* was dedicated to her; she became a few years later the sponsor of Tagore's first painting exhibition in Paris, and she was in touch with him till his death through a series of very warm letters between them. The whiff of a probable romantic involvement, always of interest to external observers, has been often detected in this relationship. That remains a matter of speculation. However, the poems which were written about this time and collected in *Purabi* suggest a renewed engagement in this-worldly human relationship, as distinct from the other-worldly concerns which appeared to be uppermost in the poet's mind from the *Gitanjali* series onwards. There is a surge of romantic poems at this time.

Before this day ends, let my wish be granted,
Let us for the last time go out together to pick the flowers of
spring
Many springs will visit your garden, I want just one.[30]

'Forget you? Never!' I had said when, on
Tear's brink, your eyes, wordless, held my face.

. . . it was only because you came that my life was filled
with harvest of songs . . .
The light in your eyes stole out of sun-beams.
the secret in their core and made music of it all.[31]

The return to the theme of love is sometimes attributed to the
appearance of Victoria—called 'Vijaya' by Tagore in his poem—in
the poet's life for a brief while. And letters to her bear a portentous
message as well. In the last letter to 'Dear Vijaya' about a year
before his death, Tagore wrote: 'Often [there] comes to my mind
the picture of that river-side home [Miralrio, on River Plate, where
Ocampo put him up] and the regret that in my absent-minded
foolishness I failed to accept fully the precious gift offered to me.
However, the time favoured by destiny is passed and it will never
return.'[32] Earlier Tagore wrote: 'Your nearness which once was so
untrammeled and close . . . has receded into a hopeless distance.'[33]
There are many letters from Rabindranath to Victoria in this vein,
usually ending with *bhalobasa* (love) to Victoria.[34]

At the same time, the impression is unavoidable that the offer
of *bhalobasa* notwithstanding, Tagore is more in love with the
memory of it. Immediately after leaving Victoria, Tagore writes
to her from the ship and it appears to be the offer of 'friendship'
and no more than that.

> I have lost most of my friends because they asked me for themselves,
> and when I said I was not free to offer away myself—they thought I
> was proud . . . I always feel nervous whenever a new gift of friendship
> comes in my way. But I accept my destiny and if you also have the
> courage fully to accept it we shall ever remain friends.[35]

Further,

> I have often said to you that I am not free to give up my freedom—for
> this freedom is claimed by my Master for his own service I
> tell you all this because I know you love me. I trust my providence.
> I feel certain—and I say this in all humility—that he has chosen
> me for some special mission of his own and not merely for the
> purpose of linking the endless chain of generation.[36]

The notion that ordinary mortals are for procreation, while his is the task of creation does require, Tagore perceived, that he should declare his humility. At any rate, this was the reason why Tagore thought that all he could offer was friendship. That was in 1925 a few days after saying goodbye to her. The thoughts of what might have been and nostalgia for his brief 'easeful captivity' loom large in Tagore's letters only a decade later. After their meeting in Paris in 1930, Tagore writes just a thank-you letter to Ocampo who sponsored Tagore's first painting exhibition.[37] In 1934 he writes to her that he had lost her address![38] And he promises to make her comfortable if she visits India. In the late 1930s, however, nostalgia for those days with Victoria pervades his letters. He recalled, in elusive language, 'the paths that accidentally had reached some preciousness', and regrets that though 'the heart longs to own it back', it was lost for ever.[39] And again in July 1940, he looks back at 'the memory of happier days the value of which enhances with time'.[40] A few weeks before his death Tagore wrote a poem to Victoria recalling that 'love from another land', 'the eyes which spoke, though she knew not the words'.[41]

Another Window into Tagore's Inner Life

In writing this narrative we have depended mainly upon Tagore's own self-reflective statements, particularly in his letters. From about 1913, i.e. the award of the Nobel Prize, the number of his correspondents increased rapidly. In the 1920s and 1930s Tagore's letters form virtually the only source because his reminiscences cover only the early part of his life. Tagore had always been aware that the letters he wrote to persons close to him were important in his inner life.

Of the great gifts we get in this world, a letter, an ordinary letter, is an extraordinary gift . . . What we gain by seeing a man, by talking to him, is different from what we gain of his personality through his letters . . . what is said in conversation is more than what is expressed in letters, and likewise what is written is more than what conversation permits. Both have an incompleteness and only when we put them together these complement each other.[42]

And again on how he could fully express himself in his letters:

The range of thoughts I have expressed in my letters . . . was never reflected in any of my other writings. All of this I cannot give to the readers in my published writings. When I consider the readers who do not know me at all and would not try to respect and grasp what I say, readers who would not even make an honest effort to understand me, readers who would not trust and accept me as I am . . . then my thoughts do not find easy expression in language and what finds expression is often artificially dressed up.[43]

To this indefatigable writer of letters all those letters mattered. He was given to writing letters which were often intended for readers other than the person to whom it was addressed. Some of these are essays pretending to be letters. Such for instance were many of his letters to his friend C.F. Andrews, letters which were promptly published in *The Modern Review* and other literary journals. And, on the other hand, there were numerous letters which throw an intimate light on Tagore's private world. Since Tagore's death in 1941 the enormous corpus of his correspondence has been available to researchers. Some bits and pieces have been printed in Bengali literary periodicals and in the series published by Visva-Bharati (less than twenty slim volumes in the course of the last sixty years). A lot remains unpublished and unseen. Tagore's correspondence in English language has received even less attention. His correspondence with William Rothenstein was published in Mary Lago's *Imperfect Encounter* [44] and his letters to Elmhirst;[45] recently I was able to put together the Tagore–Gandhi correspondence from 1915 to 1941.[46] The best collection of letters till now is Dutta and Robinson, *Selected Letters of Rabindranath Tagore* (1997). But the greater part of the wealth of information and insights into his life in Tagore's correspondence has not been accessible to readers.

Considered as a historical source, Tagore's correspondence in the 1920s reveals some things which are new in his inner life. A new interest he developed late in life was his passion for painting, which was almost a secret he carefully kept out of the view of the public. In 1893 he wrote to his niece Indira about his secret ambition to be a painter.

> I have to make a confession, casting off a sense of shame: the art of painting has always attracted me, I have eyed it like a disappointed lover—but I have no more hopes, the time has gone when I could learn the art. Like the other Muses to gain the favours of that art is not easy . . . Perhaps I should be content with the Muse of Poetry, perhaps she is the one who has favoured me most—she has been my companion from my childhood.[47]

Tagore's flirtations with graphic art took the form of pen and ink sketches and doodles on his manuscripts for the greater part of his life. Perhaps his interest was also reflected in his involvement in and active patronage of the art school in Santiniketan and his intimate interaction with artists like his nephew Abanindranath Tagore and Gaganendranath Tagore as well as Nandalal Bose, Mukul Dey and other practising artists. He writes to Gaganendranath in 1928 that he was rather worried about possible adverse criticism if he were to appear in public as a painter.[48] It is possible that in August 1928 when Tagore spent over three weeks as the guest of Mukul Dey, who became principal of the Government School of Art in Calcutta, Tagore acquired some preliminary acquaintance with the practitioners' techniques.[49] In the middle of 1928 Tagore suddenly writes to various correspondents that he was into painting, a new phase in his artistic evolution. He wrote to Gaganendranath, poet Sudhindranath Datta, his admirer Nirmal Kumari Mahalanobis, and others of his new adventure. He found a kind of freedom in the graphic arts after his engagement with words.[50] Writing letters and making a picture, he says, are similar activities.[51]

> I am ensnared by the mystery of lines. The Muse of poetry has abandoned me since I favoured this new and untimely affair of

mine with another art . . . When I write poems the theme is clear
in my mind right at the beginning . . . In my efforts in painting
the process is just the opposite—the lines come from the tip of
my [sketching] pen, and gradually as the picture forms the theme
reaches my mind. The mind is moved by the mystery of creating
forms . . . The graphic art has captured my mind. I cannot escape
from its snare. I find time and again new aspects of that art. There
is no end to this mystery.[52]

These letters from Tagore suggest that he found an intellectual
pleasure in sketching and painting. What was their worth as works
of art?

A Debut at Seventy

There is no doubt that Tagore was so diffident about his works
of art that he resolved not to exhibit his pictures till 1930. It is
possible that there was a reflection of his innermost emotions in
his paintings—and that was something he refrained from displaying
in public. 'I have no wish to acquaint the people of my province
[sic] with my work as an artist . . . Alive or dead I have no desire
to make this creation of mine public here. My pictures will not be
allowed to commit the same offence as my other creations.'[53] That
was Tagore's letter to Suniti Kumar Chatterji in 1929. However,
it appears that many artists associated with Santiniketan expressed
their appreciation of whatever they saw of Tagore's paintings and
so did some foreign artists visiting Tagore.[54]

And Tagore sought the opinion of William Rothenstein: 'I have
suddenly been seized with the mania of producing picture. The
praise they had won from our own circle of artists I did not take
at all seriously', but there were others outside the circle who also
liked those paintings, Tagore wrote. 'I still feel misgivings and I
want your advice. They [the paintings] certainly possess psychological
interest, being products of untutored fingers and untrained mind.
I am sure they do not represent what they call Indian Art . . .'[55]

It so happened that Rothenstein was either unwilling or unable to come to see Tagore's paintings at a place near Nice in France. But Tagore's friend in Argentina, Victoria Ocampo, was an enthusiast who did not wait for certificates from a second-rank painter in England, and she arranged an exhibition in Paris.

Actually, it is a little embarrassing to see, in contrast to Ocampo's confidence, Tagore's diffidence and his anxiety to collect certificates of appreciation from acquaintances in Europe at this time. It was true that he had had little appreciation of his art in his own country—but did that justify his anxiety for European appreciation and his low evaluation of response in India? For instance, this letter to Sudhindranath Datta from Tagore in France in 1930:

> There is a German gentleman here with his wife—he is a diplomat. Seeing my paintings he became really excited and said I must show them in Berlin— 'absolutely'! I am hoping they will attract the attention of connoisseurs. I vow not to take them back to my motherland: no more of this crude handling by unsuitable and unworthy fellows.[56]

Possibly Tagore was deeply disappointed by the adverse remarks on his pictures, whatever was known of them in India, and he was unable to rise above that on this particular occasion when what was involved was the youngest and the most vulnerable of the projects in his life. Further, Tagore was aware that he had cut himself off entirely from the then dominant 'Indian art' school. As he wrote to Rothenstein, he was an intruder in the Indian art world. 'With the ruthless freedom of an invader, I have been playing havoc in the complacent and stagnant world of Indian art and my people are puzzled for they do not know what judgement to pronounce upon my pictures.'[57] Some of these judgements, towards the end of his life, were pleasing to him. For instance, he thanks the painter Jamini Kanta Roy in 1941 for his appreciation of Tagore's paintings.[58] But, by and large, Tagore was apprehensive of and indeed somewhat condescending to Indian art connoisseurs because he feared that they did not understand his approach in art.

In Europe he was certain of appreciation after a series of exhibitions in 1930 in Paris and almost a dozen other European cities. Contemporary critics found in Tagore's pictures, when they were exhibited in Gallerie Pigalle in Paris in May 1930, much to praise. A critic in Paris looked upon him as a surrealist, another in Birmingham fancied he saw in those paintings an 'oriental' sense of pattern and rhythm, a third in Berlin saw parallels with German Expressionists and artists like Emil Nolde and Paul Klee.[59] These critics as well as Ananda Coomaraswamy, in the introduction he wrote for the exhibition in Boston, emphasized the quality of 'modern primitive art' in Tagore's paintings. Some recent critics have argued the opposite and attribute to Tagore sophistication and familiarity with the latest Western art forms. In fact in 1922 Tagore sponsored an exhibition of contemporary European arts, particularly the work of German artists, in the annual exhibition of the Indian Society of Oriental Art.[60] Whatever might have been the affinities with European school which contemporary critics attributed to him, there is no doubt that he was not unfamiliar with modern European art and his exhibitions secured for him critical acclaim—at least for the time being.

Tagore's Theory of Art

It is important to appreciate the fact that in his paintings in the 1920s Tagore was not only venturing into a new medium, but also deliberately departing from the path hitherto followed by most contemporary Indian artists. Thus his was indeed an adventure towards a new direction. Tagore made a departure on at least two levels. First, he criticized and broke away from the school of 'Oriental' art, then dominant in India. Second, he developed a theory of art on new aesthetic postulates. As regards the first, evidence has been noted by art historians in recent times. In the 1920s he was sceptical of Oriental art which at one time received his patronage in the person of Abanindranath Tagore and his followers; he now said that artists must look beyond the replication of Ajanta murals or

Mughal miniatures. In 1929 he was decisively of the opinion that a young artist must look towards Western art, without however, losing Indian individuality.[61] Earlier, in 1926, he delivered a tirade against 'Indian Art' in a lecture in Dhaka, East Bengal. His critical attitude to art that subsisted on the past and appealed to the 'national' imagination was, one can surmise, connected with his critique of nationalism from 1917. Why should art remain only national, and not universal? This approach in the 1920s was new and far from being popular with artists of the Bengal School. Incidentally, Tagore seems to be aware of a certain defect in his colour vision when he writes to Amiya Chakravarty, 'I do not see all colours with the same intensity, I am partial to some, who can say why?'[62] At the end of the day, Tagore was reconciled to that. He was content as an artist with the thought that, as he wrote to Jamini Roy shortly before his death, after all a full life demands that man uses all the sensory organs given to him.[63]

Tagore wrote a good deal on what we may call his theory of Art, more particularly painting: 'What is Art', a chapter in the book *Personality* (1917); 'Construction versus Creation', an Address to the Gujarati Literary Conference (1920); 'Religion of an Artist' (in various versions in 1924, 1926, 1936); 'The Meaning of Art' (1926), a lecture in Dhaka University; and a series of brief essays on 'My Pictures' (1930). The latter set of essays is more relevant for this biography, than the other writings which are generalized statements. In 1930 Tagore writes an introductory note for the exhibition of his paintings in Boston, curated by Ananda Coomaraswamy, 'People often ask me about the meaning of my pictures. I remain silent even as my pictures are. It is for them to express and not to explain. They have nothing ulterior behind their own appearance for thoughts to explore and words to describe . . .'[64] This was almost a rebuke to any attempt to offer explanations theoretically, for 'It is enough that a flower exists as a flower'. About this time in 1930 Tagore wrote two other brief essays by way of introducing his paintings: 'There is one thing common to all arts . . . the principle of rhythm.' 'My pictures are my versification, in lines. If by chance they are entitled to claim recognition, it must be primarily for some rhythmic significance of forms which is ultimate and not for any interpretation of an idea or representation of a fact.'[65] Tagore insisted that the sole inspiration behind the pictures was 'pleasure in harmonious combination of lines and colours'. And he also writes that 'the scattered corrections and scratches in my manuscript cause me annoyance' and therefore he tried to bring the scratches on those pages 'in a rhythmic relationship and transform accumulation into adornment. This has been my unconscious training in drawing'.[66] From that originated an interest 'how lines find their life and character', and how there emerged 'apparitions of non-deliberate origin', or perhaps 'a probable animal that had unaccountably missed its chance of existence'.

While this was his simple confession in respect of his paintings— he might have been persuaded by his appreciative critics to believe otherwise—Tagore had also produced an elaborate credo in the other writings mentioned above. We need not in this biography go into the details of his theory. He made three basic points, often re-stated in different beautiful phrases and metaphors. First, art 'has come out of some impulse of expression, which is the impulse of our being itself'—it has no other purpose. Unlike animals, man has 'a fund of emotional energy which is not all occupied with his self-preservation. This surplus seeks its outlet in the creation of Art, for Man's civilization is built upon his surplus'.[67] Secondly, Tagore tried to define time and again the act of creation in art. 'Creation is the revelation of truth through the rhythm of forms'—and we have seen earlier that to him 'rhythm' is the common element in all arts from literature to painting. 'Creation' is distinguished from 'construction' which is always 'for a purpose, it expresses wants' while 'creation is for itself, it expresses our very being'. Construction caters to necessities; creation belongs to the domain of the superfluous and unnecessary from the material point of view. And creation reveals a truth: 'What is the truth of the world? Its truth is not the mass of materials, but their universal relatedness.'[68] Thirdly, apart from these general propositions, in the world of painting Tagore made an important point in terms of the practice.

Art is not a gorgeous sepulchre immemorially brooding over a lonely eternity of vanished years. It belongs to the procession of life . . . Art represents the inexhaustible magnificence of creative spirit . . . I strongly urge our artists vehemently to deny their obligation carefully to produce something that can be labelled as Indian art according to some old world mannerism.

There was a time when 'human races lived in comparative segregation' and thus art settled into narrow grooves of certain traditions, but in modern times artists should have 'greater power of receptivity' to the world at large and not get 'browbeaten into conformity with a rhetoric manufactured by those who are not in the secret of the subtle mysteries of creation'.[69] This essay reads like a manifesto announcing the liberation of the artists. Indeed, Mulk Raj Anand saw it in this light when issuing the essay as a tract years later. It was perhaps a prelude to Tagore's coup in 1930, the exhibition in Paris and the triumphal march of his painting exhibition through Europe and North America.

It is given to very few to enter a new area of creative work at the age of seventy. Tagore succeeded against heavy odds. His attitude to the new art he took up was almost like that of a mother towards the most vulnerable of her children. He jealously defended it and mistrusted Indian response to his art almost till the end. India would have to wait for a later generation of artists and critics to respond adequately to the Tagorean intervention in Indian art history.

Santiniketan and Creative Writings in the 1920s

If one looks at Tagore's engagement in the 1920s in debates with Gandhi, his travels abroad for one third of the decade, his flirtation with art, and a romantic involvement, was there much space left for his creative work? A close observer as a student and teacher at Santiniketan, and a relative by marriage, Krishna Kripalani, did not think so. From the early 1920s, according to him, 'the poet was losing to the prophet, the singer to the preacher' and Tagore's efforts to preach all over the world the message of international harmony was at the cost of 'his spiritual and creative progress . . . Something was missing in his later works, that rare something which comes from exclusive devotion to one's art, from ceaseless striving for perfection, something that cannot be defined and categorized'.[70] As regards Tagore's image as a prophet there is a delightfully mischievous comment of Jacob Epstein (1880–1959), the British sculptor who made a famous bust of the poet: Tagore, he perceived, was 'conducted about as a holy man . . . aloof, dignified and cold', who 'inspired in his followers awe and a craven obedience. . . It has been remarked that my bust of him rests upon the beard, an unconscious piece of symbolism'.[71]

However, it is not entirely true that the prophet prevailed over the author in Tagore. In *Lipika* (1922) a new genre of 'prose-poems' was opened up while *Mukta-Dhara* (1922) continued the Tagorean type of dramatic symbolism. *Purabi* (1925) struck a new note of romanticism, inspired by Victoria Ocampo. After fussing over the manuscript for three years Tagore published *Rakta-Karabi* (1926) along with *Natir Puja* (1926). In 1927 he began to write the massive novel entitled *Tin Purush*, to be published later as *Yogayog* (1929). In the last years of the decade he wrote the poems of *Mohua* (1929) and surprised everyone with a novel in the 'modernist' style, *Sesher Kabita* (1929).

Moreover, these were the years when the idea of Visva-Bharati crystallized into an institutional form. In December 1921 the institution was formally established, and the land and properties at Santiniketan as well as copyright and royalties of all of Tagore's books in Bengali were transferred to it. The old and new members of the faculty Tagore gathered included an expert in music from Maharashtra; in dance from Manipur; in Sanskrit from Banaras; in painting from the Bengal School, etc.[72] In the 1920s the effort by Tagore to build bridges between India and the world is described by a contemporary observer who taught in Santiniketan.

Besides the three remarkable Englishmen, Andrews, Pearson and Elmhirst, there was the French savant Sylvain Levi and his wife.

He was soon followed by another eminent Orientalist, Professor Moritz Winternitz of the German University in Prague and later by Professor V. Lesny of the Charles University. Among other distinguished visiting scholars may be mentioned Stella Kramrisch, art historian and critic (later on the staff of the Universities of Calcutta and Pennsylvania), F. Benoit, a French-Swiss linguist, L. Bogdanov, a Russian scholar of Persian and Pehlevi, Arthur Geddes from Scotland, Stanley Jones and Miss Gretchen Green from the United States, and Miss S. Flaum, a Jewish lady who had graduated from the University of Columbia.[73]

Finally, the 1920s witnessed the beginning of the rural reconstruction and educational initiative at Sriniketan, which was then called simply by the village name Surul. In September 1921 Leonard Elmhirst joined Tagore with a considerable fund donated by his future wife, Dorothy Whitney Straight. He writes in his reminiscences: 'Early in January 1922 Tagore sent for me: "Stop your Bengali lessons . . . How soon can you . . . move to Surul?" Three weeks later, we loaded our Ford lorry with cooking pots and set off for Surul . . .' In March 1922 Tagore wrote to Elmhirst: 'Everyday I am getting more and more envious of your Swaraj at Surul . . . Plato had no place for poets in his republic. I wish I were young enough to be able to join you . . .'[74] With a small band of helpers Elmhirst began the work that ultimately led to the development of Sriniketan.[75]

These varied experiences and especially his international contacts fed the mind which created some of the most innovative writings of Tagore in *Mukta-Dhara*, *Rakta-Karabi*, *Yogayog*, and *Sesher Kabita*.

The Monster Machine: 'Free Current'

In 1922 Tagore wrote a play, *Mukta-Dhara*, which demands our attention more than many of his others. This play has been singled out here for it echoes and anticipates many of the vital issues which came to the surface in intellectual discourse in the future. First, a central issue in the play is the dichotomy between environmental concerns and the political economic agenda of the state regarding exploitation of nature. Second, it touches upon the antinomy between machine and man, or so to speak, the hegemony of mechanization and the human values. Third, the subtext of the play echoes the Gandhian agenda of non-violent non-cooperation in its depiction of the resistance to the ruler.

The story in this play is the simplest possible. Mukta-Dhara, a mountain spring, is the source of a river and a huge dam has been constructed by the great engineer (*yantraraj*) Vibhuti to divert water away from Sivatarai to another country which rules over it, Uttarakut. It is to the advantage of the king of Uttarakut to control the water that feeds cultivation in Sivatarai, hence he and his people are, in the opening scene, celebrating the creation of the dam. In the meanwhile the subjects of the king in Sivatarai face famine due to lack of water. However, the crown prince of Uttarakut, Abhijit, stumbles on the fact that he was actually not born into the royal family but a foundling who was found near the stream Mukta-Dhara. Abhijit thus identifies himself with the mountain spring that the dam had imprisoned. He gets to know of a weak point in the dam and also that only at the cost of one's life, can one attack the dam to bring it down. And that is what shows the way to save the people of Sivatarai. He attacks the dam at its weak point, destroys it, but he himself gets washed away by the flood of water that again begins to irrigate Sivatarai.

Damage to environment has emerged today as a matter of global concern particularly in relation to the future of the planet. This theme is touched upon in the very first scene: the people of Sivatarai 'cannot believe that god-given water can be denied us by man'. Their crops would dry up and they might die of famine, but Yantraraj Vibhuti says, 'the purpose was to secure the victory of man's cleverness over sand and water and stones. We have no time to think of some farmer's corn field.' What is the background to Tagore's critique? One is reminded of the pantheist tone of Tagore's writings and his emphasis on the importance of the forest and the *tapovan* in ancient Indian culture. He also gave appreciative support to Elmhirst's environmentalist tract on the *Robbery of the Soil*. His ideal of human relationship with nature was reflected in the education in natural surroundings at Santiniketan. As early as 1905 he underlined the need to develop small-scale irrigation managed by local villagers, in place of government-controlled large irrigation works. His premises in his environmental thinking were moral, social and aesthetic. In later times, especially in the beginning of the twenty-first century, environmentalism acquired a more elaborate grounding in techno-scientific knowledge than in Tagore's times. Nonetheless, there is a notable parallelism between *Mukta-Dhara* and the battle environmentalists fight today, inter alia against gigantism of dams on rivers.

Another significance of the play is that it reopens the age-old issue, man versus machinery. The builders of the dam sing an anthem to the machine. '*Namo yantra, namo yantra*' and their credo is that the machine is more powerful than man and can take the place of the gods. Tagore writes in a letter in 1922 soon after the play was published: 'Those who harm man with machinery are victims of a tragedy' because they are acting against the grain of their own human-ness, but among them there are some who stand up for man against machines. 'In my play Abhijit is one such soul' and he, therefore, gives his own life to defeat the machinery of the dam that would have harmed the people of Sivatarai. Tagore presents here an allegory of the prostitution of science for purposes of domination: the king of Uttarakut wanted the dam because control of water would allow him to control the contumacious people of Sivatarai.

Rakta-Karabi (1926) began to be written a few months after *Mukta-Dhara*. It was another allegory expressing Tagore's deep concern with the reduction of man into a mere tool in a vast machinery for mining gold. In many poems Tagore, likewise, condemned the depredations of the *Yantra danava* i.e. monster machine. At the same time, Tagore's position was different from that of Mahatma Gandhi who declared war on machinery and the materialism of the West in *Hind Swaraj* (1909). The difference was that Tagore believed that science and technology, including that of the West, was necessary for the advancement of civilization and human welfare—it was the abuse of science which he opposed. 'If the cultivation of science by Europe has any moral significance', he wrote in course of his debate with Gandhi, 'it is in its rescue of man from outrage by nature, not its use of man as a machine but its use of the machine to harness the forces of nature in man's service. One thing is certain, that the all-embracing poverty which has overwhelmed our country cannot be removed by working with our hands to the neglect of science.'[76]

The third idea that inspired the play is that diabolical machinery and the cruel oppression of the rulers can be effectively fought with moral force, not physical force or violence. The mantra of *abhaya* which Gandhi had brought seems to be replicated here. However, the character of the ascetic Dhananjay, carrier of this message, as well as his dialogues and songs were actually written in 1908–09; these passages, originally in the play *Prayaschitta* (published in 1909), were transplanted from there by Tagore to *Mukta-Dhara* in 1922. The passages are remarkable because they anticipate some basic notions of Gandhian techniques of non-violent resistance. Incidentally, in March 1922, the play was about to be staged when news came of the Mahatma's arrest. As a mark of protest, Tagore abandoned the preparations for the play.

Man's interference with nature to the detriment of man's well-being, the abuse of science to impose machine over man, and the possibility of resistance against oppression without resort to violence—these are the core ideas at play in this allegory. In fact the articulation of these ideas constitutes the text of the play. Of actual action little happens on the stage—whatever takes place is reported on stage, as in Greek classical dramas. Tagore himself wrote a commentary on the play to point to the fact that the central theme is the crown prince Abhijit's renunciation of his place in the royal house and his own life in order to regain freedom for the stream, *Mukta-Dhara*, with which he felt 'a spiritual relationship'. Tagore further comments: the name 'Free Current' may lead readers to believe that 'it has a symbolic meaning', and indeed 'the play has some symbolic element in its construction'.[77] Tagore considered the play important enough to undertake a translation of the play into English. There is another translation by Marjorie Sykes.[78]

In Mammon's Land: 'Red Oleander', 1926

Tagore wrote to the novelist Upton Sinclair, known for his socialist sympathies, in September 1923:

> You asked me my opinion of your books. I have not as yet had the opportunity to read them all, but it was *The Brass Check*, read when it was first published [1919], that made me feel that I should like to know both the man and his works. Your fearless stand for truth, for the things that are right, your viewpoint of the humiliation that worship of money brings, its stifling quality, its empty arrogance, its insidious undermining of self-respect, its valueless-ness, all the attributes which are its curse when dollars own the man; these ideas which you inculcated in this particular book immediately made a bond of sympathy. For years I have thought over these things, this especial phase of our modern civilization, and only a few weeks ago I have myself finished a drama on the same subject.[79]

The work Tagore refers to is perhaps *Rakta-Karabi*, which Tagore himself translated under the title *Red Oleander*.

In 1924 Tagore wrote a speech introducing that play; the speech was never delivered because the play could not be staged in Tagore's lifetime.

> There is an antinomy between men as individuals and men as members of a class . . . My play is about the individual man and man as member of a class. If the audience will like my advice, they might forget that class aspect. Just bear in mind that the play *Rakta-Karabi* depicts a woman named Nandini. See her emergence as an individual in the middle of the oppression that surrounds her. See the tears and the laughter which rise upwards like a gurgling fountain forced to rise by the constraint at its point of issue. If you look at that whole picture, you might find enjoyment in it. Or else you may search for meanings hidden under the petals of

the red oleander and if that causes a problem the responsibility is not mine.[80]

In these two statements, the agenda of, the themes at the core of *Rakta-Karabi*, are touched upon by Tagore. His own statement at the beginning of this play may suffice to give an idea of the storyline of the play. The events in it he says, 'are decidedly not what happened in ancient times', and the location is also indeterminate, but 'everyone knows it as Yakshapuri' (i.e. Mammon's Land). The king there stays behind a screen and his rule depends on a few sardars (satraps) who are veterans in the art of domination, as well as a number of headmen below them. All the others are 'diggers' who work in the bowels of the earth to dig up gold. They are known not by their names but the number assigned to each. Some diggers rise to the rank of headmen. There is also a Holy Man 'who often takes the name of God, but he takes his salary from his sardar' and he is of great use in Yakshapuri. Tagore goes on to say that sometimes out of the water a strange creature enters the fisherman's net and breaks through it. 'In the web of this story a girl is caught, Nandini (i.e. Giver of Joy) by name, she appears to be destined to break down the screen behind which the king hides.' Nandini and her lover and comrade Ranjan provoke a rebellion of the diggers against the regime of satraps and headmen, a system which the king himself is unable to control. She lures the king from his secret chamber and they discover that his henchmen have killed Ranjan. In the climactic scene the king joins Nandini in demolishing the regime of exploitation over which he had ruled. The representation of the head of an oppressive regime taking part in its demolition, and the stereotype of the awesome power of the eternal woman occur recurrently in many other dramatic works of Tagore. In this last dramatic allegory he wrote, these familiar stereotypes culminate in an iconic form, the king, a prisoner of his own oppressive regime, turns against it and woman, as life force, liberates. That is what Tagore projected through his allegories. That was his faith and there is no arguing with faith.

We have mentioned two interpretations of the play offered in his undelivered speech on this play. There are other interpretations elsewhere as well. For instance in his diary on his way to Europe in 1924 he wrote:

> When the joyful life-force that is in Woman, fails to inspire Man's endeavours, then the mechanical element dominates the creative. That is when the machines man creates hurt human beings . . . This is the thought which has found expression in my play *Rakta-Karabi*. In Yakshapuri, Man delves into the earth to bring out gold with relentless exertion of force. The lust for unremitting acquisition is such that there is no room there for what is beauteous in life . . . There enters Woman, enters Nandini, and thus the mechanical encounters life-force . . .'[81]

Again in 1923, Tagore wrote an essay on the growth of consciousness of unity of interest, and the strength of organization, among the exploited class. That kind of organization was no doubt the beginning of their liberation, but Tagore believed that it did not necessarily mean liberation of Man from coercive forces; it might mean just change in the locus of power.

> The Soviets were after power [in Russia] . . . And their lust for power showed signs of pitiless coercion in their circumstances also . . . I do not believe that the age-old shackles will fall away, that all the evils man suffers from will disappear, or that everyone will overnight begin to strive for the liberation of Man, only if power shifts from one stratum [of society] to another.[82]

Another significant fact connected with the composition of *Rakta-Karabi* was that while writing it, he carefully collected information from an economist who had worked on the condition of the Bombay working classes.[83] In the 1920s the new generation of Bengali litterateurs started a new trend in writing about the lower orders of Bengal society; some of them accused Tagore that he had been negligent in that respect. Socialist intellectuals were as yet few in number but the impact of the Russian Revolution (1917) had begun to create a stir. When Tagore himself visited Soviet Russia in 1930, on the one hand, he had the apprehensions cited in the above-mentioned essay of 1923; on the other hand, he was swayed by a stronger sentiment of optimism about an experiment to redress the wrongs suffered by the toiling classes at the lower end of all civilizations.

Given the ideational background we have outlined, one can understand the complexities of the play *Rakta-Karabi*. Perhaps Tagore himself found it difficult to write this play—he rewrote it at least nine times, because we have at least ten extant manuscripts containing revisions. He dithered over the title, he renamed the heroine, he translated an early version into English and published a somewhat different Bengali version a year later and then he became so fussy about the choice of an actress for his heroine's role that the play could rarely be staged in his lifetime. We know that Tagore wrote to Upton Sinclair of the completion of this play in September 1923 and the first Bengali edition of *Rakta-Karabi* came out in December 1926. Why did Tagore take more than three years working on it? Was it due to his difficulty in putting across the ideas he wished to express? We do not know. Another possible explanation is in terms of personalities: Elmhirst records that in creating the character Nandini, Tagore had in mind a teenaged girl, Ranu Adhikari (later Mukherjee), daughter of an acquaintance and frequent visitor to Santiniketan. Tagore told Elmhirst that this girl vividly brought back to Tagore the memory of his 'boy-hood companion', i.e. Kadambari Devi. Tagore acknowledged that Ranu Adhikari 'knows, and I know that she is the figure around whom the whole theme revolves'. Between Tagore, Elmhirst and Ranu there developed a friendship in which Elmhirst often served as a foil with which she could 'tease Tagore'. Elmhirst had first-hand knowledge of all this and he kept his distance because he was courting Dorothy Straight who eventually accepted his proposal in 1924. In the meanwhile the play was undergoing revision repeatedly.[84] It is possible that Tagore delayed the completion of the play because of a passion for perfection in the projection of Ranu into the character of Nandini in the play and as Elmhirst put it, Tagore's unwillingness to say farewell to the characters of his invention with whom he had 'lived so long on such intimate terms'.

Rakta-Karabi is commonly regarded as a landmark because it was Tagore's severest indictment of the injustice and oppression the toiling classes suffered in systems based on acquisition of wealth by another man's labour. However, that was an ethical judgement. When it was the question of the realities of socialism as a system, Tagore was torn between two perceptions. Four years after the publication of this play Tagore visited Soviet Russia (October 1930). In *Letters from Russia* (1931) Tagore looked optimistically at the drastic diminution in the difference between living standards of various strata of society, the effort to incorporate in the mainstream of the polity the previously marginal colonized ethnic groups, and the elimination of a leisured class and their conceit of wealth. On the other hand Tagore had doubts on the score of suppression of free discussion especially of economic matters, 'rumours of cruelty of the present administration', and the danger of dictatorship. Already 'many persecutions were taking place in Russia'. Further he says that 'time is not yet to say whether the [Soviet] economic doctrine is completely valid'.[85] Tagore had received negative and critical reports about the USSR from, among others, Professor P. Vinogradov, an émigré intellectual from Russia. In May 1922 he along with some colleagues of his at Oxford wrote to Tagore of their apprehensions about 'the intellectual leaders and brain-workers of Russia who are threatened with destruction . . .'[86] The opposite side also courted Tagore's attention; for example, the Soviet Minister of Education Lunacharsky came to Berlin to meet the poet in 1926 to invite him to visit the USSR. On the basic question of the economic dispensation under socialism in Russia, Tagore was cautious:

My only fear is that in a scripture-ridden and priest-led country [India], the natural bent of our ignorant mind is towards accepting a foreign dictum as biblical truth. Guarding ourselves against this danger, we must say that a doctrine can be tested only by its application: the end of the experiment is not yet.[87]

On the whole, on some issues he was not very familiar with, Tagore thought that it was too early to judge—it was after all only thirteen years after the Revolution. What impressed him was the courage demonstrated in Russia in casting out the past, the rapidity of advancement in popular education and public health compared to India, and above all the potential of the moral effect of the Soviet revolution. 'The important thing is that suffering humanity has a nobler vision of itself on the world stage than before . . .'[88] The awareness of Tagore of these various dimensions, and his cautiousness in delivering judgement, show perhaps an unexpected acuity in evaluating an unfamiliar political economy. If one looks to *Letters from Russia* seeking clues to read meanings in *Rakta-Karabi*, one must bear in mind the fact that Tagore suspended his judgement on the socialist system. While as a poet Tagore's opposition to exploitative systems was absolute, as a distant observer, his support in respect of some vital aspects of the alternative system that he encountered in Russia was highly qualified.

Marriage without Love: 'Relationships'

The novel *Yogayog* (1929) is a complex work where Tagore explores with a cruel scalpel gender relations in Hindu society, in particular, in conjugal life. It ends in a tragic denouement: the wife, in a loveless marriage, is forced to stay on in a relationship she hates because she is made to feel that that is her duty as a Hindu wife, and also because she has conceived a child. She has conceived against her will; it was almost, as Tagore put it in a letter at that time, a rape legalized by the institution of marriage.[89]

About two years before Tagore started writing this novel, he wrote an essay which may be considered to be a prelude to the novel. He said that 'in every country marriage is still more or less of a prison house for the confinement of woman—with all its guards wearing the badge of the dominant male . . . [Man] by dint of his efforts to bind woman, has made her the strongest of fetters of his own bondage' and 'the married state is still one of the most fruitful sources of the unhappiness and downfall of man'. This Tagore believed, was due to the failure of man to appreciate the *shakti* in the woman, and man's tendency 'to use it for the purposes of his individual enjoyment, corrupting it, confining it, like his property within jealously guarded limits'. In this essay on 'The Indian Ideal of Marriage', Tagore put in a few words the essence of the human situation in *Yogayog*.[90]

Kumudini is to her husband Madhusudan a piece of property for his delectation, and although in course of the story he has moments of realization of a love beyond the pleasure of possession, the bottom line for him is that being a successful money-maker he has acquired that woman. The irony is that Kumu accepts her god-given duty to play the role of a Hindu wife devoted to a husband not of her own choice. But she too has her rebellious moments, clouded as it is by her conception of traditional prescriptions and proscriptions binding a Hindu woman in holy matrimony. Here again Tagore's commentary is incisively relevant: 'The Hindu ideal of marriage has no regard for individual taste or inclination' and therefore 'there is danger in allowing marriage to pursue the path of self-will.' Hence 'the marriage system is walled around with a protective embankment'.[91] The Hindu prescriptions in texts ranging from Manu's *Dharma-shastra* to Kalidas's poetic creations are examples that Tagore cites in this context. This essay, read together with the novel *Yogayog*, illuminates Tagore's critique of the reality of the institution of marriage, as distinct from the ideal.

Another idea which pervades the novel is the counter-position of the acquisitive instincts which drive Madhusudan to gain wealth as well as power over his wife, as opposed to the ideals which Kumu had imbibed from her upbringing in an aristocratic family which valued money far less than 'the higher things of life'. This is a cultural dissonance often depicted by Tagore, almost a stereotype in his writings. Perhaps, it is a recurrent theme because he was born in a family which represented high culture in many ways while their fortunes had declined. Here are Kumu's reflections at the moment when she faces the fate of bearing a child of the husband she does not love:

The differences between one person and another are often very subtle but difficult to overcome. Words, body language, the signal of little habits, the unintended expressions in moments of inactivity, tone of the voice, taste, quotidian practices, ideals of life—all of them carry hidden signifiers of difference. There was something in Madhusudan which not only hurt her, but made her feel ashamed . . . Worship of money was often in Madhusudan's conversation and often he belittled Kumu's paternal family [i.e. their present poverty]. The meanness of that which was part of his nature, coarseness of his language, his discourteous showing-off, and over-all gracelessness, physical and mental as well as in the inner life of the family,—all of that made Kumu recoil physically and mentally . . . She had tried hard to fight her mental distaste for all that. Perpetual was her effort to keep unsullied her faith, her duty to be devoted to her husband, but now she realized that she was defeated.[92]

That was her and Tagore's perception of a cultural dissonance with people who are 'not like us', people with different values, habits, and background. Moreover, the story also hints at Madhusudan's extramarital relationship.

But what was the resolution of this problem and the problem of Madhusudan's perception of his wife as a piece of property? Tagore fudged that issue a little at the end. Vipradas, Kumu's brother and mentor, reminds her of the fact that when Shakuntala left her ashram, she meets with king Dushyanta's refusal to recognize her. She gets insult instead of a welcome at her husband's palace. Vipradas says, after all Shakuntala went through grief and insult eventually to attain 'abiding peace'—and that is the future he holds up for his sister. Kumu has to reconcile herself to her fate and returns to her duties as a Hindu wife.[93] Perhaps in 1929 that was realistic. The novel ends with Vipradas seeing before him 'only an abyss without end'.

People have often said that it is strange that the novels *Yogayog* and *Sesher Kabita*, totally different in style, were being written simultaneously in 1928–29. Perhaps this is not inexplicable. There is indeed a huge difference in the temper and the style of these novels. But common to both is Tagore's exploration of the idea whether marriage as an institution is beyond question. In *Yogayog* he questions that institution ruthlessly—the ideational basis of it was already explicated in the essay on the Indian ideal of marriage we have cited. In *Sesher Kabita* he addresses the same issue from a different angle. Kumudini's story is about marriage without love and Labanya's story in *Sesher Kabita* is about love without marriage. One narrative is the obverse of the other.

Love that Liberates: 'Farewell Song'

The novel *Sesher Kabita* (1929) created a sensation and remained for years one of the most popular of Tagore's fictional works. It was a sensation because it was perceived as Tagore's response to the challenge of a 'modernism' which had pretensions to opening a post-Tagorean era. This novel was popular because it is a good read, a brilliant instance of Tagore's literary craftsmanship. The novel has only two major protagonists: Amit Raye and Labanya Datta and there are two other protagonists, who are by and large kept in the wings, Ketaki or Katy Mitter and Shobhanlal, The romantic encounter between Amit and Labanya ends in her decision that she was ready to be a friend but not a wife to Amit. Thus fate neatly pairs off Amit with Katy, and Labanya with Shobhanlal. In this narrative Tagore looks quizzically at the younger generation of Bengali intellectuals with aspirations for 'modernity' and creates in Amit a protagonist who outdoes the best of that species. Outwardly he is a brilliant and amiable snob who plays effortlessly the games intellectuals play. He shows off his ability to put words together to versify in a playful engagement with the Muse of poetry, his originality as a literary critic, his social grace in playing the 'romance' game with suitable girls, and his skill in honing his innate contrariness in debates on subjects in which he feigns an interest. If Amit, thus seen outwardly, has an inner life it is unknown to us, until he meets Labanya.

> Labanya's beauty was like the morning; instead of an allure of mystery, it was suffused with intelligence . . . This, for Amit, was

her chief attraction. For in Amit's nature there was intellect, but no mercy; judgement, but no patience; a great deal of knowledge and learning, but no inner peace. In Labanya's countenance, he had glimpsed a peace that did not arise from the contentment of the heart, but rested motionless, in the depth of her intellect.[94]

There is born 'a new Amit Raye', he says.[95] The dream-like story of their love cruises along and they are talking of the ring he would gift her and the nest that will be theirs when reality intervenes in the form of Katy Mitter.

Her impending visit is a disaster to Amit and to Labanya because it brings a message: 'Amit's social world was a thousand leagues from her own . . . Labanya understood that the home which the two of them had been building in their imagination would perhaps never materialize.'[96] But social status was a factor in the outer world. In Labanya's innermost thoughts much more important was her idea of love that liberates. She quotes Tagore: 'I did not bring you joy, but gave you freedom', adding that love may not necessarily claim happiness, 'it liberates because it is free . . . What more can one offer?'[97] That is what she offers to Amit. He is not, she thinks, one of the mortals born for domesticity, and 'it is not me he wants . . . he has merely constructed an image of me'. If they were to be married some day she might 'emerge a very ordinary woman; not his own creation'.[98] Thus Labanya is ready to be a friend but not a wife to Amit. Her farewell letter to him:

Do you hear the chariot wheels of Time?. . . I float away on a
tide of change
In the journey of time.
My friend, farewell.
Of mortal clay I am made; if you saw in me
An image eternal, then let it be . . .
Free of burdens, free of any claims
My friend, farewell.[99]

Superbly crafted, *Sesher Kabita* is a good read, but it is not a great novel. For an author to produce such a work at the age of sixty-seven was an achievement. Departing from his usual practice

Tagore locates his narrative and character in this novel in the contemporary terrain, not in the near or distant past. That was new, but being contemporary is not necessarily being modern. It was perceived as 'modern' by literary persons of those times because it seemed to be in Tagore's own way his response to the challenge of the 'modernists'. The language in this novel drew attention to itself—perhaps to an excess; it established a style in Bengali language which attracted many imitators. There was a rare combination here of satire with lyricism. The satire is benign—except when it targets the anglicized Bengali stratum of society in those times. The lyrical element is infused in the prose and, of course, numerous verses interspersed throughout the text. The novel shared some of the stylistic features of the 'prose-poems' Tagore began to write in the last years of his life. In letting Amit deride Robi Thakur or invent an imaginary poet, Nibaran Chakraborty, who was playfully set up as the rival to Rabindranath Tagore, was the author indulging his ego or making fun of many a poet manqué? On questions such as this, heavy-handed attempts at explanation by literary critics seem inappropriate to the light-heartedness of the author.

> The greatest complaint against Robi Thakur is that in imitation of old man Wordsworth, this gentleman has lived unfairly long . . . If he does not voluntarily make a dignified exit, it would be our collective duty to withdraw from his literary circle . . . I have vowed to publicly expose the illicit conspiracy of the Robi Thakur faction.

The poems which the modern world needs, Amit says, should be not like flowers, but like streaks of lightning. 'Like the pain of neuralgia . . . From now on discard the artistry of rhyme and metre designed to charm the reader's heart . . . Poets who are not ashamed of surviving to be sixty or seventy invite punishment by cheapening themselves. Ultimately they find themselves trapped, hemmed in by the mimicry of a band of imitators. Their writing becomes warped; beginning to steal from their own earlier works, they become receivers of stolen goods.'[100]

Complete confidence in his ability to negotiate with the 'modernity' of a new generation—in fact to beat them at their own game—allowed Tagore to write in this manner.

Finally, there is no getting away from the fact that this book is about ideas, but the brilliance on the verbal surface is dazzling. Two ideas Tagore was concerned with were: What is modernity? What is love without consummation in marriage? Tagore reflected upon the relationship between theoretical ideas and the 'magic' of literary artistry. He wrote in a letter to the poet Sudhindranath Datta shortly before he began writing this novel: 'Thoughts can be so arrayed that the outcome is a meaning beyond the syllogism of reasoning, so that there emerges that beauty which gives us a joy (*ananda*) beyond reason . . .'[101] This was the hidden art in *Sesher Kabita*. He expounded his views on modernity in literature elsewhere in essays, for example, '*Adhunik Kavya*' ('Modern Poetry', 1932) or '*Sahitye Navatva*' ('Modernity in Literature', 1927)—but in this novel he demonstrated in practice what he preached with his accustomed virtuosity. That is why Buddhadeb Bose, a leading modernist of the new generation of writers wrote in appreciation of this novel: 'All that we had attempted without success Rabindranath had accomplished—with such ease, so completely, and in such a beautiful way!'[102]

New Directions in the 1920s

Tagore often said that his life as an author underwent seasonal changes and there were from time to time periods of fecundity. The decade of 1920s was certainly such a period when Tagore's creativity found its way towards new directions. As we have seen, in these years he negotiated with issues such as the abuse of science for purposes of domination (*Mukta-Dhara*, 1922), the systems of economic exploitation and suppression of the spirit of freedom (*Rakta-Karabi*, 1926), the subordination of women behind the façade of marriage (*Yogayog*, 1929), and the challenge of the modernists in literature (*Sesher Kabita, Mohua*, 1929), and he also broke into a totally new field of creativity in painting. He travelled through four continents for a total of over three and a half years in this decade and in Argentina he came closer than he ever did since his youth to a romantic relationship, though it was a relationship fraught with ambiguities. Tagore re-entered the public sphere, after many years of isolation at Santiniketan, with his bold renunciation of his knighthood in protest against the government's atrocities in Punjab. He remained active as a public spokesman through this Gandhian era of nationalist politics, articulating views which sometimes converged with and sometimes diverged from the Mahatma's approach. These were the years when these adversaries in debate became the closest of friends.

In Tagore's many-faceted activities in this decade one can perhaps sense a spirit of restlessness in his inner life, something that is sublimated in and hidden from view in the polished writings. It found expression in one of his poems soon after the end of this decade.

> That black stallion inside my mind, panting hard, through the night,
> That is my dark desire.
> . . . . Like the dark flame of an apocalypse,
> a black storm
> In a sudden awakening of its despair
> Through the door unguarded at night
> Sallies forth unbound.
> It bears on its back my love, a figure of sorrow,
> My love who found no space in my outer life
> And took all the space in my soul.[103]

'Kalo Ghora' is an obscure poem, not easy to read, nor widely read. But probably it is one of the rare writings which hold the key to that unrest in Tagore's mind which will probably ever remain tantalizing, unknowable.

CHAPTER SIX

Towards the Religion of Man
1930–1941

The decade of the thirties, with historical hindsight, appears to move with the inevitability of a classical drama towards the climactic moment, the Second World War. To people in those times, however, this was not so clear and as the world moved towards a catastrophic clash, Tagore's oft-repeated warnings against the dangers of aggressive nationalism tended to be dismissed as baseless doomsday predictions. His message upholding 'the religion of man' had few takers.

When we look back, the pattern of events emerges clearly. The Nazi party scores electoral success in Germany (1932) soon to be followed by Hitler's bid for dictatorial powers (1933) and eventually the title of Fuhrer (1934). Japan captures Manchuria (1931) and Mussolini's Italy attacks Ethiopia, then called Abyssinia (1935). In Germany concentration camps begin to be set up for Jews and political suspects (1933) while in Spain persecution of communists and political dissent slowly leads to Civil War and the dictatorship of General Francisco Franco (1936). The alliance between Italian Fascists and German Nazis is formalized in the Berlin–Rome Axis (1936). In the meanwhile, Chinese nationalism begins its long battle against Japanese aggression. Chiang Kai-shek becomes President of the Republic of China (1935), declares war on Japan (1936) and Mao-tse Dong joins hands with him to fight foreign aggression (1937). On the other hand in Europe the leaders of Europe are mute bystanders as the Belgrade Treaty is forged between Italy and Yugoslavia (1937), Prime Minister Neville Chamberlain's appeasement policy leads to the Munich Pact with Hitler (1938) and dictator Franco's regime is recognized by Britain and France (1939). Tagore's words about the West being untrue to their own vaunted values seemed to be more than ever true now. Germany's invasion of Poland (1939) at last awakens Britain and France to the impending threat to their very existence and they declare war on Germany. Undeterred, Germany invades Denmark and Norway (April 1940). Soon after Churchill becomes prime minister, France falls and the Battle of Britain begins (June 1940). Shortly before Tagore's death Germany invades Yugoslavia (April 1941) and the USSR (June 1941).

The course of events was no less tempestuous in India. On the one hand the militant or revolutionary nationalist activities reached a high pitch. Jatin Das's hunger strike and death and an attempt to assassinate Viceroy Irwin occurred in 1929. There followed the raid on the Chittagong Armoury in East Bengal by Surya Sen's Indian Republican Army and the assassination of the inspector general of prisons in a gun battle in the Bengal government secretariat in Calcutta. The Lahore Conspiracy Case ended in the sentence of death for Bhagat Singh and his associates. These events in 1930 marked the high-water mark of militant action. On the other hand those pursuing the Gandhian path raised their movement to a higher level. The year 1930 witnessed the spectacular demonstration of violation of the salt law in the Dandi March and the Congress's boycott of the Round Table Conference called by British authorities. The Congress was banned by the end of 1930 while the Muslim League's idea of Pakistan began to find favour with the government. The Congress eventually entered negotiations with the government and the outcome was a scheme of communal representation and eventually the Government of India Act of 1935 which allowed elected provincial governments to be formed. In 1937 the Congress won the election to form such governments in all but two states, but administration of provincial affairs by elected governments was hemmed in by various laws which left the real control in the hands of the 'central' Government of India. Moreover the provincial governments formed by the Congress had a very brief tenure of power. In late 1939 the fact that India was forced to join the War without any effort by the British government to consult Indian opinion and obtain Indian leaders' concurrence, led to the resignation of the provincial Congress governments. Thus the brief interlude of limited self-government ended. The powers retained by the Government of India enabled it to practise various repressive measures to control political dissent and unrest and Tagore was often very vocal against that policy.

Tagore and the World

Rabindranath Tagore's perception of the world has commonly suffered from reduction to the simplest terms in the hands of his interpreters. His attitude to the world is reduced to his attitude to the West, his attitude to the West is reduced to his dire pronouncements on the eve of his death in *Crisis in Civilization,* and those adverse pronouncements are reduced to a kind of spiritual revulsion against the West. This tendency of reductionism is unhistorical in that it homogenizes his views although they had many qualifications and underwent many changes in different stages of his intellectual evolution.

There is a deeper problem as well. An unproblematic and usually undisputed narrative of the life and philosophy of Tagore often focuses on Tagore as a sage or a prophet. Actually, it is quite possible to argue that there are two Tagores. There is Tagore seen as a prophet and thus iconized by his admirers, especially in Bengal, as an oracle. And then there is also another Tagore, an intellectual who had a fair bit of knowledge of the history of the world in his own times. This other Tagore as an observer was more balanced in judgement than prophets need to be. Tagore, to be fair to him, was himself quite sceptical of the icon of a prophet. He saw, at the peak of his success in 1939[1] that 'the icon (*putuli*) that the multitude created . . . cannot escape the hunger of the eternal dust,' that it would turn into dust 'under the wheel of Time'. But his scepticism notwithstanding, Tagore as a prophetic icon outgrew in the imagination of his contemporaries the other Tagore.

In the 1920s and 1930s contemporary world history was very much on Tagore's mind. His correspondence reveals that his contact with various countries through his travels around the world, his friends and admirers abroad, and in some ways his philosophy of universalism meant a deep and lasting engagement with the global course of events. It was an inescapable engagement though he might have wished, as he wrote more than once, to be away from it all, leading the life of a poet in seclusion.

Sometimes world politics impinged on his life in small things. For example, in 1920 his lecture tour in the United States, to raise funds for Santiniketan, was cancelled because the lecture organizers or agents thought he was unwanted in North America since he was seen as an anti-Allies agitator during the World War. He wrote to Andrews, almost in relief, 'the atmosphere of our mind has been cleared, at a sweep, of the dense fog of the contemplation of five million dollars'.[2] A problem of a much larger dimension was his totally uncalled for acceptance of Benito Mussolini's invitation in 1926. He realized the unwisdom of that action and of his uninformed and vacuous comments on that dictator, only after Romain Rolland and others told him of the true role of Mussolini and Fascism.

It took a long time to live that down, though Tagore published in *Manchester Guardian* a kind of apologia: 'the principles of Fascism concern all humanity and it is absurd to imagine that I could ever support a movement which ruthlessly suppresses freedom of expression, . . . and walks a bloodstained path of violence and stealthy crime.'[3] Tagore was misled by Professor Carlo Formichi, a Fascist enthusiast, who brought Mussolini's message to Santiniketan. Later, when Nazism was getting a grip over Germany, we see Tagore warning his grandson, then a resident of Germany as a trainee in printing technology: the young man must keep away from the 'cannibalistic' political culture that Nazism had given birth to.[4] Tagore had friends in Germany and he was probably kept informed of the activities of the Nazis. In 1934 he refers to 'the insults offered to my friend Einstein' which shook his 'faith in modern civilization'.[5] This was in a letter to a Jewish journalist and the incident mentioned was a raid by Nazi Brown Shirts on the house where Albert Einstein entertained Tagore in 1930. Einstein who had received the Nobel Prize in 1921 was dismissed by Nazis from his academic position in Berlin in 1932, and thus he was forced to migrate to Princeton, New Jersey, where he worked till the end of his life. The persecution of Einstein moved Tagore, but there is no major statement from him on the plight of the Jews in general in Germany, perhaps for lack of information.

However, when the appeasement of Nazi Germany was revealed to the world at Munich, Tagore did not keep silent. He reacted with a poem which he sent to his friend Professor Vincenc Lesny, an Indologist in Prague who had translated Tagore into Czech. Tagore's own translation of the poem: 'God will never suffer to be cheated of His due / by the miserly manipulation of diplomatic piety / carefully avoiding all cost to itself'—and Tagore predicted 'an awful retribution' in the ultimate end.[6] And he wrote to Lesny: 'I feel so keenly about the suffering of your people as if I was one of them'; presumably speaking of Austen Chamberlain he wrote, principles at the core of Western civilization were being sold by their 'cowardly guardians . . . [who are] saving their own skins'. And then in his wonted prophetic mode: 'When men turn beasts they sooner or later tear each other.'[7]

Since he was fully aware of Japan's depredations in China, Tagore declined an invitation to visit Japan, ostensibly from Rash Behari Bose—in future a colleague of Subhas Chandra Bose in securing Japanese support for Subhas's endeavour in the form of the Indian National Army. The invitations in 1937 and again in 1938 were ostensibly from Rash Behari but it is almost certain that the sponsor was the Japanese government. Having learnt his lesson in his trip to Mussolini's Italy in 1926, Tagore decisively declined the invitations and wrote: he had 'genuine love for the Japanese people' but he was doubtful whether 'the military authorities of Japanese, which seem bent upon devastating China' would allow Tagore to freely speak his mind, had he visited Japan.[8] China figured inordinately prominently in Tagore's imagination. He believed, as Nehru did later, that these two oldest civilizations of Asia were linked by destiny in some manner right from the times when Buddhism spread to China.

> In my visits to China and Japan, and to Siam, Java and Bali, I felt profoundly moved to find how the communion of our cultures had persisted even up to our own days . . . [O]ur peoples have maintained an Asiatic tradition of cultural exchange: we have not fought with each other in the name of hungry nationalism as the Western countries have been doing in Europe. Japanese aggression [in China], therefore, seems to me essentially a case of borrowed pugnacity . . .[9]

Needless to say, the signs of 'Asiatic unity' that Tagore thus perceived was in civilizational terms. When it came to the discourse of nationalism, the situation was different. But the imagined unities remained closer to Tagore's heart. And it was not just his imagination; there were quite a few individuals who shared his vision. Professor Tan Yun-san teaching at Santiniketan raised funds for building the China Hall in Santiniketan solely from individual contributions.[10] Tagore had invited Nehru to inaugurate the China Hall in 1937, not perhaps because Nehru was the president of the Congress but because Tagore was aware of the outlook they shared on China and Asia at large. In *The Discovery of India* in 1946 Nehru expounded that outlook in a manner very similar to Tagore's.

The mismatch between Tagore's ideal of universalism and the reality of conflict between national interests became obvious in the last days of Tagore's life. The world the generation of Rabindranath Tagore knew was in a turmoil that changed it forever. Tagore's response could only be in poetic mode. Thus in 1937:

> Hissing serpents poison the very air.
>   Here fine words of Peace ring hollow.
> My time is up; but before I go, I send out

My call to those who are getting ready in a
Thousand homes to fight the demon.[11]

Or again writing in 1941 on the long run of history: 'Aeon on aeon, in the lengthening past have marched masses of men proudly, with victory's arrogant speed' but their empires collapse and on their ruins the common people carry on their lives.

Royal sceptres break, war-drums cease
Victory towers gape, stupidly, self-forgetful.
Bloodstained arms and blood-shot eyes are lost in children's tales.
The people work. In every country, go where you will . . .
The hum and roar of their toil link nights and days, made vibrant
by work. Sorrows and joys, from day to day, orchestrate life's great
music.[12]

In other words, the poet says to himself, of the tragedy of lives lost and creations of civilizations destroyed: This too shall pass.

There were conjunctures in the stream of events which might have inspired such hopes in Tagore. Significantly, sitting in a remote corner of north-east India, he heard on the radio the broadcast of André Gide's translation of his play 'Post Office' (*Dakghar*), on the night before Paris fell to the German invaders on 14 June 1940.[13] Such an event, forgotten in history, may be read as the symbol of the universalism of human civilization at a moment when it was threatened with extinction. Perhaps equally significant was Tagore's message to Franklin D. Roosevelt, President of the United States from 1933 to 1945. Tagore surmised that all the problems of the world 'have merged into one supreme world politics'.[14] That was a crucially important moment of realization that the ideal of universalism is inseparable from the domain of global politics where it needs to be worked out in real time.

Tagore faced an immense disillusionment: the faith his generation had once reposed, as inheritors of the traditions of Enlightenment, in the civilization of Europe was exposed to be untrue and unreal in the light of the history of aggrandizing nationalism, imperialist expansion, economic exploitation, and the mindless violence of the Western powers. What had Tagore and his peers found in European civilization as worthy of admiration and emulation? The best exposition of that view is in a piece of writing that was somehow overlooked by the editors of his works and hence excluded from his 'Collected Writings'. This was Tagore's Convocation Address at the University of Calcutta in 1937. It is an important document to explicate the complexities and ambiguities in Tagore's perception of Western civilization. In his mind there was perhaps the memory of thinkers like David Hume or J.S. Mill or Herbert Spencer, fighters for human welfare like William Wilberforce or Abraham Lincoln, the countless scholars who built a fund of knowledge of nature and human beings, and the progress of culture which admitted of further development or a critique to push it to new terrains. Tagore had mentioned these contributions to civilization time and again in his writings from his youth. In 1937 he reiterated that:

Europe has provided the world with the gifts of a great culture—had it not the power to do so, it would never have attained its supremacy. It has given the example of deathless courage, ungrudging self-sacrifice, it has shown tireless energy in the acquisition and spread of knowledge, in the making of institutions for human welfare . . . When in the beginning or middle of the nineteenth century we made our first acquaintance with European civilization, our joy and admiration freely went out to it in the belief that it had come into the world animated with a genuine respect for man . . .[15]

That was Europe as it was in the perception of Tagore and his peers in his youth. But the course of history revealed another truth. Tagore went on to say: 'Within the short span of our own life time, we have seen this love of humanity, this sense of justice, growing feebler and feebler' and thus 'a bitter protest has gone forth from the Eastern World against the claim of greatness of European civilization and culture.' At the same time in India we must not 'delude ourselves with home-made claims to superiority', we must search within to find whether 'the seeds of our downfall are within us, deeply embedded in our character, our society, our habits, our unreasoning prejudices'. In particular Tagore pointed to 'communal separation and dissension' and 'maladies born of our poverty, of physical and mental starvation' eating away the vitality of Indian society and culture.[16] Thus Tagore highlighted the problems threatening within as well as the threat from without. He recognized that European Enlightenment had at one time enriched India's reawakening and at the same time he pointed to the disillusionment that his generation experienced.

Tagore's last response to this theme, the crisis in his conception of universalism, came a few weeks before his death, his last public pronouncement, 'Crisis in Civilization'. Here Tagore addressed not just the crisis that is mentioned in the title, he addressed a personal crisis. His personal philosophy had been based since the 1920s upon humanist universalism, and he witnessed in his last years its collapse like a house of cards in the global history leading to World War II. Likewise, he had postulated a syncretic Indian civilization from 1902, a civilization that united diversities. The communal and casteist mindset did not match that construct, particularly from the 1920s onwards. That was Tagore's crisis.

The crisis in Tagore's personal faith merges with the global crisis he describes in the *Crisis in Civilization*. He makes three points, reiterating what he had said in his Convocation Address at Calcutta University in 1937. First, Western civilization had at one time carried in its core humanist values; that is what inspired the reawakening of India in the nineteenth century. Second, by the end of the nineteenth and in the early twentieth century Europe was revealed to be untrue to those values and principles; nationalist aggrandizement and the inexorable urge to accumulate wealth, drove imperialist state power and that threatened the basis of human civilization and well-being. Third, notwithstanding that trend in the hegemonic powers of the West, there were individuals who fought that trend from within and there was also the potential of resistance from the hegemonized peoples of the world; hence, one must not underestimate, in the task of addressing the crisis in civilization, the potentialities of mankind. Tagore declares his faith in Man. Apropos of making these points, Tagore recalls his own experiences.

> During my boyhood days, the attitude of the cultured and educated section of Bengal, nurtured on English learning, was charged with a feeling of revolt against rigid regulations of society . . . Then came . . . a painful feeling of disillusion when I began increasingly to discover how easily those who accepted the highest truths of civilization disowned them with impunity whenever questions of national self-interest was involved . . . I had at one time believed that the spring of civilization would issue out of the heart of Europe. But today when I am about to quit the world that faith has gone bankrupt altogether.[17]

A Syncretic Civilization?

Tagore's agonizing reappraisal of his notion of a syncretic civilization in India, his disillusionment from the middle of the nineteen twenties with the ability of the political leadership to withstand the onslaught of communalism and to keep India on the track of assimilation and unification, has been discussed already in the previous chapter. Tagore touches on these themes in his essay, 'Hindu Musalman' (1931). 'When we find that the Namashudras [an untouchable Hindu caste] joined the Muslims, should we not ask why they were wanting in the spirit of familial loyalty?' The evils of casteism as well as Hindu communalism were highlighted by him.[18] He also touched upon the threat to unity due to regional identities being prioritized over the people's identity as Indians. In an essay on the 'Congress' (1939) and another on the notion of 'Mahajati' (1939) he refers to the exclusion of Subhas Chandra Bose from the Congress and the consequent feeling in Bengal 'that the Bengali people are being pushed around or sidelined'. He adds, 'To believe this complaint is a sign of weakness. To believe in a conspiracy theory and to allow that to influence your judgement is a sign of mental sickness.' However, the fact was that in popular perception the unity between one province of India and another was not alive and strong; there were signs of parochialism and conflict. These were some of the fault lines in the emerging nationhood of India which deeply concerned Tagore.[19] His last message to the people of Bengal was perhaps in the address he gave at the invitation of Subhas Chandra Bose on the occasion of the foundation of Mahajati Sadan: 'Confidence in herself should enable Bengal to form an inseparable bond with India, self-pride and disastrous parochialism should not lead to her severance [from the mainstream] . . . In India's struggle for freedom Bengal must not break away towards a path of futility.'[20] In these writings of the nineteen thirties we see none of that self-confidence Tagore once had of the syncretic character of Indian civilization. It was for Tagore a moment of tormented rethinking.

Mahatma and Tagore shared the same concerns about the recrudescence of communalism and another national level leader with whom Tagore shared his thoughts was the young Jawaharlal Nehru. To the latter, Tagore became a sort of father-figure—in fact Tagore and Jawahar's father Motilal were born the same year. Jawahar was attracted by Tagore's intellect and Tagore found in Nehru a bridgehead into the mind of the younger generation of Congressmen. When he was thirty-one, Nehru, in the retinue of Gandhi, first visited Santiniketan and after that they met intermittently. Nehru wrote in his autobiography that in 1934 he and Kamala planned to send their daughter Indira to Santiniketan. In 1936 we find that Nehru sought Tagore's patronage to build and promote his Civil Liberties Union. Tagore wrote back, with his consent to be president. About that time he also sought Tagore's intervention in the debate on *Vande mataram*.

That patriotic song fell a victim to the communalist trend and M.A. Jinnah on behalf of the Muslim League demanded that the Congress drop the song from meetings of the legislature and various public bodies. The objection was on the grounds that the song was idolatrous and Hindu. Originally, the poem had been purely a description of the beauties of the motherland. That was what the first stanza was about. But in 1881 the poem was included by Chatterjee in the novel *Anandamath* and in the expanded version the poem was endowed with militant Hindu accoutrement in the context of the novel.[21] The All India Congress Committee had to make some response to the Muslim community's objection. Nehru decided to consult the oracle of the cultural world, Tagore. Subhas Bose, in the meanwhile, approached Tagore with the report that Hindu opinion in Bengal was strongly against any move to discard *Vande mataram*.[22] Tagore's judgement was that the first two stanzas of the song were unexceptionable for they are about 'the beautiful and beneficent aspects of our motherland'. But of the rest of the song Tagore wrote: 'brought up as I was on the monotheistic ideals of my father, I could have no sympathy'. Further that last part of the song and the context in which it was placed in the novel *Anandamath* was 'liable to be interpreted in ways that might wound Moslem susceptibilities'. However, the first two stanzas have 'inspiring significance of its own in which I see nothing to offend any sect or community'.[23] The Congress Working Committee decided to accept Tagore's recommendation in favour of the first two stanzas, and dropped the latter portions of the song. The song's historical associations with the nationalist movement were recognized by Tagore: he himself had first sung the song at the Congress session in Calcutta in 1896, he recalled, and he also reminded Nehru of the fact that in the anti-partition agitation of 1905 it had 'caught on as a national anthem'. This was recognized by the Congress Working Committee in a resolution of which the draft written by Nehru survives among the Congress papers. 'The Working Committee feel that past associations, with their long record of suffering for the cause, as well as popular usage, have made the first two stanzas of this song a living and inseparable part of our national movement . . . '[24]

Tagore's published opinion that only the first two stanzas of the *Vande mataram* song were universally acceptable was against the grain of popular sentiment among the elite in Bengal.[25] He was attacked in the media as an unpatriotic man and Tagore wrote bitterly in a letter to a literary friend: 'Since I have been born in Bengal the typhoon of name-calling is like the accustomed breeze of my homeland to me. I have made no complaint or protest. Those days are over when I was sensitive to all that . . .'[26]

On the whole, the 1930s formed a critical period in Tagore's life-long conviction in the unifying spirit of Indian civilization, the syncretic character of that civilization. He was now confronted by the fault lines in evidence in the relationship between religious communities, the disprivileged castes vis-à-vis the upper castes, and the parochially defined provincial identities. In the manner of Mahatma Gandhi, shaken to the core by the evidence of disunity, he repeatedly reasserted his faith in the possibility of overcoming the divisive forces ultimately. But the confidence that there was in his earlier assertions, from 1902 onwards, of the fundamental unity of Indian civilization was greatly impaired in the last days of his life. Likewise, Tagore's faith in the unifying tendency of human civilization was threatened by the evidence he saw in the global trends leading to the World War. His answer to these crises in his convictions was to turn his mind to the message of universal humanism inherent in what he called the 'religion of man'.

The 'Religion of Man'

What Tagore described as 'the religion of man' was the subject of three of his works in this period. *Manusher Dharma* (1933) was the text of his professorial lectures in Bengali at Calcutta University. The second work, *Religion of Man* (1931) in English was entirely different from the Bengali lecture text. The English work was an expanded version of the text of Tagore's Hibbert Lectures in Oxford University in 1930. There was a third work entitled *Man* (1937), the lecture delivered at Andhra University, in 1933, by and large a synopsis of the Calcutta lectures. Apart from these publications of 1931, 1933 and 1937 Tagore touched upon this theme in his other works also, most notably in his tribute to Raja Rammohan Roy in 1933.

Why did the 'religion of man' assume importance towards the end of Tagore's intellectual life? Tagore wrote in 1930: 'Religion of Man has been growing within my mind as a religious experience and not merely as a philosophical subject. In fact a very large portion of my writings, beginning from the early products of my immature youth down to present time, carry an almost continuous trace of the history of this growth.'[27] In the beginning of this book we have noted that the 'Inner Life' of Tagore was characterized by a pervading consciousness of the inner unity of his ideas and writings. This unity in man's creativity and the unity of the individual with the Universal are two major themes in the writings on religion of man. This book was not one of his best. The three lectures delivered in Oxford were elaborated in not less than twenty-five chapters and still more after-thoughts and incidental reflections were added in seven appendices. However, the core of the argument is clear in the initial six chapters on 'Man in the Universe', the universal 'Creative Spirit', and the union between the Universal and the individual in varieties of religious experience ranging from the example of Zarathustra in ancient Iran to the sect known as Bauls in modern Bengal.

> The idea of the humanity of our God, or the divinity of Man the Eternal, is the main subject of this book. This thought of God has not grown in my mind through any process of philosophical reasoning. On the contrary, it has followed the current of my temperament from early days . . .[28]

Tagore believed that his own experience showed him that beyond the 'ever changing phases of the individual self there dwells the Eternal Spirit of human unity beyond our direct knowledge'. He points to the fact that he was 'brought up in an atmosphere of freedom—freedom from the dominance of any creed' and 'it was an idiosyncrasy of my temperament that I refused to accept any religious teaching merely because people in my surroundings believed it to be true.'[29] Obviously Tagore is speaking of religion in its institutional form. He had a faith which he believed was that of his 'Vedic ancestors', a kind of pantheistic faith inspired by a joy in the beauty of nature. 'It is evident that my religion is a poet's religion, and neither that of an orthodox man of piety nor that of a theologian.'[30] This religion of a poet, Tagore says, was revealed to him in his early days through his 'keen sensitiveness . . . [to] the world around me, natural and human' and later in life he had flashes of consciousness of 'the religion of Man, in which the infinite became defined in humanity', 'a profound organic unity with the universe comprehended by the human mind'.[31]

The idea of evolution towards organic unity is explained very well by Tagore, but the concept of the universal mind may not be so clear to every reader of the *Religion of Man*. In this book as well as in *Manusher Dharma* (1933) Tagore resorts to the biological analogy of the cellular structure working towards organic unity.

A multitude of cells were bound together into a large unit, not through aggregation, but through a marvelous quality of complex interrelationship maintaining a perfect coordination of functions. This is the creative principle of unity . . . Creation has been made possible through the continual self-surrender of the unit to the universe.[32]

As regards the Universal Mind, Tagore ventures to postulate it, though in his discussions with Albert Einstein the scientist had rejected it. We shall look at that debate later in these pages. Tagore believed that just as there is an organic unity among numerous cells which constitute a biological unit, human minds are part of a unity, an entity which may be called the Universal Mind. Albert Einstein had objected to this category and in his discussions with Tagore he maintained a strictly empirical position. For example, he said, a table is no doubt perceived by our mind but the table continues to be in existence even if no man is in the room to perceive it. That physical truth does not depend for its existence on the human mind. Tagore maintained the opposite position: 'Men of science tell us that truth, unlike beauty and goodness, is independent of our consciousness.' But Tagore believed that truth is also dependent on consciousness but 'that ideal truth does not depend on the individual mind of man, but on the universal mind which comprehends the individual'. Thus the table exists, even if no one is in the room to perceive it, because it is within the perception of the universal mind.[33] Science represents 'the rational mind of the universal Man' and it 'belongs to the human universe'; to maintain that 'truth, as we see it, exists apart from humanity is really to contradict science itself, because science can only organize into rational concepts those facts which man can know and understand'.[34]

Having thus postulated the 'creative unity' of humanity and a 'human universe', Tagore went on to develop the idea that Man possesses a 'Spirit of Life' which has 'a surplus far in excess of the requirements of the biological animal in Man'.[35] This is what enables human beings to rise above the struggle for existence and 'take his right seat as a creator'. In a chapter called 'The Surplus of Man' Tagore argues that it is the excess of Life Spirit which finds expression in the growth of culture and civilization.

It is significant that all great religions have their historic origin in persons who represented in their life a truth which was not cosmic and unmoral, but human and good. They came as the messengers of Man to men of all countries and spoke of the salvation that could only be reached by the perfecting of our relationship with Man the Eternal, Man the Divine. Whatever might be their doctrines of God, or some dogmas that they borrowed from their own time and tradition, their life and teaching had the deeper implication of a Being who is the infinite in Man, the Father, the Friend, the Lover, whose service must be realized through serving all mankind. For the God in Man depends upon men's service and men's love for his own love's fulfilment.[36]

The concept of 'religion of man' is a reassertion of Tagore's faith in humanism and universalism. In the chapter on his 'inner life' in the beginning of this book we have cited his earlier writings in Bengali on this theme. The Hibbert Lectures allowed Tagore an opportunity to present those ideas to the English-speaking readership. At that stage of his life none of his associates ventured to edit what he wrote and thus the book became an amalgam of many disparate pieces of writing, detracting from the thrust of his assertions. But the spirit of universal humanism comes through loud and clear. That was perhaps his last message to the world he was to leave very soon.

Santiniketan: the Educational Philosophy in Retrospect

We have mentioned the development of Santiniketan in the previous chapters but an attempt to examine that experiment in the light of Tagore's theoretical approach to education needs to be addressed. This is useful for two reasons. To those who do not know the Bengali language, Tagore's thoughts need an introduction. Most of his writings on education were in Bengali and only a few of these are available in translation in English. For example, some of the early writings, in particular those written during the Swadeshi agitation of 1905–07 and of formative importance in the history of the National Education movement have not been translated. His educational ideas of the latter period, however, are partly available in English; for example, *Personality* (1917), *Creative Unity* (1922), and *The Centre of Indian Culture* (1919).[37] There is another reason why it is important to re-examine his educational ideas and to try to historically situate Tagore's writings in the context of his times. The commentaries by a number of scholars on his writings are unfortunately insufficiently sensitive to the evolution of his ideas in interaction with the intellectual and social environment.[38] An undifferentiated continuity and changelessness is assumed in the random selection of ideas from out of a large corpus of his writings spread over about four decades. Such an approach, without regard to chronology and context, encourages us to ignore the fact that Tagore's ideas underwent substantial changes over time in response to the need for intervention as he perceived it.

Tagore's educational philosophy was a creative intervention in the conventional discourse of education in his times.[39] Tagore wrote his first essay on India in 1892—when he was only thirty-one years of age and had no claim to be considered an authority on education. In this essay in Bengali, entitled 'The Mismatch of Education', (*Shikshar Her-fer*) Tagore made a searing critique of the colonial pattern of education.[40] Basically he saw, from his own experience in school in his childhood and from his observation in later life, the system instituted by the British government as an incompetent imitation of the English model which educated only a few and that too inadequately. This critique constituted an agenda for developing a truly Indian educational institution. It took the shape of the ashram he founded in Santiniketan in 1901: the object was to locate the school in the lap of Nature, away from the colonial metropolis of Calcutta, to build a cultural ambience that would be responsive to the culture of the country and its people, and to offer education in the mother tongue to promote the acceptance and diffusion of modern knowledge. Tagore took under his care only five students in the first instance and hoped to build a microcosmic society complete in itself, moulding the personality of the students. In this first phase, Tagore thought the alternative to conventional education lay in the ashram concept of classical India.

Tagore's ideas underwent a change in 1905 with the beginning of the Swadeshi and National Education movement in Bengal.[41] In this second phase, roughly from 1905 to 1915, he took a leading role in articulating the nationalist ideas on education. However, he retained his individuality and soon it became clear that his ideas were not always congruent with those of the political leaders of the Swadeshi agitation. He became sceptical whether merely boycotting of government institutions and setting up institutions under the banner 'National' was enough to create an alternative to colonial education.[42]

When we see a foreign University, we see only its smaller body—its building, its furniture, its regulations, its syllabus; its larger body is not present to us. But as the kernel of the coconut is in the whole coconut, so the university, in the case of Europeans, is in their society, in their parliament, in their literature, in the numerous activities of their corporate life. They have their thoughts published in their books, as well as the living men who think those thoughts and criticize, compare and disseminate them. This organic unity of their mind and life and culture has enabled them to seek truth from all lands and all times, and to make it vitally one with their own culture which is the basis of their civilization. On the other hand, those who, like our present Indian students, have to rely upon books, not truly for their mental sustenance, but for some external advantage, are sure to be anemic in their intellects, like babies solely fed with artificial food.[43]

This is the phase when he began moulding the school at Santiniketan on lines which he later described in *My School*:[44]

The young mind should be saturated with the idea that it has been born in a human world which is in harmony with the world around it. And this is what our regular type of school ignores with an air of superior wisdom, severe and disdainful. It forcibly snatches away children from a world full of mystery of God's own handiwork, full of suggestiveness of personality. It is a mere method of discipline which refuses to take into account the individual . . . I believe that the object of education is the freedom of mind which can only be achieved through the path of freedom—though freedom has its risk and responsibility as life itself has. I know it for certain, though most people seem to have forgotten it, that children are living beings—more living than grown-up people who have built their shells of habit around them. Therefore it is absolutely necessary for their mental health and development that they should not have mere schools for their lessons, but a world whose guiding spirit is personal love. It must be an *ashram* where men have gathered for the highest end of life, in the peace of nature; where life is not merely meditative, but fully awake in its activities.

We can discern a third phase in the evolution of Tagore's educational philosophy in the period 1914 to roughly the early thirties. The First World War turned his mind towards an aspect of European nationalism: he thought that the global struggle between imperialist powers was the outcome of aggressive and exploitative

European nationalism and that kind of nationalism was alien to Indian civilization which had always been syncretic, pluralistic and open to inter-cultural exchange and understanding. He thought that India needed 'an institution where knowledge will be exchanged and compared, where India's knowledge can be located and analysed in the perspective of the knowledge acquired by the entire mankind'. Thus the concept of Visva-Bharati took shape and it was formally founded in 1921. The central idea was captured very well in the words Tagore made the motto of the university: *Yatra visva bhavati ekanidam*, i.e. this is where the entire world meets in a single nest. The educational thoughts in this phase are touched upon in Tagore's *Centre of Indian Culture* as well as 'An Eastern University' in *Creative Unity*.[45] In the latter Tagore expounded his new approach:

> Mind, when long deprived of its natural food of truth and freedom of growth, develops an unnatural craving for success; and our students have fallen victims to the mania for success in examinations. Success consists in obtaining the largest number of marks with the strictest economy of knowledge. It is a deliberate cultivation of disloyalty to truth, of intellectual dishonesty, of a foolish imposition by which the mind is encouraged to rob itself . . . A most important truth which we are apt to forget, is that a teacher can never light another lamp unless he is still learning himself. A lamp can never light another lamp unless it continues to burn its own flame. The teacher who has come to the end of his subject, who has no living traffic with his knowledge, but merely repeats his lessons to his students, can only load their minds; he cannot quicken them. Truth not only must inform but inspire. If the inspiration dies out, and the information only accumulates, then truth loses its infinity.

Further, Tagore believed that the generation of knowledge was as important a function of a university as the transmission of knowledge.

> In education, the most important factor must be the inspiring atmosphere of creative activity. And therefore the primary function of our university should be the constructive work of knowledge. Men should be brought together and full scope given to them for work of intellectual exploration and creation; and the teaching should be

like the overflow water of this spring of culture, spontaneous and inevitable. Education can only become natural and wholesome when it is the direct fruit of a living growing knowledge.[46]

From the early 1930s we see the last phase when the focus of his attention was on *Loka-siksha* or people's education. The beginning of this phase is marked by two essays published in 1933 and 1935 on 'the spread (*bikiran*) of education' and on the 'internalization (*swangikaran*) of education'[47]. The indigenous premodern educational system had been allowed to die by the colonial administration. The modern schools and colleges, even those inspired by nationalist ideals, had failed to spread education beyond their walls and gates, among the people.

In 1936 Tagore elaborated on this theme in his inaugural address to the Indian chapter of an international organization called New Education Fellowship which included many educationists influenced by John Dewey's innovative thinking.[48] Modern education, particularly science and a scientific world-outlook, Tagore said, must be naturalized in the Indian soil and the opportunity for education must not be limited to the top of society leaving untouched layers below. Tagore made a concrete suggestion which anticipated the idea of the Open University—a syllabus to be announced, and examination to be conducted by the University of Calcutta without requiring school or college attendance and payment of fees. The plan, needless to say, was rejected by the University authorities of the day. In pursuance of the idea of popular education Tagore initiated the People's Education Book Series (*Loka-siksha Granthamala*).

At about the same time, the Wardha Scheme (1937) was launched by Mahatma Gandhi; he had visited Tagore's village school in Sriniketan in 1925 and now he called upon A. William Aryanayakam, the principal of Tagore's village school from 1926 to 1934, to take part in drafting the scheme and to run a Gandhian experimental school in Wardha. Tagore felt that the Wardha pattern put an overwhelming emphasis on practical training in crafts to the exclusion of the element of 'play' and artistic creativity. However, he recognized a convergence between his idea of *loka-siksha* and the

Gandhian scheme for 'basic education'. In 1940, in his last public pronouncement a few months before his death, Tagore tried to focus public attention on the inequality in education which stood in the way of social equality.[49] Some of Tagore's ideas are reflected in his debate with Gandhi in the 1930s.[50]

We have tried briefly to outline the evolution of Tagore's thought from the paradigm of the *ashram* in the first phase, and the Swadeshi or National Education model in the second phase, to the idea of Visva-Bharati in the third phase, and finally to the agenda of *loka-siksha* in the last years of his life. As we said earlier, in this evolution of ideas there was creativity in action and Tagore said so in his inimitable way:

> I am often asked what is the idea upon which my school is based? The question is a very embarrassing one for me, because to satisfy the expectation of my questioners I cannot afford to be commonplace in my answer. However, I shall resist the temptation to be original and shall be content with being merely truthful. In the first place, I must confess it is difficult for me to say what is the idea which underlies my institution. For the idea is not like a fixed foundation upon which a building is erected. It is more like a seed which cannot be separated and pointed out, directly it begins to grow into a plant.[51]

Thus he looked upon his idea of education as an organic creation that grew over time.

Some of the key elements in his approach were: freedom is required for allowing development of the pupil's individuality that needs opportunity for exposure to and harmony with nature; the pedagogic process in school must work towards the removal of false values, like pursuit of success in examinations to the detriment of real acquisition of knowledge; teachers should participate in creativity by way of producing knowledge, rather than being mere transporters of knowledge as a commodity; and, finally, there is need for that organic relationship between agencies of learning and the society as a whole which alone can bring about a creative engagement. It is sad to reflect on the fact that much of Tagore's implicit critique of the teaching system remains valid almost a century later in this day and age.

Institutional Problems of Santiniketan

While Tagore tried to apply these ideas in the pedagogy and overall intellectual development path that was projected in Santiniketan, he was keenly aware of the distance between the institution there and his ideas. It is mortifying to see in some of his speeches at Santiniketan, how despondently and lovingly he looked upon his own creation, Visva-Bharati. He suffered a drain on his energy and resources for four decades. Towards the end of his life, he found it was difficult to bear the cross any longer. Without any governmental support and with only spasmodic support from occasional donors, Santiniketan depended on Tagore's book royalty and income from the land estates.

All said and done, he depended on his income as a landlord of the properties he inherited. The bottom line was that he recognized the fact that he and his family were 'zamindars, which means collectors of revenue under British government'. This he wrote to Charles Andrews on 5 March 1921. Further, he said:

Until the time comes when we give up paying revenue and allow our lands to be sold [under the Permanent Zamindary Settlement Act of 1793] we have not the right to ask . . . anybody else to make any sacrifice [of incomes] which may be all they have. My father was about to give up all his property for the sake of truth and honesty [to repay his father Dwarakanath Tagore's liabilities and debts]. And likewise we may come to that point when we have to give up our means of livelihood. When I put to myself this problem the answer which I find is that by temperament and training all the good that I am capable of doing presupposes certain amount of wealth. If I am to begin to earn my living, possibly I shall be able to support myself, but nothing better than that. Which will mean not merely sacrificing my money but my mind . . . But so long as I do not feel the call, or respond to it myself, how can I urge others to follow the path of utter renunciation? Let the individuals choose their own responsibility of sacrifice, but are we ready to accept that responsibility for them?[52]

What a strikingly clear-sighted recognition of the moral constraints of a beneficiary of the system of landlordism or *zamindari* in colonial Bengal.

The brutal frankness of Tagore's evaluation of the situation was brought out even more clearly in his correspondence later. The World Depression of the early 1930s hit hard the landlords or zamindars of eastern India. Rabindranath writes to his son Rathindra on 31 October 1930:

In the era that is upon us, we can no longer depend on our *zamindari* for income. My mind has been rebelling against it from way back and the feeling is now definite . . . the whole business of zamindari makes me ashamed . . . I feel sad to think that from childhood we have been raised as parasites . . . At certain historical conjunctures everyone must suffer; indeed everyone is already experiencing this; it is wrong to expect to remain comfortable by evading the crisis.[53]

To anticipate the later developments, let us look at 1934 when the Great Depression affected the income of the Tagore estates:

These are very hard times. In the first place, my *ryots* [rent-paying peasants] are destitute, the price of their crops being hopelessly low, and so the revenue [of the Tagore estates, as landlords] is almost nil. The interest on the Nobel Prize money has ceased. [The Prize money, as mentioned earlier, was invested in an agricultural cooperative bank] . . . The expenses of my family and my Visva-[Bharati] family are being met from the dregs of my income and from loans . . . I have been importing money from abroad to maintain a steady flow [of cash]. But I will not live forever . . . We have driven our work [at Santiniketan] close to the abyss of bankruptcy, we may still go under. We are, so to speak, in the grip of an obsession [i.e. building Visva-Bharati]—and such delusion is always more alluring than reality.[54]

Tagore was remarkably frank and forthright: he was part of an exploitative system, it was impossible for Visva-Bharati to survive on the incomes from that system, and he had to devise ways and means of shoring up that institution by other methods in those years of world economic crisis. One of those means was the income from the royalty on his books and book sales, but even that declined in the West because of the Depression and also because Tagore's message against aggressive nationalism was unpalatable to the Western world. In September 1935 Tagore writes to Mahatma Gandhi and follows it up with another letter to Jawaharlal Nehru: the 'constant begging excursions' produced meagre results, while they were 'a hateful trial for me' for it was like 'laboriously picking minute crumbs of favour from the tables of parsimonious patrons.'[55] At the same time, when Gandhi objected to the indignity of his begging excursions in the guise of presentation of Tagore's songs and dramatic performances, Tagore reacted sharply. Those were not just begging expeditions, he said, but they were an expression of that artistic self which was part of the culture and personality of Santiniketan. 'It is part of a poet's religion.'[56] Shortly before his death, in one of his last letters to Gandhi, Tagore appealed to him to 'accept this institution under your protection'. 'Visva-Bharati is like a vessel which is carrying the cargo of my life's best treasure and I hope it may claim special care for my countrymen for its preservation.'[57] Mahatma Gandhi replied that this letter had 'gone straight into my heart,' and assured Tagore of his best efforts to assure the future of Visva-Bharati.[58] That was Gandhi's last visit to Santiniketan in Tagore's lifetime.

Encounter with Science

In the higher levels of study in Visva-Bharati the natural sciences were conspicuously absent because due to lack of government funding and the uncertain flow of donations Tagore could not afford to install laboratories and employ scientists. But there is evidence of his keen awareness of the importance of scientific attitude in his debates with Gandhi in the 1920s as well as in his personal interactions with top-ranking scientists like Albert Einstein, the bio-physicist Jagadish Chandra Bose, and the physicist Satyendra Nath Bose. The same interest is also in evidence in his writings. Among the works published by Tagore in the last years of his life was a totally new venture, *Visva-Parichay* ('An Introduction to the Universe'). He begins the work, in a long dedication to his young friend the physicist S.N. Bose (known as the co-author of the Bose–Einstein statistics), with the remark that the Indian mind was yet to internalize the scientific attitude.

> In the forest leaves fall from the trees and that fertilizes the soil. In countries where science is cultivated little bits of that knowledge are spreading all the time. That fertilizes and animates a scientific mind. In the absence of that our mind remains unscientific. It is a poverty in the domain of knowledge as well as all the areas of our life and work.[59]

Tagore wrote this book as the first publication in a series he began, the Popular Education Books. Many experts contributed to the series of small booklets, each on his specialization, in simple Bengali accessible to general readers. Tagore was, as he admits in the preface, no specialist in science but he wanted to offer an interpretation in his own light. He had been, he said, like a mendicant collecting fragments of knowledge from the scientists' works, to the extent he understood it, and that gave him an aesthetic pleasure. The poet's sense of joy in looking at the expanding universe in the light of astrophysics of his times and the quality of prose continue to attract readers, though the information content is naturally out of date now.

Tagore traces his interest in astrophysics to the lessons in astronomy he received in his childhood from his father. His readings in popular science in later times, he writes, fed his mind; it did not constitute education in science in the proper sense of the term, but it helped develop an awareness of science and 'an ability to see through the stupidity of blind faith'.[60] What seems to matter to Tagore was above all the need to promote in India a scientific attitude. Even Mahatma Gandhi was criticized by him severely when he saw the Mahatma wanting in that respect. A well-known incident that illustrates this was Tagore's protest when Gandhi made a press statement after the Bihar earthquake of 1934 to the effect that it was 'a divine chastisement' for the sin of casteism. Tagore drew Gandhi's attention to the implications of 'this kind of unscientific view of things'.[61] He apologized for stating the truism that 'physical catastrophes have their inevitable and exclusive origin in a certain combination of physical facts'. To 'associate ethical principles with cosmic phenomena' will only serve to 'promote elements of unreason' in the public mind.[62] Another instance was Tagore's critique of the Gandhian position on modern technology in connection with the charkha. Tagore argued that 'the all-embracing poverty, which has overwhelmed our country cannot be removed by working with our hands to the neglect of science'.[63] On both occasions Mahatma Gandhi declined to accept Tagore's position, though he cordially conceded Tagore the right to express his dissent.[64]

A superficial reading of Tagore's play *Mukta-Dhara* might suggest that there is an anti-science message in it, but actually it is against the abuse of science for purposes of exploitation and oppression. The same is true of *Rakta-Karabi* where it is not so much science involved as crude technology. Earlier in life, Tagore had criticized exponents of the 'Hindu' view of science and condemned them in no uncertain terms.[65] That was in the 1890s when there was a neo-Hindu wave in Bengal, an attempt to revive Hindu orthodoxy feeling imperilled by the growing strength of Brahmaism. Tagore had a good command over Sanskrit and exposed to ridicule the pseudo-scholars who tried to give a 'modern' rationalization of traditional Hindu practices and to reinterpret old texts. He wrote in a letter to a friend about that time: 'It is time to speak out boldly and harshly. Because the mist of spiritualism is rising and obscures everything.'[66]

Virtually from the 1890s to the 1930s we see Tagore carrying on a campaign for the scientific attitude in India and against ignorant obscurantism and slavish faith in the infallibility of the shastras among the educated. Sometimes such pronouncements have been seen as Brahma Samaj propaganda against Hinduism. That is an error. There is evidence that Tagore, as he grew to maturity, ceased to be a devout member of the Adi Brahma Samaj, although in his early life, motivated by his father, he played a prominent role in the organization and its propaganda. In 1910 Tagore lectured at the Sadharan Brahma Samaj on 'The significance of the Brahma Samaj'. His argument, upholding Rammohan's Brahmaism, did not go down too well, specially because Tagore's message was that Brahma Samaj must break out of Brahma sectarianism.[67] In 1930 he wrote frankly to his niece: the Adi Brahma Samaj was dead and 'I don't feel enthused to carry the corpse—we should respect the past, but we should not pretend that it is not the past'.[68] Tagore's was not a Brahma Samajist agenda against orthodox Hinduism, the agenda was to promote a scientific attitude in his country.

Compared to this central purpose consistently pursued by Tagore, the book *Visva-Parichay* he wrote or his contacts with scientists may be considered trivial. He was one of the closest friends of Sir Jagadish Chandra Bose, a physicist by training who made important research contribution in the area of biology. Bose was the second Indian scientist to be elected Fellow of Royal Society, the first being the mathematician Srinivasa Ramanujan. Tagore not only provided Bose moral support but also funds donated by his friend, Maharaja of Tripura, to finance Bose's research in Europe. However, Bose and Tagore did not have much to share in the discourse of science.

Between Tagore and Albert Einstein we have records of fairly long discussions in the philosophical vein. They met first in 1926 and four times, July to December, in 1930. Of the first meeting there is no record of the conversation, of the second set there are two versions, one carried by the *New York Times* after correction by Einstein, and another slightly different version which Tagore edited and published along with his Hibbert Lectures. They formed high regard for each other. That is evident from Einstein's letter to Tagore and Tagore's refusal of an honorary degree from

Berlin University as a mark of protest against the persecution of Einstein in Nazi Germany. However, instances of mutual regard notwithstanding, some observers have doubted whether there was significant intellectual exchange between the two. Einstein's future son-in-law, a journalist, was present at some of the conversations and he thought that it was 'as though two planets were engaged in a chat . . . Tagore the poet with the head of a thinker, and Einstein, the thinker with the head of a poet'.[69] Einstein wrote to Romain Rolland: 'My conversation with Tagore was rather unsuccessful because of difficulties in communication.'[70] A young contemporary, Isaiah Berlin surmised that there was not 'much in common between them'.[71] Thus perceptions differ a good deal.

Instead of speculating in that fashion, one might look at the central points of divergence and convergence between Tagore and Einstein in the recorded conversation. They both agreed that 'beauty is not independent of man', i.e. human perception. The divergence was on the question whether, as Tagore put it, 'truth is realized through man'. Einstein maintained that there is a reality independent of human observation. 'We attribute to truth a super-human objectivity—this reality which is independent of our existence and our experience and our mind . . .' Einstein posed the standard question to confront philosophical idealism: 'nobody may be in this house, yet that table remains where it is.' Tagore's answer: 'Yes, it remains outside the individual mind but not the universal mind.' Einstein did not accept the postulated 'universal mind'. Thus the basic divergence was between Einstein's position that there was a reality 'out there' regardless of human perceptions, and Tagore's position that if there is such a reality it is unrelated and irrelevant to man and thus 'for us non-existing'. Contemporary physics touched on this question but that need not detain us here.[72] It was an old and well-known epistemological issue, the contra-position of a notion of objective reality, regardless of human perception or knowledge of it, and the view that only human constructs makes reality knowable. Two of the greatest minds of the early twentieth century puzzled over this classical philosophical problem, revived again in the frontiers of science.

Thoughts on Music and its Language

The heart feels shy to bring to your vagrant mind
The lyric of my secret, lest its meaning be missed
And its rhythm.

Tagore wrote thus (his own translation) of his songs.[73]

It is quite difficult to talk of Tagore's songs dispassionately. That is the task to which we must turn now, avoiding the profusion of superlatives which characterizes discussion of that subject when the author happens to be Bengali—to non-Bengalis that often makes little sense. The reason for this difference in perception is, as everyone knows, that Tagore's role as a poet is as important in creating these songs as his as a music composer. If you break the magical marriage of the lyric and the music, you tend to lose the essential quality of these songs. Tagore developed a theory about it, when he was as yet an obscure poet and unknown as a lyric writer or music composer, in 1881 in an essay entitled 'Music and Poetry'.[74] 'Mankind has two means of self-expression—words and music. In fact even words depend upon the tone . . . When we write poetry we depend more on words and in songs we depend on the language of music.' But there is a difference between the two: words must add up to express an idea; music can attain expression without words. As a result, poetry has been compelled to cultivate the art of expressing ideas; music has fallen behind in that respect. Tagore was evidently aware that there were stereotypes of association between a *raga* and a *bhava*. Nevertheless he thought that the cultivation and expression of bhava had declined in music as compared to the poet's world where the poet cannot do without bhava to be expressed in words. Tagore concluded that music ought to be open to bhava; that is to say, poetry should be a close companion of music.

In arguing in this fashion Tagore, then aged twenty, might have been a little dogmatic but the statement was important not so much as a description of the status of music and poetry, but as a statement of his agenda as a writer and composer of songs. He believed that a union between these two creative functions was a necessity. Thus the lyric he wrote mattered to him as much as the music he composed, neither was complete without the other.

Another interesting and original characteristic of Tagore's thinking on music was his effort to understand and situate the practice of producing music in its social context. For instance, he reflects on the decline in the appreciation of classical music in early twentieth century north India. At one time the wealthy would patronize musicians and there was an appreciative audience in the durbar. 'Today we have plenty of public meetings,' he writes in 1915, 'but the *majlis* for music is a thing of the past. Among the young people today it is difficult to find anyone who will willingly face the full-length performance of a classical musician . . . Our musical tradition is now a sleeping beauty incarcerated in the midst of her limitless wealth . . .'[75] On the other hand he believed that music in Europe drew sustenance from contemporary culture and social support.

> At one time in every country the rich aristocracy patronized art and literature and music. In Europe today the commoners have taken the place of those traditional patrons . . . But the wealthy in our country today have no sense of their obligation. . . And the commonalty have neither the money nor the taste [for that music] . . . We have lost the contact between our life and our arts.[76]

Tagore believed that the proud exclusiveness of the classical tradition and its practitioners and patrons stood in the way of opening up the world of classical Indian music.

Another point Tagore made, more than once, was the potential of allowing a creative encounter between the musical traditions of India and the West. He particularly underlined this during his visit to England in 1912–13, when he witnessed the Handel festival at Crystal Palace, London, where four thousand performers played his music. Probably this was the celebration of the two-hundredth anniversary of Handel's migration from Germany to England in 1712. Tagore was impressed with the organized energy of so many musicians performing together. He recognized that there were basic differences between the European and Indian musical tradition. European music is based on the principle of harmony, Indian music on melody; Europe's music celebrates life here and now, Indian music addresses the individual's quest for the eternal.[77] Nonetheless traffic between the two was desirable. He maintained: 'In literature the impact of the West has been vivifying, likewise India needs to take music out of the iron chest of *dastur*' (customary practice). Tagore went on to say that Indian music would be appreciated in India again if it were to receive appreciation in the West. 'Once we send our music overseas we will then welcome it back and begin truly to appreciate it. We have been far too long in our domestic corner to know the true value of our own things; we are unfit now to evaluate what is our own and to understand its glory.'[78] These were prophetic words in more senses than one.

In 1917 in an essay entitled 'Liberation of Music' (*Sangiter Mukti*) Tagore developed the argument further. He read out the text at a meeting in Calcutta and created a controversy with proponents of 'purity' of Indian music. Tagore argued that in Bengal there had always been a tendency to question the infallibility of shastric prescriptions and it was inevitable that music too would claim freedom from rigid formats and forms. True creativity requires such a freedom for self-expression. (This essay was later published in a collection entitled *Sangit Chinta*). Tagore returned to the subject again in his essays on metre which he compared with the beat in music; the innovation he made in the early 1930s, the form of 'prose-poem', led to this discussion with music experts.[79]

These were not just theoretical points to Tagore. Many of his innovations in music emanated from there. Building upon folk tradition Tagore virtually created a new genre of 'musical drama' in Bengal. This reached an audience wider than the audience at mehfils or majlis. He also made commercial stage shows 'respectable'. Earlier his brothers and relatives had pioneered participation of upper-class members of the gentry (bhadralok) in stage performances. In order to raise funds for his school in Santiniketan, Tagore began to stage performances by his students, men and women, on the public stage. Then, Tagore synthesized music of different traditions in the music he composed. This practice crossed the conventional boundaries between Western and Indian music, folk and classical traditions, and within classical the regional boundaries. Needless to say, approximation between different musical traditions was not unknown in earlier times, *khayal* and *dhrupad* found acceptance as classical, or exponents of north Indian music were to be found in the south as well, there was cross-fertilization between different *gharanas*, and music had travelled with musicians who went from one prince's durbar to another. Tagore deliberately widened the range of such crossings across boundaries. Finally, in presenting dance with his songs Tagore created a unique art form where dance styles of Manipur or Java or Kerala blended in an operatic form which paralleled the European operas of the nineteenth century. He developed what came to be known in Bengal as 'dance-drama' (*nritya-natya*).

The details of these innovations by Tagore need not detain us. But no one who looks at Tagore's writings can fail to notice the importance he attached to his musical creations, known initially as *Rabi-babur gan* and later as *Rabindra-sangit*. He said often that all his other creations might be forgotten, but his songs would be his enduring memorial. His eclecticism was evident from the very beginning in his use of Western tunes in the earliest musical dramas he composed, *Valmiki-Pratibha* (1881), *Kal-Mrigaya* (1882), and *Mayar Khela* (1888). Tunes like 'The Vicar of Bray', 'The British Grenadier', 'Ye banks and braes', 'Go where glory awaits thee', 'Nancy Lee', etc. were used along with semi-classical Indian music. Tagore's own commentary:

I cannot claim that I have entered the core of European music. But what I gathered of European music as an outsider attracted something deep in my heart. I used to sense the romantic in that music . . . I never composed anything with the kind of the enthusiasm with which I composed *Valmiki-Pratibha* and *Kal-mrigaya*. These two were written in a state of mad delight in breaking all conventions in the fiesta of a musical revolution. Hence that had harmony and dissonance and no discrimination between Bengali and English tunes.[80]

In those days, Rabindranath's brother, Jyotirindra played an important role as the pianist and as a composer of tunes.

Tagore's early training in classical music, of the Bishnupur gharana, showed in his range of pickings from classical schools. He picked portions and not the whole of a composition and hence he called these *bhanga gan* or pieces of songs. A recent compilation of such songs lists over 230 such songs taken from Haridas Swami, Meera, Thyagaraja, Dikshitar, et al.[81] These are acknowledged by the author or associates as musical pieces from a specified source; there were many other songs inspired by other composers but that remains unrecorded. This practice of picking a piece to work it into a new composition can be seen in the early years of Tagore's life. Statistics are not very useful in this regard but there is an estimate that up to age twenty-six, Tagore thus composed from borrowings nearly 190 songs; on the other hand in the last twenty-five years of his life there were only twenty-two instances recorded. Needless to say, a common classical base shared by Tagore and the earlier composers helped in the transformation of the borrowings into something new.[82]

In the middle period of his life Tagore drew upon folk songs extensively, particularly of the Baul school. This was also the period, roughly between 1900 and 1920, when Tagore wrote the largest number of *swadeshi* or patriotic songs which were ideally suited to the folk idiom of music. He entitled his earliest collection of patriotic songs *Baul* (1905). The folk tunes were derived from *baul* (songs of a sect of mendicants with affinity to Vaishnavism and Sufism), *kirtan* (Vaishnava songs about Radha and Krishna), *Ramprasadi* (songs in praise of the deity Kali, known by the name of the eighteenth-century author of the genre, Ramprasad), *bhatiali* and *sari* (boatmen's songs) in origin. We may connect this development in Tagore's creations with what we have noticed earlier—his increasing involvement with the supervision of the Tagore estates and tours in rural areas from the 1890s. That is when he seems to wake up to the wealth of folk songs in Bengal.

The first wave of swadeshi songs and music composition was provoked by the Partition of Bengal but such composition continued unabated even after Tagore drifted away from the rest of the nationalist leadership from about 1907–08. Some of the patriotic songs were based on classical ragas, e.g. *Jana-gana-mana-Adhinayaka*, composed in 1911 and destined to be our national anthem.[83]

Incidentally, a myth regarding this song needs to be refuted and laid to rest. It is on record that the song was written in December 1911. On 12 December 1911 the Delhi Durbar met to honour King Emperor George V. Presumably a poem written a few days before could not be intended for such an august event. The song was actually sung at the twenty-seventh session of the Indian National Congress, Calcutta, on 27 December 1911, as the opening song at the beginning of the day's proceedings. Thereafter it was also sung at the foundation day anniversary of Adi Brahma Samaj in February 1912 and included in their collection of psalms, *Brahma Sangit*. Many years later fertile and malicious imagination connected the composition of the song and the Durbar and it was rumoured that Tagore's poem was meant to be sung in the Delhi Durbar. Pulin Behari Sen, a careful bibliographist and editor of Tagore's works, asked him to throw light on that story. The reply of 20 November 1937 has been preserved in the Tagore archives.[84] Tagore wrote that it was obvious that 'neither the Fifth nor the Sixth nor any George could be the maker of human destiny through the ages'. He said 'I had hailed in the song *Jana-gana-mana Adhinayaka* that Dispenser of India's destiny who guides, through all rise and fall, the wayfarers, He who shows the people the way . . .' Tagore had in mind parts of the poem where we see no mortal, but a divine entity: 'Eternal charioteer, thou drivest man's history / Along the road that is rugged with the rise and fall of nations.'[85] And that is why it was promptly included among the Brahma Samaj hymns. To see George V as the object of worship in place of the 'Dispenser of India's destiny. . . Thou King of all Kings' was not only absurd, but sacrilegious to Tagore. Asked to write to welcome the emperor, he declined and wrote this poem and he did not write it for the Congress either. It was a hymn to his Maker, the guardian of the country's destiny.

In his earlier publications Tagore used to indicate the *raga* and the *tala* as custom demanded. That is what you will see you if you look up his *Rabichhaya* (1885), *Kavya Granthavali* (1898), *Kavya Grantha* (1903) edited by Mohit Chandra Sen, or *Rabindra Granthavali* (1904) of the Hitabadi edition. In course of time Tagore gave up these traditional markers. The synthesis he often aimed at did not accommodate rigid classification. *Rabindra-sangit* exponents are generally of the view that the truest characteristic of that music is its freedom from the constraints that govern other genres of music. More important than the conventional markers was the bhava in the songs. Significantly, he recast the first edition of *Gitabitan* (1931–32), which followed a chronological order, to rearrange songs so as to underline the bhava. Tagore brought out a second edition under his own supervision and wrote in a preface:

> When *Gitabitan* was first published the compilers, due to a pressure to expedite publication, were unable to arrange it thematically. Not only did that cause problems to its users, but from the literary point of view it was detrimental to aesthetics. That is why in this edition the songs have been arranged in terms of *bhava*. This way, even when the music is not rendered, a reader can read the songs as lyrics.[86]

Tagore himself edited the volume and sectionalized the songs into parts entitled: Prayer, Motherland, Love, Nature, Varieties. There were further subdivisions; for example, within 'Prayer' songs were arranged under subtitles like Friend, Awakening, Joy, Beauty, etc.

As regards the lyrics some of Tagore's finest poems are in his books of songs. Some were translated by Tagore: 'Thou will dwell in my heart / Like the full moon in the summer night' (1896). 'My heart, like a peacock on a rainy day, / spreads its plumes tinged with rapturous colours of thoughts' (1900). 'Forgive my langour,

O Lord, / If ever I lag behind upon life's way' (1914). 'I shall not wait and watch in the house for thy coming / . . . For the petals fall from the drooping flowers / And time flies to its end' (1918). 'My heart sings at the wonder of my place / In this world of light and life / At the feel in my pulse of the rhythm of creation / Cadenced by the swing of endless time' (1922). 'We two lay sunk in the dusk of dreams' (1931).[87] According to the estimate made by Prabhat Kumar Mukherjee, an authority on Tagore, the total number of songs written by him was 2232. These are the songs included in the collection of *Gitabitan* of which the second edition Tagore himself edited in 1938–41. However, the songs with musical score, mostly in the sixty-four volumes of *Swarabitan* number only 1721. There are some lyrics without traceable scores.[88] Tagore said a few weeks before his death:

> I don't know where they [songs by Tagore] originated . . . They came to me and I sang . . . When I listen I say to myself 'Your song will endure, Time cannot steal it'. . . Music has this characteristic—it preserves momentary joys and sorrows, for ever.[89]

What was the cause of this self-confidence and why it seems justifiable are questions which one cannot even pose without any means of translating to the readers the quality of the music and the lyrics in his songs. Therefore we have limited our discussion to the ideas which inspired the musician Tagore.

Theory of Literature

In 1936 Tagore published a collection of essays on literature (*Sahityer Pathe*, i.e. 'On the Path to Literature'). He never wrote a systematic exposition of his theoretical position vis-à-vis literature. However, he had written early in life a large number of essays in literary criticism which he collected in 1907. These were four volumes of essays on ancient Indian literature in Sanskrit, modern Bengali writings, and folk-literature of Bengal (*Prachin Sahitya, Sahitya, Adhunik Sahitya,*

Loka-sahitya all published in 1907). In fact these essays were far superior to the ones on literary criticism collected in 1936: the latter were often *obiter dicta*, reiterating ideas which were already expressed in his earlier writings with a more persuasive style of exposition. Tagore himself made this comment on his writings on literature, addressing a reader: 'I have often restated my opinions, I have refined them at each restatement, which makes it difficult to fix a particular position attributable to me.' And, further:

> 'you will be impatient with my metaphorical language. That you know is an old weakness of mine. When I am keen to express an idea, my mind dresses it up in metaphors, avoiding wordy expositions. It is like using hieroglyphics instead of letters of [the] alphabet.' But this style is sanctioned by very old literary practice—to express ideas indirectly through representative surrogates. 'At the same time this style hampers the application of the logical method of reasoning. I admit this failing in me.'[90]

This self-critique in a letter to his friend is valid for a great deal of Tagore's theoretical writings, on the aesthetics of literature.

The collections published in 1907 comprised essays written between 1891 and 1902 and they mark the birth of a new literary sensibility. The comparison he makes between Sakuntala and Miranda in Shakespeare's *Tempest* is not a part of traditional appreciation of Kalidasa. When he writes of *Meghadutam* again, Tagore puts himself in the position of a modern Indian reader and looks at 'the life which flowed at one time in India from which we have been exiled'. No literary critic earlier to him took folk literature seriously the way Tagore did in *Loka-Sahitya*, a commentary on a collection of nursery rhymes, folk songs, rhymes current among women in their domestic interiors, and the verses of plebeian versifiers (*Kabi-wallahs*) of the eighteenth and nineteenth century. Of modern writings Tagore's criticism is unusually alive to the social and historical context of literary men. Almost half of his book on modern literature is devoted to Bankim Chandra Chatterjee and his times. An example of his thought-laden appreciation:

Vidyasagar [Ishwarchandra] staked his all and entirely by himself triumphed over impossible odds, by virtue of his unstoppable energy . . . In his efforts for the welfare of countless thousands he was as alone as he was in struggle with the opposition of thousands.

In his social reform activities in his 'lethargic, debilitated, ungenerous country' he was as alone as Bankim Chandra was in the literary field in his effort to bring in a 'new vitalizing element'. Bankim reconstituted the foundations of Bengali literature and in doing so he wielded a merciless critic's broom to clear out of the way all that was unfit for survival. Tagore admired Bankim the critic as much as Bankim the creative writer. Perhaps Tagore's admiration for Bankim and his 'merciless pursuit of the highest standards, commitment, and masculine majesty' was all the greater because Tagore himself often fought shy of engaging in that task because he detested crossing swords with the lesser folk around him.[91]

In these early writings Tagore's basic approach to literature emerges. In the lead article in *Sahitya* (1907) he writes: 'To sum up what we have to say, literature is about the heart and the mind of human beings . . . The symphony created by the heart and the outer world and the human mind, when represented through language in word-pictures and poesy, is literature.' There is a divinity at work in the joy of creation, and the human heart is in that creative activity to express its own self. The innate human desire for self-expression, the desire to reach out to other human beings, the desire to keep the message alive beyond the here and now—that is at the core of writings ranging from ancient inscriptions to the latest literature. However, all that is expressed is not literature. It is literature when the expression of an idea or a feeling or whatever is expressible, takes a form which allows effective transmission to another mind so as to recreate the same idea, feeling, etc. in that other mind. The artifices of literature enable things in one man's mind to be internalized in other people's minds.[92]

Another important point Tagore makes is that literature speaks not only to the present times but to the future as well. 'That which tries to claim immortality in the heart of man for ever' is literature. Tagore almost echoes Bhavabhuti, '*Vipula prithvi kalascha nirabadhi*', and postulates that literature addresses not just the contemporary reader but 'the human society of all times'.[93] Thirdly, in his early essays as well as in later writings Tagore declares his faith in the maxim 'Truth is beauty; beauty truth'. What looks like a cliché is rescued by Tagore with invocations of the authority of the Upanishads. He goes back to the Upanishadic pronouncement: '*ananda rupamamritam yadvibhati*', whatever is expressed or revealed is divine ecstasy and life eternal. Or again, '*raso vai sah*'[94] and so forth. Finally, Tagore makes a point that was entirely his own.

> Only when we realize that Literature reveals the universal man (*visva-manab*) we shall see what is the essence of literature . . . When an author's thoughts resonates with the thoughts of the whole mankind, when he expresses in his writings the anguish of all men, that is what finds a place in literature . . . Consider how man has extended his self in the tangible world into an intangible self . . . Confined as he is in his location in the outer world, in his intangible creations he enlarges his self, and this second universe is his own creation, that is what literature is about.[95]

Tagore goes on to say that it was not for him to show the way to this ultimate aim of literature, but he wanted to liberate literature from the parochialism that fails to perceive the universalism inherent in literature.

These basic ideas about literature expounded in *Sahitya* are reiterated over and again in Tagore's later writings (*Sahityer Swarup*, 1943, posthumous collection; *Sahityer Pathe*, 1936). The new element that is seen in the later writings is Tagore's approach to 'modernism' in literature in the 1930s. Many of the later writings are in the form of letters to various literary personalities of those times and what Tagore writes is often like Tagore 'talking down' to them. Some of these writings in the 1930s are commissioned by favoured editors and the like and are not of Tagore's best. The other problem is that some of the pronouncements in the 1930s are *ex cathedra* judgements which Tagore did not care to defend or explain in that last phase in his life. Thus Tagore's writings on the subject in these years, hailed by admirers around him, do not match the quality of his earlier writings in literary criticism. Krishna Kripalani was a close observer who married Tagore's granddaughter. He recalls that Tagore 'was writing for an uncritical clientele who applauded whatever he did. Gradually he came to be surrounded by a flock of admirers, many of whom were little better than courtiers and sycophants, who were like a wall between him and the real world'.[96] Kripalani also quotes Rothenstein who felt uncomfortable to see Tagore's band of followers who pretended to share his spiritual idealism and tended to 'weaken his artistic integrity by flattery'. Tagore's essays in literary theory appear to be particularly prone to fall prey to the tendency to uncritically acclaim whatever fell from the great poet's lips. However, Tagore continued to give his best to poetry and creative writing.

What are the new themes Tagore writes about in the late 1920s and 1930s? First, he writes about the genre he virtually creates in Bengali, the prose-poem (*gadya-kavya*). He tried that form in *Lipika* (1922), but 'did not have the courage' to do that again till the 1930s (*Punascha*, 1932; *Sesh Saptak*, 1935; *Patraput*, 1936; *Shyamali*, 1936; and poems elsewhere which verge upon prose-poems). Tagore cites the examples of the psalms of David and Solomon which possess a poetic quality that is evident in the English translations of King James's version of the Bible. *Yajurveda*, he says, is also a prose-poem and the English version of *Gitanjali* likewise. Popular taste might not be ready for it, but Tagore declared that he was ready to risk it.[97]

The other important issue in Tagore's later writings is 'modernism'. In 1927 we see him welcoming the advent of new authors in Bengal marching under the banner of modernism; he saw 'a new wave of creative energy'. At the same time he said:

These modernists claim that only we know what is life, only we deal with reality,—this has become an easy and cheap prescription. Yet they have done very little for the poverty-stricken masses; they are prosperous, they enjoy a comfortable living style; poverty to them is only a hot spice to impart pep to modernist literature. This curry powder of imagination is an ingredient in cooking up a cheap and artificial literature.

Likewise, the stress on the sex urge in literature, he said, is not necessarily commendable. It is one of the easiest ways of showing off a kind of courage.

Courage in writing, or for that matter in society at large, is a good thing. But courage may be of different types, of different qualities. 'We do not care a damn' is an attitude of courage, but to have courage because we care is another kind, a greater kind of courage.[98]

In the early 1930s Tagore addressed the issue of modernism in English poetry. He began with saying that when he was young, Burnes, Coleridge, Shelley, Keats were considered modern; in the 1930s it became customary to call all that 'mid-Victorian' and a new modernism took the place of the old. What are the marks of modernity in poetry? Tagore thought its characteristic was the poet's trying hard to avoid being 'poetic'. There was an effort to eschew ornamentation, to bring things down to the barest form.

Tagore cited examples from Amy Lowell, T.S. Eliot, et al. to come to this final conclusion:

If you ask me what is pure modernism, I would say it is to perceive the world dispassionately, as a person uninvolved and objective. This perception is pure and illuminating, there is joy in perception in a dispassionate way. Just as science today examines the world in an objective way, modern poetry would look at the whole world objectively, that is what is classically modern.

But Tagore went on to argue that this perception called modern in the early twentieth century, existed in earlier times too—he cited as examples works of the ninth-century Chinese poet Lih Po. The only new feature of twentieth century modernism, he said, was the proclivity to look at only the distaff side of life. In this it differed from the older poetic tradition and it was also artificial.[99]

But it is not the subject of writing which makes it modern; a subject relevant to the times makes a piece of writing valuable, but it is not necessarily good as literature. Moreover, he said 'in India we are easily overwhelmed when we encounter a trend in European literature' and this was a source of danger to our authors.[100] Did the tone of Tagore's critique of modernism, despite the profession of willingness to welcome the generation of modernist authors, suggest that he felt a little insecure? Be that as it may, the outcome was a spectacular achievement. Tagore outdid the modernists in the novel *Sesher Kabita* ('The Farewell Song'). His works in the thirties in fiction (*Char Adhyay*, 'Four Chapters', 1934; *Tinsangi*, 'Three Companions', short stories, 1940) as well as in poetry (*Punascha*, 'Post Script', 1932; *Senjuti*, 'The Evening Lamp', 1938; *Nabajatak*, 1940) mark a new turn in his creative writings.

It is difficult to define what is new in these poems of the 1930s. Examples are telling. From 'Night Express':

This heart of mine, a night express, is on the way
The night is deep, the carriages are loaded with sleep.
. . . Moments aglow in flashes are instantly left behind
Unknown lands hurl through the speechless night
Towards the unthinkable, far away, the final destination.[101]

In *Sesh Saptak*:

When the desert covering of thousands of years was
lifted, there was revealed the mammoth skeleton of a dateless human
habitation which once had life in the void behind the backdrop
of history.
Its resonant centuries have consigned all this poetry and song to
the depths of an unplumbed silence
. . . Nowhere was felt their loss.[102]

In *Shyamali*:

My perception coloured the emerald green and the ruby red
The east and the west were lighted when I turned my eyes to the sky
I said to the rose 'You are beautiful' and beautiful it became.
That is metaphysics, you say, not poetry. Truth, that is what poetry
is about, is my answer.[103]

In *Parisesh*:

Once again I wake up when the night has waned
When the world opens all its petals once more,
And this is an endless wonder . . .
The centuries on which have flashed and foundered
kingly crowns like bubbles,
have left their signature on the bark of this aged tree,
Where I am allowed to sit under its ancient shade for one more
day
And this is an endless wonder.[104]

Many of the 'modernist' poets acclaimed the new turn in Tagore's writings from the late twenties. Tagore in turn patronized and contributed to the modernists' literary journals, (e.g. *Kabita*, *Parichay*), corresponded cordially with young poets of the school,[105] and as one of them, Samar Sen recalls, 'his certificate of a line or two was something they hankered for.'[106] Thus Tagore remained a dominant though distant presence.

A New Turn, Old Genres

Other than poetry, Tagore contributed in the 1930s to three different genres: musical drama, prose fiction, and nonsense literature. The latter consisted of nonsense rhymes as well as a surrealistic kind of fiction (*Khapchhara*, 1937; *Chharar chhabi*, 1937; *Shay* (1937); *Prahasini*, 1939). These are highly enjoyable to read and their appeal is not limited to the child to whom these are ostensibly addressed. It is interesting that at the time when Tagore was writing so often on the theme of death, his mind found release in the realm of magical unreason. However, more attention has been commanded by the musical dramas *Chandalika* (1933), *Taser Desh* (1933) and *Shyama* (1939). That is partly because these have often been enacted with great success on the stage, and partly because they bring to the viewers some of Tagore's abiding ideas very effectively.

Taser Desh ('The Land of Playing Cards') is virtually a manifesto of rebellion against the rule of authority and tradition—a theme on which Tagore often wrote, castigating India's stagnation in modern times. He uses a familiar literary device—strangers invade a land of hierarchic gradation like a pack of playing cards, routinized habits inherited from the past, and a cast of mind opposed to change. The play *Chandalika* (The Untouchable Girl') is also a rebellion of another kind: the untouchable girl is made conscious of being a human being, not an object of contempt as an outcaste, when a passing Buddhist monk takes water from her hands. Tagore's deep concern with the inhumanity of casteism in India was reflected in this drama. And Mahatma Gandhi's struggle against untouchablity seems to take a visible form and life. A secondary theme was that sublime love triumphs over carnal love—a denouement foreordained in the story of an untouchable girl's love for the monk, which Tagore found in a Buddhist text. The last of the great musical dramas (written in 1936, rewritten 1939) is also on the theme of carnal and sublime love. The main protagonist, Shyama, sacrifices one of her devoted admirers in order to save the life of Vajrasena with whom she is infatuated; but Vajrasena, once he knows of that, is repelled by her inhuman conduct and rejects her at the end. The theme of infatuation contrasted to true love occurs in many of Tagore's creations, right from *Mayar Khela* (1888), but in this play the woman's infatuation is depicted in the starkest form.

In fiction, short stories and novels, Tagore was not spectacularly productive during these years. Three of his short stories were published at the end of the decade (*Tinsangi*). In 1933–34 two novels and a play were published, *Dui Bon* ('Two Sisters'), *Malancha* ('The Orchard'), and *Bansari*. All of them are mainly focused on psychological analysis of love in conjugal life and outside of it. There was something wanting in them. It has been said that Tagore's treatment of love now was intellectualized and ineffective in conveying its feeling; the protagonists seemed to be unreal artefacts, not flesh and blood creatures.[107] This is perhaps true. But that cannot be said of the last novel Tagore wrote, *Char Adhyay*.

The novel is remarkable for its intensity of gaze and ruthlessness in thinking through to judgements. Its focus is on political violence in conflict with human values. The historical context is, of course, the militant nationalist (*biplabi*) programme of activity through secret societies and acts of individual violence in Bengal and in India at large in the early decades of the twentieth century. In political essays like 'Path o Patheya' ('Ends and Means', 1908) Tagore had dealt with the question but that was without the emotional charge notable in this novel. He had touched on it in the play *Visarjan (1890)* (1909) but that was in allegorical form. He had delved deep into the question in *Ghare Baire* (1916) but much of that was drawing-room conversation compared to this novel. It is evident that Tagore had thought long and hard about the issue. It is not known why he returned to it in 1934. The action of militant nationalists in Chittagong in April 1930 and the eventual execution of its leader Surya Sen in 1934 may have provoked Tagore's thoughts once again.

There are only three major protagonists in the novel: Indranath, the brilliant evil genius of a secret society of militant nationalist youths who believe in violent means towards attaining the country's independence; Atin, an idealist young man who took to that path but found it revolting to be part of inhuman crimes committed in the name of national interests; in the fringes of the secret society, Ela, a woman whose romantic attachment to Atin, dedicated to a cause that allows no other commitment, is destined to a tragic end.

Atin looks into his mind. An untimely end to his life is near, the curtain is quivering, the light is flickering. At the beginning of life he was in the clear light of the morning, and today he has come far from there. What could have sustained him in that journey has been wasted to nothing; he had been cheating his own self . . . where is the truth, where is the valour, where is the glory in the path leading to the muck he was into—this dark abyss of theft and robbery and murder by men in masks can never be the foundation of a lighthouse that will illuminate the course of history. Soul-killing crimes have been fruitless, the certainty of failure lies ahead.[108]

There came a day when Atin encountered the miracle of love. He had imagined at one time how Dante and Beatrice had dedicated their lives to a cause, but was there such a noble cause uniting Atin and Ela? To Atin the 'disgusting path of secret terror' meant the 'defeat of the soul'. 'A web of lies, base shoddiness, mutual mistrust, lust for power, espionage, will one day drag all these people to the depth of abasement,' Atin began to realize. 'Throughout the world nationalism thunders a false message that we can bring life to the country at the cost of the country's soul—and my mind has often inwardly rebelled in protest'. Ela says: 'Turn back', and Atin: 'The arrow may miss the target but it cannot return to the quiver'. Ela: 'This path is not yours.' Atin: 'The path is not mine, now I belong to this path.' There was no space for love in that path.

There was a huge outcry in Bengal against Tagore's depiction of the militant nationalists. The reaction against the novel might have been in part a reaction against Tagore's treatment of sexuality in this novel. Perhaps for the first time in Tagore's prose writings the woman's body appears in a manner unknown till then. Ela to Atin: 'I am yours, wholly yours—yours in death as well. Take me . . .' Or again: 'My body is yours . . . I have not known till today how much I love you. For the sake of that love, kill me.' The militants possibly thought that this was trivializing the holy relationship of comrades in arms.

The critical reception compelled Tagore to write an 'explanation' which was printed as an appendix to the novel from the second edition onwards.

From the point of view of literature it is irrelevant whether *Char Adhyay* contains any message or judgement. It is plainly about the love of the hero and the heroine for each other in a story situated in modern Bengal. The dramatic element in the love story comes from the militant [or revolutionary] nationalists' endeavours in Bengal. The stormy atmosphere of that turmoil, the intensity and the pain that it caused, that is what literature is about. Debates and sage advice belong to the domain of newspapers.

Tagore went on to say that it was best for him as the author to remain indifferent to the criticism of the book. He had no doubt that he and his readers in the 1930s were too near the political events in the background of this story. He looked to the distant future. 'When the excitement of the present times will recede and it will be a subject of cool historical judgement, then the readers' imagination will no longer find it difficult to accept the story in a natural light, this is what I hope for.'[109] As regards the main story, Tagore thought that apart from the tragic end to the love between Atin and Ela, there was a poignant tragedy in Atin's failure to keep true to himself, true to his *swabhava*, in the political path he had chosen.

In the 1930s Tagore spoke up against the government's policy of incarceration without trial and he protested against torture suffered by militant activities in the hands of the police and jail authorities. At the same time, Tagore was keenly aware of the futility of militant acts of individual heroism—acts which attracted popular admiration. However, Tagore's agonizing dilemma, his admiration for heroism and his consciousness of its futility, does not explain the emotional energy at work in writing this novel. Tagore himself provides a clue in recounting an episode that seems to touch upon a canker in his soul. In 1934 he recalled an incident that happened long ago. Brahmo Bandhab Upadhyay (1861–1907) was his first colleague in building the school in Santiniketan but he left there to join the militant nationalists.

He founded the journal *Sandhya*, his spirited writing and intoxicating message set ablaze a fire in the national mind. In the journal the hidden signs of the tactics of terrorism first appeared . . . Then we did not meet each other for a long time. I thought that he had turned away since he had scornfully perceived that my path in politics was different from his. In those days of blind excitement one day I was sitting in my room on the third floor of our house in Jorasanka [Calcutta], when Upadhyay walked in suddenly. We talked about this and that, things in our past. Then he ended the conversation to bid goodbye. He walked up to the threshold and then he turned back. 'Rabi-babu, I have fallen to the depths.' He blurted it out and left that moment. I sensed that he had come just to say those soul-searing words. He was then so ensnared in his web of activities there was no escape open to him. This was my last encounter with him, these were his last words to me. It is relevant to recount this incident at the beginning of this novel.

This was Tagore's 'Introduction' to the novel in its first edition.[110] That Tagore remembered this incident thirty years later and thought this to be an appropriate bridgehead into the theme of the novel suggests that this was something that bothered him, something that deeply engaged his thoughts and emotions: how politics parted two friends, that desultory conversation at an unexpected reunion, the sudden turning back at the threshold, the blurting out of a painful thing that had to be said, and the parting for ever like 'ships that pass in the night'. It is one of the most moving accounts of an episode in Tagore's life. Perhaps it is the key to a secret chamber in Tagore's inner life—the scorn he felt when trusted friends left him, his anguish when he was just an onlooker while admirable men and even lads staked their lives, his desolation in the belief that all that was futile. We will never know for sure.

When the novel was published in 1934, for the time being Tagore's stock in some political circles fell drastically. The *biplabis* (i.e. revolutionary or militant nationalists) were deeply offended.[111] In the years leading to the publication of this novel Tagore's warm sympathy and admiration for them was demonstrated on many occasions. Tagore spoke at a mass meeting in Calcutta in September 1931 to protest against police atrocities, particularly the plight of prisoners in jail.[112] In May 1931 on the occasion of Tagore's seventieth birthday the political prisoners at Buxa Fort sent him their felicitations and in reply Tagore wrote a memorable poem addressing them: 'Your song to the sun shames the dark night around you / They can cage the bird, but they cannot cage the song.'[113] Another celebrated poem entitled 'The Question' written in 1932 expressed Tagore's anguish: 'Does God forgive His enemies?'[114] A few months before *Char Adhyay* was published Tagore issued a political statement on the imprisonment of militant activists without trial: will the British in India claim 'dignity which is based on its claim to appreciation of human values and not on mere assertion of power'?[115] Tagore's empathy with the militant nationalists is manifest here. His heart was with them but his mind was against the means they were wont to use to attain undoubtedly noble ends—hence the relentless tragic trajectory in *Char Adhyay*. That tragedy continues to be relevant, because in Tagore's unfortunate country the protagonists of that story reincarnate time and again till our times.

Three Waves of Poetry

Tagore's poetic creativity seems to be driven by three great waves in the thirties. The *first wave* wafts to us the prose-poems of *Punascha* ('Post-script', 1932), *Sesh Saptak* ('The Last Octave', 1935), *Patraput* ('A Platter of Leaves', 1936), *Shyamali* ('The Dark Maiden', 1936)—mostly prose-poems, a form Tagore began to experiment with—and *Bithika* ('The Avenue', 1935) which carried conventional rhymed verse. *Parishesh* ('The End', 1932) also is in rhymed verse and it was published in 1932, but almost all the poems were written in the late twenties.

We have seen earlier that Tagore opened up the new genre of prose-poems with great deliberation in *Punascha*. He wrote a special 'Introduction' there to say that his aim was to serve poetry in the form of prose, to instil in prose the *rhythm* of poetry without forcing it into *rhyme*, and also to discard antiquated words which were exclusively in poetic usage.[116] Thus in his seventies Tagore entered into a new experiment in form, though he continued to write rhymed verses as well. The themes were often quotidian and prosaic life. The very first poem was on the humble stream near Santiniketan, and its cadence was in time with what it depicts—the tribal boy tramping along with bow and arrow, the lumbering bullock cart, the potter carrying his ware, the pariah dog, the village school master holding an old torn umbrella. The stream 'finds its semblance in the rhythm of my poet's verse . . . crowded with the jarring trivialities of the work-a-day hours'. The poem following that was translated by Tagore and likewise the next.

An oldish upcountry [i.e. north Indian] man, tall and lean, with shaven shrunken cheeks like wilted fruits . . . I imagine he has a cow in his stall, a parrot in the cage, his wife with bangles on her arms grinding wheat, . . . and somewhere my own indistinct self, only as a passing person.[117]

A poem on the tribal women employed in building Tagore's own house:

The building of my mud house has commenced and labourers are busy raising the walls . . . I sit on my terrace watching the young woman toiling at her task hour after hour. My heart is touched with shame when I feel that the woman's service, sacredly ordained for her loved ones, its dignity soiled by the market price, should have been robbed by me with the help of a few pieces of copper.[118]

Some of the poems are almost like short stories. 'A Sudden Encounter' is about meeting a girl and reviving memories of a friendship; 'Those days which are gone, are they truly gone?' she asks. 'The stars of the night remain in the light of the day'—did he juggle with words when he answered thus?[119] Another story in a poem: the man revisits his unrequited love after many years and finds her as distant as ever, now married to another man. He had carried the gift of a diamond broach that remained in his pocket, for the precious stone seemed to 'sparkle with ironical laughter'.[120] The prose-poem was the form that the poet chose to address themes like this.

However, the grand themes Tagore was wont to address are also there in the prose-poems. He wrote not less than three versions of a poem on Africa, published in 1936, 1937 and, posthumously, in 1944. Tagore's own translation of the version in *Patraput*:

You are hidden, alas, under a black veil
Which obscures your human dignity
to the darkened vision of contempt . . .
The savage greed of the civilized stripped naked its unashamed inhumanity.

You wept and your cry was smothered,
Your forest trails became wet with tears and blood . . . .
And all the time across the sea
Church bells were ringing in their towns and villages,
the children were lulled in mother's arms,
And poets sang hymns to Beauty.[121]

Or the poem 'Forever Wayfarers':[122]

Since the first day-break of human age misted with myths
they walk wonder-eyed on strange shores, the seekers
and the fighters march at the drum-beats of storm gods
towards an ever-distant time
along an endless stretch of battle-fields.

Tagore evidently counted himself among those seekers, 'the wreckers of patterns' responding to 'the drum-beats of eternity'. This identification comes out more clearly in a poem where he talks of his own evolution, 'the series of many Rabindranaths', on the occasion of his birthday in 1936. 'Carrying the stream of many birth-days towards the final day of death, moves *Vaisakh* [the month of Tagore's birth] Twenty-fifth', Time has strung 'a garland of many Rabindranaths'. Tagore recalls, 'Once I was a boy. He would sit by life's little window and look at the beyond . . . Another age came . . . The young minstrel tuned his lyre' and sang love-songs in a sylvan garden. A change came again when the world called him and the poet found himself on 'the shores of the human sea where waves swelled and roared . . . I had to give up the lyre and take up the trumpet instead'. That was the battlefield the poet was about to quit and 'be lost in the silent nameless solitude beyond all description'.[123]

After the wave of those prose-poems, a *second wave* begins in late 1937. It is different in nature in that the verses in *Prantik* ('Terminal', 1938) and *Senjuti* ('Evening Lamp', 1938) carry the shadow of the near-death experience of Tagore in September 1937. He was unconscious for more than two days and Tagore looked upon this experience as a forewarning of impending death. The first poem he wrote after this incident is the first poem in *Prantik*:

This body of mine – the carrier of the burden of a past – seemed
to me like an exhausted cloud slipping off from the listless arm of
the morning.
I felt freed from its clasp
in the heart of an incorporeal light
at the farthest shore . . .[124]

This was Tagore's own translation; there is another poem of that
kind, written a few weeks later, translated by a different hand. 'In
the tired twilight of consciousness, I saw this body floating adown
the dark stream of oblivion, carrying away all sensations . . .'[125]
In some poems of this period Tagore looks on the times after his
death.

When I shall cease to be on this earth
Should you wish to remember me
Come to the shady solitude
Of this grove in spring time.[126]

Tagore's translation of one of these poems in *Senjuti*:

My birthday!
with Death's passport in hand
it has emerged from dive into the chasm of nothingness
to breathe a while on the outskirts of existence . . .
With this newest birthday
begins the counting of the days of a new-born life.[127]

Not all the poems of 1937–38 are sombre with the near-death
experience. Tagore reflects on being a prisoner in the public domain,
'entangled in the meshes drawn by countless gazing eyes'. 'He lives
in his solitary cell among the crowd . . . Take pity and free him.'[128]
Or again, he imagines that the youth of a new era asked about him
"who is it that sails in his boat towards the setting sun?" I tuned
my harp and sang once again, "Let my only description be that
I am one of you."[129] An interesting point to note is that most of
the poems of his second wave, in *Prantik* and *Senjuti*, are verses

in rhyme, not prose-poems. Actually the prose-poems sometimes display repetitious mannerisms, for example, shifting the verb in the sentence towards the beginning of each sentence, and using a profusion of hyphenation to create compound words to replace the Sanskritic *samasa*.

The *third wave* of poems—written in the late 1930s—were totally different in nature from the second. The poems published in *Akash-pradip* (1939), *Nabajatak* (1940), *Sehnai* (1940) speak in Tagore's accustomed language and mood known to us in the twenties. He no longer makes a fetish of writing prose-poems. In fact from his manuscripts we learn that he sometimes preferred the rhymed to the prose-poem versions.[130]

Tagore, in his dedication of the first of these books to the modernist poet Sudhindranath Datta, expressed the hope that his new poetry would touch the heart and mind of the young generation. And once again in his preface to *Nabajatak* Tagore very self-consciously underlined the new turn his poetry had taken. Reflecting on his poetic self, Tagore said, his creativity underwent changes like the change of seasons in nature. Some of his distinctly 'modernist' poems belong to this period, e.g. the 'Night Train' where he compares life to a train going through the dark to destinations unknown. In another poem the poet describes the 'Ishteshan', i.e. the railway station, in cheerful onomatopic rhyme:

Rattle, rattle, all the day
A storm of crowded coaches,
Changing motion, swing and sway
now east, now west approaches.[131]

In a mystic vein, of 'My Fated Kingdom': 'My fated kingdom lies in the east, remnant of a timeworn and ageless land'; among the debris of the past, 'the inscriptions on stone ask in a tired voice, Is there any more to be said, isn't our message over and done with?' A proud confession in the poem 'Romantic': 'They call me Romantic. My love, I admit that.' I bring to you the fragrance of spring time, I sing to you the melody that resonates your thoughts . . . 'They say, this is not Realistic, Right, I say, for I am a Romantic.'[132]

Some of the best romantic lyrics of Tagore appeared in *Sehnai*. Over twenty of them became songs, with music composed by him. One of the memorable love poems:

> Love came, silent,
> Just a dream it seemed
> I did not usher love in.
> I woke up when love went out the door
> And as I ran after that body-less dream
> It melded into the dark
> And love's distant light
> Was but a blood-red mirage.[133]

In *Akash-pradip* Tagore wrote an 'Introduction' in verse. It indicated the philosophical outlook which helped him get over the sombre phase in his inner life after the near-death experience of September 1937. Life, he wrote, tries to defeat death and makes images to outlast the limited life of the mortals. If after his death, Tagore said, his works of imagination survived, however briefly, that would be for him life beyond death.[134]

Thoughts of Death and the Last Days

In Tagore's writings in the last decade of his life the theme of death recurs frequently. Even the titles he gave to his books of verse reflect that tendency of thought: 'The End', 'The Last Octave', 'Terminal', 'The Evening Lamp', 'Sick Bed', between 1935 and 1940. Needless to say the death theme has always been a part of romantic imagination from the early nineteenth century and Tagore's poems do touch on that theme in earlier years. But in advanced age thoughts of death inevitably acquired a new significance. And with thoughts of death there came a new concern with the meaning of life—in evidence in his work *The Religion of Man* (1930) as well as other writings.

A beast's bony frame lies bleaching on the grass.
Its dry white bones—Time's hard laughter—cry to me:
'Thy end, proud man, is one with the end of the cattle that graze
no more.'
. . . Death, I refuse to accept from thee
That I am nothing but a gigantic jest of God,
A blank annihilation built with all the wealth of the Infinite.

The sudden turn at the end is characteristic of Tagore's mode of thinking about death. This poem, entitled 'The Skeleton', was inspired by Tagore's conversation with Victoria Ocampo on a poem with a similar theme by Baudelaire.[135]

A last series of poems starts from September 1940 when Tagore fell a victim to another spell of illness which eventually led to his death in less than a year. In *Rogsajyay, Arogya* ('Recovery', 1941), *Janmadine* ('On the Birthday', 1941), *Sesh Lekha* ('Last Writings', poems dictated by the poet during illness, some published posthumously, 1941)—small collections of writings, often left unrevised because Tagore did not live to revise them into a publishable form—Tagore's last words are inscribed.

Some of the poems in the last series of poems are touching in their simplicity. 'When I do not see you, in sick imagination, I think the earth under my feet is conspiring to move away . . . I wake with a start and at once see you are still there beside me: sitting with bent head, knitting wool, with a look of invincible peace about you.'[136] A poem to a sparrow that used to peck at his window: 'When the sleepless night drags on, I wait for your first pecking to bring the simple and fearless message of life and the light of day calling to me, O my sparrow of early dawn.'[137]

Then again: 'It's not my achievement that I trust. I know the constant waves of Time will break upon it day by day and obliterate it. My faith is in myself, this cup I have filled with the universe and drunk. And filled it too with every moment's love.'[138] 'I know that my poetry, though it has wandered on many paths, has yet not found its way everywhere. I wait for the message of the poet who is close to the soil . . .'[139]

Most of the poems are addressed to basic existential questions. Some of his memorable poems in the last few years of his life are on death.
In 1934:

The time has come when the bird shall leave the nest.
Soon the nest bereft, song-less, shall be scattered by forest winds,
And drift with dead leaves, flowers, of all yesterdays
To a pathless oblivion.[140]

In 1937:

'In the twilight of consciousness, I saw
This body floating adown the dark stream of oblivion . . . [141]

In November 1940: 'Once you had lent to my eyes a generous portion from your limitless store of light, now at the day's end you have come to reclaim it, my Master'—reminds one of Milton's 'On His Blindness'.[142]
Further:

Momently I feel
The time comes near for me to leave.
Let the time be peaceful, let it be silent.
Let not any pomp of memorial meeting create sorrow's trance.[143]

After September 1937 when Tagore was gravely ill and remained unconscious for over two days, his recovery was slow. And in the four years left to him he lost some of his close associates and friends: a friend of his youth Jagadish Chandra Bose (1937), the artist Gaganendranath Tagore (1938), his closest confidant Charles Andrews (1940), Surendranath Tagore (1940) his nephew and the son of his mentor Satyendra Nath, Kalimohan Ghosh (1940) who had served Santiniketan and Sriniketan since 1907. The loneliness that characterized his personal life was perhaps never more intense than now.

Perhaps towards the end the only companion in thoughts and endeavours was Mahatma Gandhi. There were many people surrounding him in the last years of his life but, as Krishna Kripalani, a close observer and husband to Tagore's granddaughter, recalls they were a 'flock of admirers, many of whom were no better than courtiers and sycophants.'[144] Judging by his letters, after the death of Andrews, Gandhi was a friend he could turn to. Gandhi was reticent about his personal relationship with Tagore, while praising in public his 'poetic genius and singular purity of life' and the inspiration he received from Tagore since 1916. 'The other ties and memories are too sacred to bear mention in a public tribute.'[145] They supported each other at times of crises. When Gandhi was about to undertake fast at Yervada Jail, Pune, in 1933 he asked for Tagore's blessings and Tagore rushed to Pune to be by his side.[146] In 1940 when Tagore, anticipating his impending death, requested Gandhi to take under his wings Visva-Bharati—'a vessel which is carrying my life's best treasure'—Gandhi wrote back within a few hours to assure Tagore that he would protect Santiniketan, 'my second home'.[147] They were also given to teasing each other. On Tagore's eightieth birthday, Gandhi cabled Tagore: 'Four score not enough, may you finish five.' Tagore cabled back: 'Four score is impertinence, five score intolerable.'[148] Upon hearing of the grave illness of Tagore—the last spell of illness that led to his death—Gandhi wrote a touching letter, 'stay yet awhile'. That was Gandhi's last letter to Tagore.[149] The poet died on 7 August 1941.

Notwithstanding the companionship that Gandhi and perhaps a few others offered, Tagore's loneliness was all too evident in his last days. Perhaps it was the ultimate loneliness of a man facing death. 'The Great Unknown' he spoke of in a famous poem was to be encountered.[150] Tagore wrote about ten days before his death:

The first day's Sun asked
At the manifestation of being –
'Who are you',
No answer came.
Year after year went by,
The last Sun of the day
The last question utters

As the western sea shone in the silent evening –
'Who are you'
He gets no answer.[151]

This was not a fear of the unknown; it was rather a sense of wonder comparable to that of some of the Upanishadic hymns. Tagore repeatedly asserted till the end the undefeated spirit of man facing pain, sorrow, death.

Sorrow's dark night, again and again,
has come to my door
Its only weapons, I saw,
. . . was fear's hideous gestures . . .

Man must see through 'the mask of dread', 'the varied fears—Death's skilful handiwork'.[152] Or again:

In words writ in blood
I saw my being manifest
My own self I knew
Through repeated hurts and pain.
Hard is truth
That hardness I loved,
Never it deceives.[153]

In the last poem he wrote, a week before his death, there is again that sense of wonder about the meaning of existence:

Your creation's path you have covered
With a varied net of wiles,
Thou Guileful One.
False belief's snare you have
Laid with skilful hands in simple lives.
With this deceit have you left a mark

On Greatness:

For him is kept no secret night.
The path that is shown to him by your star

Is the path of his own heart, ever lucid,
Which his simple faith makes eternally shine . . .
Truth he wins
In his inner heart washed with his own light . . .
He who has easefully borne your wile
Gets from your hands
the unwasting right to peace.[154]

Epilogue

Looking Back

Rabindranath Tagore happened to be born at a time when history was crowded with events which marked a transition from an old political order, social dispensation and lineaments of culture. The uprising of 1857, the end of the rule of the East India Company in 1858, and the new regime directly under Queen Victoria marked the end of an epoch. Rabindranath Tagore's grandfather built his fortune under the shadow of the East India Company and his father belonged to a class of landowners who were pillars of the Queen's Empire. In the meanwhile another momentous change came upon mid-nineteenth century India with the emergence of a new intelligentsia, the product of the new universities founded in Calcutta, Bombay and Madras in 1857–58, a generation whose cross-cultural education extended beyond the range of the traditional intellectuals. Despite his awareness of the limitations of colonial education and his lifelong effort to build an alternative to that system, undeniably the audience the poet addressed belonged to the middle class who were dependent on and supportive towards the colonial system of 'English' education. In his times despite all the limitations of a colonial regime that evolved, the new aesthetic sensibilities, the opening up of opportunities to introduce new genres of literature, and above all exposure, however limited, to the humanist and liberal bourgeois ideologies of Europe, created the intellectual space which accommodated a mind like Tagore's. There was another agency of change in the 'social reform' movements. The achievement of Raja Rammohan Roy and Ishwarchandra Vidyasagar and social reformers in other parts of India was not limited to the objects of the legislation or social action they brought about. The discourse of social reform, despite certain inconsistencies and contradictions between rhetoric and action, served a larger purpose of loosening the hold of obscurantism and tradition on the Indian mind. It will be perhaps a mistake to view that discourse in isolation, although commonly 'social reformers' are so treated in works of history. The entire gamut of associative activities needs to be considered because agendas of social reform shaded off into manifold activities pertaining to other areas of civil society including the proto-political.

The decades from the middle to the end of the nineteenth century witnessed the initiation of a wide range of associative activities which aimed to address a broad spectrum of social and political agenda framed by the colonial intelligentsia. On the one hand the old religious bodies began to split and also to proliferate: Rammohan Roy's Brahma Samaj was re-named Adi [Original] Brahma Samaj (1866) to which Debendranath and his youngest son Rabindranath belonged—while Keshub Chandra Sen set up the Bharatvarshiya Brahma Samaj (1868) and dissidents from that created the Sadharan Brahma Samaj (1878). Bombay Presidency had its own Prarthana Sabha from 1867, and there were messengers of a new religious reformism elsewhere in India as well. Traditional Hinduism responded with their own organizations like the Arya Samaj (1875) founded by Swami Dayananda Saraswati, and the Ramakrishna Mission (1897) founded by Swami Vivekananda. While too fine a typology will be inappropriate, another family of associations centred around social and cultural agendas, sometimes closely related to and overlapping with the socio-religious activities of the kind mentioned earlier. Such were the Bengal Social Science Association in Calcutta (1867), the Indian Association for the Cultivation of Sciences in Calcutta (1876), Social Reform Association (1878) founded by Veeresalingam in present-day Andhra Pradesh, the Poona Sarvajanik Sabha (1870), the Hindu Social Reform Association (1892) of Madras, the Bengal Academy of Literature (1893) later known as Sahitya Parisad. A third family of voluntary associations may be identified as those which were more explicitly political associations. To this family belonged the Hindu Mela (1867), the Indian Association (1876) founded by Surendranath Banerjea, the National Conference (1883), the Mahajana Sabha (1884) founded by P. Ananda Charlu in Madras, and the Indian National Congress which held its first three sessions in Bombay (1885), Calcutta (1886) and Madras (1887). There is evidence that Tagore attended and sang the song 'Vande mataram' at the Indian National Congress in Calcutta in 1896. Whether he was present at the 1886 session of the Indian National Congress in Calcutta when he was twenty-five years old is less certain; we have evidence that he attended and presented national songs at a meeting of members of the Brahma Samaj who attended the Congress as delegates in 1886 in Calcutta.[1] There were many other associative activities and institutions which would have merited mention if our aim had been to make an exhaustive list, but our aim is different: our aim is to point to the intellectual climate of those times when Tagore was maturing from his boyhood to manhood. Young Tagore was a participant in almost all the institutions based in Calcutta mentioned by us, and in course of his extensive tours in later life he developed contacts with most of the other ones located elsewhere in India, with the exception of those which became religious sects within the fold of orthodox Hinduism.

Along with these great changes in the areas of British administration, the intellectual orientation of the educated middle classes, and socio-political activities in civil society, a transformative change was in the offing in the domain of literature. It is interesting to reflect on the fact that in the first thirty years of Tagore's life, creators of modern literature in most Indian languages were born. Who were these younger contemporaries? Among these were Munshi Premchand (b.1880), Purushottam Das Tandon (b.1882) and Maithilisharan Gupta (b. 1886) in Hindi literature; Hari

Narayan Apte (b.1864), Krishnaji Keshav Damle (b.1866), Keshavsut (b.1866),Vishnu Sastri Chiplunkar (b.1882) in Maharashtra; in Kerala, Vallathol Narayana Menon (b.1878), Chandu Menon, and Ulloor Parameswara Iyer (b. 1877); in Kannada, B.M. Sreekantiah (b. 1884), T.P. Kailasam (b. 1885), D.V. Gundappa (b. 1888), and Masti Venkatesha Iyengar (b. 1891); Subramania Bharathi (b. 1882) in Tamil; Kakasaheb Kalelkar (b. 1865) in Gujarati, Mohammad Iqbal (b. 1877) in Urdu; and there were stalwarts in the making, Gopabandhu Das (b. 1877) in Orissa; Lakshminath Bezbarua (b. 1864) and Nilmani Phookan (b. 1933) in Assam; Bhai Vir Singh (b. 1872) and Hira Singh Dard (b. 1889) in Punjab.

Among the litterateurs who passed away while Tagore was young there were some eminences in Tamil and Gujarati literature, as well as in Hindi (Bharatendu Harishchandra died in 1885), in Urdu (Mirza Ghalib died in 1869) and in Bengali (Michael Madhusudan Dutt died in 1873). The list of names could have been expanded but our purpose is only to mention names indicative of the trend. The younger contemporaries of Tagore, born before he reached the age of thirty years, transformed Indian literature in the last years of the nineteenth century and early decades of the twentieth. Some languages of India had an early start in this regard, but the rest joined the current in course of Tagore's lifetime.

Who were Tagore's contemporaries in world literature? Some of those who were born like him in the 1860s were: the Belgian poet-dramatist Maurice Maeterlinck (b. 1862), the English author Rudyard Kipling (b. 1865), the Irish poet W.B. Yeats (b. 1865), the French novelist and essayist Romain Rolland (b. 1866), the Italian philosopher Benedetto Croce (b. 1866), British playwright John Galsworthy (b. 1867), the French author André Gide (b. 1869). Every one of them, except for Croce, won the Nobel Prize. Two of them, Yeats and Gide were among those who played an important role in making Tagore's *Gitanjali* accessible in translation, while Rolland and Croce had personal contact with him while he was in Europe. With most of them Tagore had formed a relationship of mutual admiration. It is interesting to observe that Tagore's younger contemporaries did not become a part of a circle of mutual admiration. The Nobel Prize winner of 1946 Hermann Hesse (1877–1962), or Stefan Zweig (1881–1942), came close to such a relationship, but Thomas Mann (1875–1955), or Franz Kafka (1883–1924) were quite unimpressed and privately dismissive. A prominent exception in that generation younger to Tagore was the Nobel Prize winner (1956) Juan Ramon Jimenez (1881–1958) who translated Tagore into Spanish.

It will be useful to bear in mind the changing global context. As we have seen earlier, Tagore was widely appreciated and indeed admired in the years following the award of the Nobel Prize. In the years of the World War I and in the inter-war period things began to change. First, Tagore's consistent critique of European nationalist urge towards aggression and domination reduced the following of admirers he had in the West. Second, many of those in England who had helped in the process of translating and presenting the works of Tagore to readers in the English language began to say that the translations published after the first three books were of poor quality and there was much adverse criticism of the translations. Thirdly, Tagore's early translations tended to quarry one single vein in his works in Bengali, those in spiritual mode, and this trend by and large continued later as well. Thus he was cast into stereotype, the 'sage of the East' which did not find favour with many critics later and it was obviously inappropriate for the 'myriad-minded' poet.

As far as Western readers are concerned one notices a long and steady trend of depreciation of his reputation, with possible exceptions like the Hispanic literary world. The iconization of Tagore in his own country in his last years or after his death seems to have an inverse correlation with his reputation in the West, for it underwent there a steady devaluation. It is by now well known that once the euphoria and the encomiums attending the Nobel Prize award were over, the West became disenchanted with its own creation: the Sage Poet from the East. Recently a German scholar, Martin Kämpchen, has documented Tagore's reception in the continent at the time. To Thomas Mann in 1921, Tagore was a figure 'picturesque but pallid . . . animated by a somewhat anaemic humanitarian spirit'. To Hermann Hesse, Tagore's message seemed edifying and 'banal'. To Stefan Zweig he was, though admirable, a victim of a European literary trend which treated Tagore with 'cool and distant benevolence'. And to Franz Kafka, he was an object of somewhat ironic condescension. Even earlier, Rainer Maria Rilke, while declining a publisher's offer to translate Tagore, wrote of a kind of failure of communication since Tagore's poetry was 'borne towards me on a tide of unfamiliarity whose movement I would hardly know how to reproduce without somehow doing violence to myself'.[2] As in the Continent, in England and later in North America as well, the tide turned against Tagore somewhere in the 1920s. There remained, however, avid readers of Tagore in Europe. For instance, the philosopher Ludwig Wittgenstein we are told was in the habit of reading Tagore's poems, often turning his back on his audience at seminars he addressed in Vienna! In 1938, about the time when he was writing his *Philosophical Investigations*, he translated parts of Tagore's *King of the Dark Chamber* because Wittgenstein thought that 'Tagore expresses Wittgenstein's own religious ideal'.[3] Where and in which minds Tagore's words found resonance was unpredictable. One is reminded of the poet Wilfred Owen who, when saying his last goodbye to his mother before going to the war front where he died, quoted *Gitanjali*: 'When I go from hence, let this be my parting word . . .'[4] To find such response from unknown people is an author's highest reward.

The construction of this image of the sage Tagore and its denigration in the Anglo-Saxon world becomes abundantly clear from recent research into British and North American archives and private papers. The fragility of Tagore's peculiar image in the West if not obvious in the quality of praise that came his way at the time of the Nobel Prize award, became clear in the years following. Some examples: D. H. Lawrence in 1916: 'this wretched worship-of-Tagore attitude is disgusting' considering 'how far higher, in reality, our European civilization stands.'[5] Ezra Pound, a great Tagore enthusiast before the Nobel Prize, in 1917: 'Tagore got the Nobel Prize because, after the cleverest boom of our times, after the fiat of omnipotent literati of distinction, he lapsed into religion' and the award was 'a matter of convenience for the Swedish Academy in the face of conflicting claims of European authors'.[6] An impatient Beatrice Webb in 1920: 'Whilst he [Tagore] resents any criticism of Hindu tradition or of Hindu rites, still more of Hindu mysticism, he is a bitter and uninformed critic of Western industrial organization, and of Western nationalism, Western science . . .'[7] At the same time, to be fair to Webb, she also had due regard for Tagore as a personality, as a 'dramatic saint' and 'a perfect personification of his part in the world's history'. Even Sir William Rothenstein who played such an important role in introducing the author to the English readership, writes to Max Beerbohm in 1920: 'The strong wine of praise, and the weak wine of worship' had gone 'to this man's head'.[8] And W.B. Yeats to Rothenstein in 1931: '[T]hrough entire lack of judgement . . . he published intolerable and interminable volumes of mistranslated verse', instead of remaining content with the first three volumes which Yeats and Sturge Moore had edited.[9] Graham Greene in 1937: 'As for Rabindranath Tagore, I cannot believe that anyone but Yeats can still take his poems very seriously.'[10] Bertrand Russell in 1967: 'His talk of the infinite is vague nonsense. The sort of language that is admired by many Indians, unfortunately does not, in fact, mean anything at all.'[11] One can multiply examples. The question is: what accounts for this ebb tide in Tagore's reputation, seen from the West?

The author of the first Tagore biography in English, E.J. Thompson (less known than his son, the historian E.P. Thompson, but a prominent Indophile in his times) attributed this trend to the poor quality of Tagore translations into English since those sponsored by Yeats and Sturge Moore. Dutta and Robinson endorse this view. Krishna Kripalani chose to ignore this trend; in fact, it is difficult to accept his opinion that 'Tagore startled the West into a recognition of the real India, not the mysterious India where once shone the Light of Asia . . .'[12] The truth lies in the opposite direction. The

West preferred to construe Tagore as a sage and systematically, the poems chosen for translation were those appropriate to that stereotype. It was these two mutually reinforcing trends which led to that peculiar representation of Tagore in Europe and North America as a mystic sage. It was, it may be argued, not simply a matter of the quality of translation. Dutta and Robinson offer an explanation of the devaluation of Tagore in Europe in terms of politics as well. The society and polity of Edwardian England was such that Tagore's mystic poems were very acceptable. A reversal followed from World War I, when strong nationalistic sentiments were aroused and the universalism of the Tagorean kind was irrelevant.

Finally, how did Tagore's writings or more generally his cultural role impact the Indian national scene? There has been no systematic study of the subject but the impression is unavoidable that due to the barrier of language the specific impact of his writings was of less importance than the general impact of his presence in the cultural world. He was admired widely, but his works were not read that widely. There were translations of some of his writings from Bengali or English to other Indian languages. That was a channel, narrow as it was, that spread his impact. Second, his Santiniketan attracted many young writers and thinkers who came to visit him or to spend some time there to partake of the Tagorean cultural ambience. Third, there were those who neither had access to him in translation nor direct acquaintance with him or his institution at Santiniketan, but they were nevertheless affected by the Tagorean wave at a distance.

Some of the early translations from Tagore into Hindi appeared during his lifetime. Hazari Prasad Dwivedi (1907–79) joined the Santiniketan faculty in 1930 and worked as the director of the Hindi Bhavan there from 1940 to 1950. He translated a good deal of Tagore's writings directly from Bengali to Hindi; his pseudonym for this purpose was Vyomkesh Sastri. Kshitimohan Sen and Krishna Kripalani, teachers at Santiniketan, were also active in this field. The Tagorean impact is commonly recognized as a formative factor in the growth of the Chhayavad school in Hindi literature. Among others Surya Kant Tripathi, better known by his pseudonym Nirala, having been educated in Bengal had direct access to Tagore's writings. Mahadevi Varma, Sumitranandan Pant, and Maithilisharan Gupta were also inspired by Tagore's writings. A little later, Dr Ramdhari Singh Dinkar brought Tagore's philosophy to the forefront in his critical writings.

Urdu at that time had a flourishing literature and one of the first translations of *Gitanjali* was into Urdu in 1914. Munshi Premchand's (Dhanpat Rai Srivastava) correspondence shows his awareness of the significance of Tagore's contributions. The influence of Tagore's short stories has been seen in Premchand's writings in that rather new genre in Hindi literature. Among the Urdu translators of Tagore were major poets like Firaq Gorakhpuri, Asrar ul Haq Majaz and Josh Malihabadi. The latter, has left in his reminiscences *Yaadon Ki Baraat* an account of his meetings with Tagore during his residence at Santiniketan for six months. It is interesting to note that Malihabadi thought that though Tagore was admirable in many other ways he had a weakness for publicity.[13]

A large number of the early visitors to and students of Santiniketan School were from Gujarat. Gandhi's influence might have been a factor. Two earliest translations were *Chitrangada* in 1915 by Mahadev Desai, later Gandhi's secretary, and *Gitanjali* in 1918 by Manibhai Desai. From then onwards the pace of translation was remarkable: according to the latest count there are eight Gujarati translations of *Gitanjali*, three of *Gora*, three of *Chokher Bali*, etc. As in the case of the Chhayavadis in Hindi, a new wave in Gujarati is attributed to Tagore's influence. Prahlad Parekh, Nagindas Parikh, Krishenlal Sridharani, Kaka Kalelkar and, to a lesser extent, Umashankar Joshi and several others since the 1930s are regarded as products of Tagorean influence. In Marathi also translations of Tagore appeared fairly early. *Mukta-Dhara* was translated in 1924, *Gitanjali* in 1928, *Dakghar* in 1930. It is generally recognized that the poet Kashinath Hari Modak (1872–1916), Narayan Gupte (1872–1947) and others, of that generation were indebted to Tagore's influence. As an evidence of reverse flow one might recall that, as we have noticed in an earlier chapter, Tagore translated a great many of Tukaram's verses when he was a teenager, a protégé of his elder brother serving in the ICS in Bombay Presidency. In Kannada literature a number of students who had a part of their education in Santiniketan played an important role. These include Masti Venkatesha Iyengar and A.N. Krishna Rao. Prahlada Naregal and Narayana Sangama translated *Gitanjali* directly from Bengali, unlike many other translators elsewhere. Likewise M.N. Kamat translated from the original. During the 1920s and 1930s, many other Kannada writers visited Santiniketan and as in the case of Chhayavadi phase in Hindi, in Kannada literature the years when Tagorean influence was direct and strong is often perceived as a distinct phase.[14]

In the south, Tamil had a good translator from Tagore in T.N. Kumaraswamil who spent some time in Santiniketan and learned Bengali, but otherwise there was a scarcity of translations till the 1950s. In Telugu a good number of works were available in translation; some of the leading writers like Rayaprolu Subba Rao and Abburi Ramakrishna Rao studied at Santiniketan. Early twentieth century romantic poetry, known as the Bhava Kavitha wave in Telugu, acknowledged the influence of Tagore. Malayalam was exceptionally fortunate that some younger contemporaries of Tagore took a prominent role in introducing him to Kerala. Kumaran Asan was younger to him by twelve years, Vallathol Narayana Menon by eighteen years. They, as well as the third great poet of that era, Ulloor S. Paramaswara Iyer, probably met Tagore in Kerala in 1922. Vallathol visited Santiniketan in 1939 and his creation Kerala Kala Mandalam was a cultural enterprise similar to Tagore's institution.[15]

On the whole, Tagore's impact was perceptible in distant regions as much as in neighbouring regions like Orissa and Assam, and the receptivity or imperviousness depended on local and historical factors—and we cannot even begin to get into all of that history. And bibliographic itemization will be pointless here. The important question is what do literary historians mean when they talk of

Tagore's 'influence'? If one examines the notion of an 'impact' or 'influence' several questions arise. Is similarity a decisive proof of diffusion or influence? Can one rely on 'parallel hunting' as a method of tracing influence, given the possibility of independent origination at different sites of literary activity? Does not the concept of 'impact' suggest a one-way traffic of ideas or forms, whereas there is often a two-way cultural exchange between literatures in different languages?

If one considers these issues one may arrive at the conclusion that literary waves like Chhayavad in Hindi, or Navodaya in Kannada, or Bhava Kavitha in Telugu grew out of deep-seated roots in those language communities. There were no doubt parallels with the Tagorean tradition in Bengal. We need not exaggerate Tagore's influence and highlight the parallelism in that light. Tagore has greater claims to fame than that. His presence in the Indian cultural world was important as a source of inspiration to many, translations helped to expand his audience, a shared environment account for many common elements in ideas and forms. To essentialize that complex process into a simple category, 'influence', may be open to question. The most important outcome of that process, an interaction occasioned by Tagore's inspiring presence, was that it opened the discourse of 'Indian Literature'. At one time, as Sheldon Pollock points out, Sanskrit was regarded as one unifying classical code. In modern times the recognition of the plurality of literatures, each rooted in their regional and cultural site, tended to obscure the possibility of a notion of 'Indian Literature' in the singular.[16] Through mutual 'influence' and exchange—at various levels from 'proper literature', that is to say products of high culture, to chap books and cheaply available imprints at the subaltern level—a new Indian identity in literature was struggling to be born. In that process Rabindranath Tagore was a common icon, unknowingly a catalytic agent. That did not make 'Indian Literature' a reality but it made it thinkable.

Notes and References

Introduction

1   '1400 Sal', *Chitra*, 1895, *Rabindra Rachanabali*, vol. II, p. 198 (hereafter cited as: *R.R.*).

2   'Janma-dinay', *Nabajatak*, 1939, *R.R.*, vol. XII, p. 134.

3   'Smaran', *Senjuti*, 1936, *R.R.*, vol. XI, pp. 134–135.

4   *Nabajatak*, 1939, *R.R.*, vol. XII, p. 134.

5   Poem no. 26, *Rogsajya*, 1940, *R.R.*, vol. XIII, p. 23.

6   'Suchana', *Nabajatak*, *R.R.*, vol. XII, p. 101.

7   Tagore, *Poems*, (ed.) Krishna Kripalani et. al., Visva-Bharati, Calcutta, 1942.

8   Tagore, 'Kavyer Tatparya', *Panch-bhuta*, *R.R.*, vol. I, pp. 924–28.

9   R.T., 'Introduction to Collected Works', dated 30.6.1939, *R.R.*, vol. I, pp. 9–11.

10 Introduction to *Nabajatak*, *R.R.*, vol. XII, p. 101.

11 R.T. to Charles Andrews, 8 February 1921, *Letters to a Friend*, edited and compiled by C.F. Andrews, 1st edn., George Allen and Unwin, London, 1928; reprint *EWRT*, Sahitya Akademi, Delhi, 1996, vol. III, p. 281; hereafter this work is cited as: *L.F.*

12 R.T. to Andrews, 10 March 1918, from Santiniketan, *L.F.*, p. 253.

13 R.T., Introduction to *Sanchaita*, *R.R.*, vol. I, p. 955.

14 *L.F.*, p. 228.

15 *L.F.*, p. 223.

16 *Path o Patheya*, *R.R.*, vol. V, pp. 664–672.

17 See Chapter IV of this book.

18   S. Bhattacharya (ed.), *The Mahatma and the Poet: Letters and Debates Between Gandhi and Tagore*, 1915–1941, National Book Trust, New Delhi, 5th reprint, 2008.

19   Buddhadeb Bose, *Rabindranath: Kathasahitya*, Visva-Bharati, Calcutta, 1955, p. 126, cited in Radha Chakravarty, translator and editor, *Farewell Song*, Srishti, Delhi, 2005.

20   'My Pictures', 1930, *EWRT*, vol. III, p. 635.

21   Ananda Coomaraswamy, cited in Krishna Kripalani, *Rabindranath Tagore: a Biography*, reprint Calcutta, 2008, pp. 398–399.

22   'The Meaning of Art', 1926; 'My Pictures', 1930; 'The Religion of an Artist', 1936, *EWRT*, vol. III, pp. 580–88, 635–38, 683–98.

23   'Sahitye Navatva', 1927, *R.R.*, vol. XII, pp. 455–58.

24   'Adhunik Kavya', 1932, *R.R.*, vol. XII, pp. 463–72.

25   R.T., *Chithi Patra*, vol. XVI, (ed.) Sutapa Bhattacharya, Visva-Bharati, Calcutta, 1995. (hereafter cited as: C.P.)

26   'The Religion of an Artist', *EWRT*, vol. III, p. 684.

27   Ibid., p. 686.

28   'Janmadine' in *Senjuti*, p.1, tr. by Tagore in *Poems*, a posthumous publication edited by Krishna Kripalani, Visva-Bharati, Calcutta, 1942, pp. 185–86.

Chapter 1

1   'Kabi-Jibani', 1901, *Sahitya, R.R.*, vol. IV, pp. 688–690.

2   In *'Bangabhashar Lekhak'*,1904, *R.R.*, vol. XIV, p. 141.

3   *Amar Dharma*, 1917, *R.R.*, vol. XIV, p. 159.

4   'Janmadine', *Atma-Parichay*, 1940, *R.R.*, vol. XIV, p. 171.

5   Ibid., p. 175.

6   Tagore's statement was published in 1904 in a miscellany on lives of Bengal's writers, *R.R.*, XIV, pp. 137–149.

7   *Atma-Parichay, R.R.*, vol. XIV, pp. 152–169.

8   Ibid., p. 156.

9   Ibid., p. 167.

10   'Ebar Phirao More', *Chitra*, tr. Humayun Kabir, (ed.), *Poems of Tagore*, p. 42.

11   Address at a reception to Tagore at Calcutta Town Hall on his fiftieth birthday, 1912, in *R.R.*, vol. XIV, pp. 149–152.

12   Ibid., p. 152.

13   Ibid., *R.R.*, vol. XIV, p. 170.

14   *R.R.*, vol. I, pp. 9–11

15   *Atma-Parichay, R.R.*, vol. XIV, p. 172.

16 *R.R.,* vol. XIV, p. 830.

17 *Letters to a Friend*, edited and compiled by C.F. Andrews, 1st edn. George Allen and Unwin, London, 1928, reprint *EWRT*, Sahitya Akademi, Delhi, 1996, vol. III, p. 300, hereafter *L.F.*

18 *L.F.,* p. 225.

19 *L.F.,* p. 228.

20 *L.F.,* pp. 239–240.

21 *L.F.,* p. 250.

22 *L.F.,* p. 234.

23 Tagore to Andrews, 30 June 1915, *L.F.,* p. 244.

24 Tagore to Rathindranath, n.d., 1914, Pal, vol. VII, p. 10.

25 Tagore to Andrews, 7 October 1914, *L.F.,* p. 237.

26 Tagore to Andrews, 18 March 1921, *L.F.,* p. 291.

27 Tagore, 'Shok-sabha', in the journal *Sadhana*, 1894, *R.R.*, vol.V, pp. 613–17; the senior poet who opposed the meeting was Nabin Chandra Sen.

28 S. Bhattacharya 'Introduction', in N.N. Vohra and S. Bhattacharya (eds.), *Looking Back: India in the Twentieth Century*, National Book Trust, Delhi, 2002, pp. xxxvii–xxxviii.

29 Tagore, 'Englander Bhabuk Samaj', *Pather Sanchay*, *R.R.*, vol. XIII, pp. 674–677.

30 Tagore, 'Visva-Bharati', *R.R.*, vol. XIV, p. 270.

31 Ibid., p. 271.

32 Ibid., p. 271.

33 Ibid., p. 277.

34 Ibid., p. 280.

35 Ibid., p. 281.

36 Ibid., p. 282.

37 Ibid., pp. 290–91.

38 R.T. to Andrews, 23 July 1915, *L.F.* pp. 246–247.

39 Detailed discussion in Sabyasachi Bhattacharya, *Talking Back: the Idea of Civilization in the Indian Nationalist Discourse*, Oxford University Press, Delhi, 2011.

40 This essay, first published in 1904, was included in *Atma-Parichay*, *R.R.*, vol. XIV, pp. 137–149.

41 *Sadhana*, *EWRT*, vol. II, pp. 281–289.

42 *The Centre of Indian Culture*, *EWRT*, vol. II, p. 486.

43 "East and West', *Creative Unity*, *EWRT*, vol. II, pp. 530–32.

44 *Talks in China*, published in 1925, *EWRT*, vol. II, p. 599.

45 Speech of Tagore at first meeting of Executive Council of Visva-Bharati, 1921, Visva-Bharati, *R.R.,* vol. XIV, p.248.

46 R. Tagore, C. F. Andrews (ed.), *Letters to a Friend*, London, 1928, *EWRT*, vol. III, p.268.

47 R.T. to Andrews, 20 December 1920, *L.F,* p. 273.

48 R.T. to Andrews, 10 May 1921, *L.F.,* p. 306.

49 R.T. to Andrews, 7 September 1920, *L.F.,* p. 263.

50 R.T. to Andrews, 13 March 1921, *L.F.,* p. 279.

51 R.T. to Andrews 13 July 1921, *L.F,* p. 317.

52 M.K. Gandhi, *Hind Swaraj,* in *Collected Works of Mahatma Gandhi,* vol. X, pp. 36–37.

53 R.T. to Andrews, 12 July 1921, *L.F,* p. 317.

54 R.T. to Andrews, 13 March 1921, *L.F,* p. 289.

55 Gandhi, 'The Great Sentinel', *Young India,* 1 June 1921.

56 R.T. to Andrews, n.d March 1921, *L.F,* p. 294.

57 Ibid., p.293.

58 R.T. to Andrews, 14 January 1921, *L.F.,* p. 277.

59 R.T. to Andrews, 9 July 1921, *L.F.,* p. 316.

60 R.T. to Andrews, 4 August 1920, *L.F.,* p. 262.

61 R.T. to Andrews, 11 October 1913, *L.F.,* p. 232.

62 R.T. to Andrews, 4 June 1921, *L.F.,* p. 311.

63 R.T. to Andrews, 13 March 1921, *L.F,* p. 289.

64 R.T. to Andrew, 20 August 1920, *L.F.,* p. 262.

65 R.T. to Andrews, 20 August 1920, *L.F.,* p. 261.

66 Tagore, 'Bangla Lekhak' in *Sadhana,* 1893, and Tagore, *Sahitya,* Calcutta, 1961, pp. 237–243, not included in *R.R.*

67 Prabhat Kumar Mukhopadhyay, *Rabindra Jibani o Rabindra Sahitya Prabeshak,* Visva-Bharati, Calcutta, 5th edition, 2008, vol. II, pp. 447–449, contains Tagore's speech on this occasion; (hereafter this work is cited as: Mukhopadhyay).

68 R.T. to J.C. Bose, 28 December 1925, *Chithi Patra,* vol. VI, p. 72.

69 *Chithi Patra,* vol. V, letter no. 53, vol. V, letter no. 52.

70 See Mukhopadhyay, vol. II, pp. 596–597.

71 Tagore to Ramendra Sundar Trivedi, 1911, quoted in Mukhopadhyay, vol. II, p. 316.

72 Mukhopadhyaya, vol. I, pp. 141–143.

73 *Benglar Jatiya Sahitya',* 1895, in *Sahitya, R.R.,* vol. IV, pp. 665–75.

74 Prasanta Kumar Pal, *Rabi-Jibani,* Ananda Publishers, Calcutta, 2nd edn., 1993, vol. V, p. 17; (hereafter this work, vols. I–IX, is cited as: Pal.)

75 Tagore, *R.R.,* vol. XII, p. 504.

76 Tagore, *Sahityer Pathe, R.R.,* vol. XII, p. 506.

77 R.T. to Andrews, undated, 1921, *L.F.,* pp. 291–92.

78 *L.F.,* p. 293.

[79]   R.T. to Andrews, 18 March 1921, *L.F.*, p. 290.

[80]   R.T. to Andrews, 24 February 1921, *L.F.*, p. 283.

[81]   R.T. to Andrews, 18 March 1921 *L.F.*, p. 290.

[82]   R.T. to Andrews, 7 July 1921, *L.F,* p. 313.

[83]   R.T. to Andrews, 6 July 1921, *L.F,* p. 313.

[84]   R.T. to Andrews, 5 July 1921, *L.F.*, p. 312.

[85]   R.T. to Andrews, 8 July 1921, *L.F,* p. 312.

[86]   R.T. to Andrews, 7 July 1921, *L.F.*, pp. 313–14.

[87]   R.T. to W.W. Pearson, 6 March 1918, *L.F.*, p. 253.

[88]   R.T. to Andrews, 23 September 1915, *L.F.*, p. 248.

[89]   R.T. to Andrews, 24 February 1921, *L.F.*, p. 283.

[90]   R.T. to Andrews, 24 February 1921, *L.F.*, p. 283.

[91]   *L.F.*, p. 241.

[92]   *L.F.*, p. 241.

[93]   *L.F,* p. 242.

[94]   *L.F.*, p. 237.

[95]   *L.F.*, pp. 234–35.

[96]   *L.F.*, p. 235.

[97]   R.T. to Rathindranath Tagore, n.d. in Pal, op. cit., vol. VII, p. 10.

[98]   R.T. to Rathindranath, *Chithi Patra*, vol. II, pp. 28–30.

[99]   *L.F.*, p. 235.

[100] *L.F,* p. 239.

[101] *L.F,* p. 237.

[102] *L.F.*, pp. 241–42.

[103] *L.F,* p. 269.

[104] R.T., to Andrews, 21 December 1920, *L.F.*, p. 274.

[105] R.T., to Andrews, 21 December 1921, *L.F.*, p. 274.

[106] Pal, vol. I, pp. 235–36.

[107] Pal, vol. I, p. 94. An account given by Birendra's wife, Prafullamayee.

[108] Pal, vol. II, pp. 25–26.

[109] R.T. to Indira Devi, 10 August 1890, *C. P.,* vol. II, p. 42. Many recent literary biographers, e.g., Jay Parini, *A Matchless Time: A Life of William Faulkner*, Harper Collins, 2004, or works of that genre which are admitted to be classics, e.g., Leon Edel, *Henry James: A Biography*, 5 vols, Lippincott, 1953–72, focus upon the intellectual life and the interconnection between the author and the history of his/her times, decidedly stepping out of the conventional day-to-day accounts of events of life.

[110] Tagore's letter to poet Buddhadeb Bose, written in May 1941, was included in the book *Sahityer Swarup, R.R.*, vol. XIV, pp. 198–200.

Chapter 2

[1] *Jiban Smriti*, *R.R.*, vol. IX, pp. 417–18, (hereafter cited as: *J.S.*); *Atma Smriti*, *R.R.*, vol. XIV, pp. 172–73.

[2] *J.S.*, 1905, *R.R.* vol. IX, pp 413–14.

[3] Pal, vol. I, pp. 191–93.

[4] *Chhelebela*, 1940, *R.R.*, vol. XIII, p.715.

[5] Krishna Kripalani, *Dwarakanath Tagore*, New Delhi, 1981, pp. 261–62; Blair B. Kling, *Partner in Empire*, Berkeley, 1976.

[6] Blair B Kling, in Anon. (ed.) Visva-Bharati, *Rabindranath Tagore in Perspective*, Calcutta, 1989, pp. 41–42.

[7] Pal, vol. I, p. 12.

[8] Pal, vol. I, p. 13.

[9] 'Ma-ke amar pade na mone', *Shishu Bholanath*, 1921, translation by R.T. in *Poems*, Krishna Kripalani (ed.), Visva-Bharati, Calcutta, 1942, p. 64.

[10] *J.S.*, *R.R.*, vol. IX, p. 446.

[11] *Atma-parichay*, *R.R.*, vol. XIV, p.172.

[12] *J.S.*, *R.R.*, vol. IX, p. 446.

[13] *J.S.*, *R.R.*, vol. IX, p. 414

[14] Pal, vol. I, pp. 81, 87, 88, 18.

[15] Debendranath to Rabindranath Tagore, 18 February 1884, Pal, vol. I, p. 189.

[16] R.T., Speech at Women's Education Society, 2 July 1940, cited in Pal, vol. I, p. 33.

[17] Pal, vol. I, p. 33.

[18] Anon., 'Europe Jatri kono Bangiya Jubaker Patra', discovered by Sajani Kanta Das, and authenticated by Prashanta Kumar Pal, vol. II, p. 90, as Rabindranath's writing, see *R.R.*, XVIII, p. 369

[19] Krishna Kripalani, *Dwarkanath Tagore*, pp. 261–62.

[20] Pal, vol. I, p. 95.

[21] Pal, vol. I, pp. 53–54.

[22] Pal, vol. I, pp. 59, 64, 102–103.

[23] *J.S.*, *R.R.*, vol. XIV, pp. 421–22.

[24] Pal, vol. I, p. 124; Tagore, *J.S.*, *R.R.*, IX, p. 432.

[25] Tagore, *J.S.*, *R.R.*, vol. XIV, pp. 450.

[26] R.T., *J.S.*, *R.R.*, vol. XIV, pp. 450.

[27] Pal, vol. I, p. 234.

[28] R.T., *J.S.*, *R.R.*, vol. XIV, pp. 450.

[29] *J.S.*, *R.R.*, vol. XIV, pp. 424.

30 Pal, vol. I, pp. 211, 234.

31 Pal, vol. I, p. 195.

32 *J.S.*, *R.R.*, vol. XIV, pp. 451.

33 *J.S.*, *R.R.*, vol. XIV, p. 453.

34 *J.S.*, *R.R.*, vol. XIV, pp. 428.

35 *J.S.*, *R.R.*, vol. XIV, pp. 456–57.

36 General (Miscellaneous) Dept., File no. 69, Progs. B-3-6, March 1878.

37 *J.S.*, *R.R.*, vol. XIV, pp. 462–465.

38 *J.S.*, *R.R.*, vol. XIV, p. 690; there are many portions of the original manuscript which were not published in the book entitled *J.S.* in 1912; these unpublished discarded pieces were found and published later, *inter alia R.R.*, vol.XIV, pp. 687–72, including the elaborate family tree.

39 *J.S.*, p. 448.

40 *J.S.*, p. 508.

41 *J.S.*, p. 447.

42 *J.S.*, *R.R.*, vol. XIV, pp. 508–09.

43 Tagore, 'Pushpanjali' or 'Flower Offerings', published in *Bharati*, 1885, a few months after Kadambari Devi's death; the above includes portions from the unpublished manuscript of the essay, in *R.R.*, vol. XIV, pp. 711–17.

44 Ibid, R.R., vol. XIV, p. 717.

45 *J.S*, R.R., vol. XIV, p. 717.

46 Krishna Kripalani, *Rabindranath Tagore: a Biography*, Oxford University Press, New Delhi, 1962, reprint UBSPD, Calcutta, 2008, p. 117; Prabhat, vol. I, pp. 194–97; Pal, vol. II, pp. 204–07. The incident was disturbing to the Tagore family: the coroner was paid special fees to conduct the post-mortem at the Tagore residence, other connected papers were destroyed under instructions from Debendranath Tagore and newspapers were silenced, according to Pal.

47 The books dedicated to Kadambari Devi are *Bhagna Hriday, Chhabi o Gan, Shaishab Sangit,* and *Bhanu Singher Padabali*

48 Debendranath Tagore to R.T., 7 September 1883, in Pal, vol. II, p. 178.

49 Pal, vol. II, pp. 177–179.

50 Pal, vol. II, p. 189.

51 Pal, vol. II, p. 212.

52 Tagore, *Smaran*, 1902.

53 *C.P.*, vol. I, p.13.

54 *C.P.*, vol. I, p.11.

55 *C.P.*, vol. I, p.40.

56 *C.P.*, vol. I, p.50.

[57] *C.P.*, vol. I, pp. 5, 42–43, 56, 57.
[58] *C.P.*, vol. I, pp. 21, 57.
[59] Pal, vol. V, p. 121.
[60] Pal, vol. V, pp. 96–97.
[61] Pal, vol. V, p. 217.
[62] Pal, vol. V, p. 94.
[63] *Atma-parichay*, *R.R.*, vol. XIV, p.172.
[64] *J.S.*, *R.R.*, vol. IX, p. 430.
[65] R.T. in his Introduction to *Sanchaita*, 1931, *R.R.*, vol. I, p. 955.
[66] *J.S.*, *R.R.*, vol. IX, p. 477.
[67] *J.S.*, *R.R.*, vol. IX, p. 489.
[68] *J.S.*, *R.R.*, vol. IX, p. 486.
[69] *J.S.*, *R.R.*, vol. IX, p. 499.
[70] *J.S.*, *R.R.*, vol. IX, p. 462.
[71] *J.S.*, *R.R.*, vol. IX, pp. 478–79.
[72] *J.S.*, *R.R.*, vol. IX, p. 479.
[73] *J.S.*, *R.R.*, vol. IX, p. 513.
[74] *J.S.*, *R.R.*, vol. IX, p. 514.
[75] R.T.'s statement to C.F. Andrews made in 1912 in London, *L.F.*, pp. 226–27.
[76] *J.S.*, *R.R.*, vol. IX, p. 492, f.n. 1, quoting from the draft manuscript.
[77] *J.S.*, *R.R.*, vol. IX, p. 500.
[78] Mukhopadhyay, vol. I, p. 129, points out that these earlier models were Biharilal Chakraborty and more particularly Akshay Chandra Chowdhury.
[79] 'Akaran Kashta', *Bharati*, 1880, p. 289, cited in Mukhopadhyay, vol. I, p. 143.
[80] 'Jathartha Doshar' or 'True Companion', in *Bharati*, 1881, in Mukhopadhyay, vol. I, p. 137.
[81] 'Bengalis are not poets', Bharati, 1880, ibid., vol. I, pp. 141–42.
[82] R.T., Introduction to *Bou Thakuranir Hat*, *R.R.*, vol. I, p. 603.
[83] R.T., *R.R.*, vol. I, p. 225, written in 1940, Introduction to *Manasi*, published in 1890.
[84] R.T., *Poems*, 1942, p.15; translation of 'Nishphal Kamana'; the English title appears in the facsimile of the poet's manuscript but not in the printed version cited here.
[85] R.T., translation of 'Ananta Prem', *Manasi*, in Tagore, *Poems*, 1942, pp. 19–20.
[86] R.T., Introduction to *Sanchaita*.

Chapter 3

1   R.T. to Nagendra Nath Gangulee, son-in-law, 27 June 1915; *Selected Letters*, p. 165, R.200 p.m.

2   'Duhsamay', *Kalpana, R.R.*, vol. III.

3   'Ebar Phirao Moray', *Chitra*.

4   'Mantri-Abhishek', *R.R.*, vol. XIV, pp. 127–36; this is part of the *Achalita Rachanabali*, which Tagore declined to include in his 'Collected Works'.

5   *Raja Praja, R.R.*, vol.V, pp. 623–42.

6   'Ingrej o Bharatbasi', 1893, *Raja Praja, R.R.*, vol. V, p. 624.

7   Ibid., pp. 631–37.

8   *Itihas*, 1955, pp. 5–15.

9   In *Atma-sakti*, 1905, *R.R.*, vol. II, p. 625.

10 Books entitled *Atma-sakti, Swadesh, Bharatvarsha, Samuha, Swadeshi Samaj*.

11 In *R.R.*, vol. II, pp. 671–83.

12 Tagore, 'Byadhi o Pratikar', *R.R.*, vol. V, p. 783.

13 Tagore, 'Path o Patheya', *R.R.*, vol. V, pp. 667, 671.

14 Ibid., p. 677.

15 They wrote articles critical of Tagore in *Bangadarshan, Bande Mataram* and *Swaraj* in 1907–08; see Sumit Sarkar, *The Swadeshi Movement in Bengal 1903–1908*, People's Publishing House, Delhi, 1994, pp. 61–62. For reasons which are none too clear Sarkar, in this otherwise perspicacious study, depicts him as a Hindu revivalist when Tagore wrote 'Swadeshi Samaj'

16 Tagore, Foreword to *Chokher Bali*, May 1940, *R.R.*, vol. II, p. 373.

17 *Poems*, p. 32.

18 *Poems*, p. 26.

19 *Smaran*, 1908, translated by Tagore in *Fruit Gathering, EWRT*, p. 179.

20 'Gan shona', *Kheya*, 1906; *Lover's Gift*, 1918, *EWRT*, p. 204.

21 'Asabdhan', *Kshanika*, 1900, translated by Rabindranath Tagore, *Lover's Gift, EWRT*, p. 200–201.

22 The poems cited above are respectively from *Chitra*, 1896; *Naibedya*, 1901; *Smaran*, 1903; *Kavyagranthabali*, 1903, later in *Gitabitan*; and *Kheya*, 1906, all translated by Tagore himself; these remained unpublished till after his death they were published in Tagore's *Poems*, edited by Krishna Kripalani, Calcutta, 1942, pp. 27, 40, 41, 42, 43, 54, 69; (hereafter this is cited as: *Poems*.)

23 'Utsarga', 1903, translated by Tagore, *Poems*, 1942, p. 59.

24 'Smaran', in Tagore's own translation, in *Fruit Gathering, EWRT*, vol. 1, poems nos. 47, 56, 46.

25 'Sunday', *Shishu*, translated by Sukhendu Ray, in Sukanta Chaudhuri

(ed.), *Rabindranath Tagore: Selected Writings for Children*, Oxford Tagore Translations, Delhi, 2002, p. 35.

26   *The Crescent Moon, EWRT*, vol. I, p. 134.

27   Ibid., p. 150.

28   'Paper Boats', in *Shishu*, 1903, translated by Rabindranath Tagore, in *The Crescent Moon, EWRT*, 1913, p. 144.

29   Vasudha Dalmia, *The Nationalisation of Hindu Traditions: Bharatendu Harischandra and Nineteenth Century Banaras*, Oxford University Press, Delhi, 1997, p. 287.

30   Translated by Tagore, *Poems*, 1942, p. 45.

31   Prabhat Kumar Mukhopadhyay, *Gitabitan: Kalanukramik Suchi*, Calcutta, 1992, p. 154; the song was first published in September 1905 and the musical score in 1908.

32   Translated by Tagore in *Gitanjali*, 1912.

33   Tagore to J.C. Bose, 18 March 1901, *C.P.*, vol. VI, no. 6.

34   Tagore, *Poems*, 1942, p. 62.

35   In *Atma-sakti*, 1905.

Chapter 4

1   R.T. to H.E. Viceroy Irwin, 30 May 1919; the original draft written by Tagore is in the Rabindra Bhavan, Visva-Bharati University. For the full text of the letter see Sabyasachi Bhattacharya (ed.), *The Mahatma and the Poet: Letters and Debates Between Gandhi and Tagore, 1915–1941*, National Book Trust, New Delhi, 5th edn. 2008 Pal, VII, p.418, RT in Calcutta.

2   R.T. to Rathindranath Tagore, Los Angeles, 11 October 1916, *C.P.*, vol. II, pp. 55–56.

3   *C.P.*, vol. II, pp. 55–56; Rathindranath Tagore's diary cited by Mukhopadhyay, vol. II, p. 619.

4   Mukhopadhyay, vol. II, p. 621.

5   See Krishna Kripalani, *Rabindranath Tagore: a Biography*, p. 251; I was unable to check the original text in *TLS*.

6   Kripalani, op. cit., p. 265.

7   T.S. Eliot spoke to Tagore's biographer Krishna Kripalani of this event many years later, Kripalani, ibid., f.n. 19, p. 265.

8   Ibid., pp. 250–57.

9   Ibid., p. 256.

10   Sujit Mukherjee, *Passage to America: The Reception of Rabindranath Tagore in the United States, 1912–1941*, Bookland, Calcutta, 1964; Martin Kampchen, *Rabindranath Tagore and Germany: a documentation*, Calcutta, 1991.

[11] Edward Said, *Orientalism*, London, 1978, pp. 67, 75–79; and *Culture and Imperialism*, London, 1993, pp. 233–35

[12] *The Outlook*, No. 106, 14 April 1914, p. 817, anonymous review of *One Hundred Poems*, cited in Sujit Mukherjee, op. cit., p. 41

[13] Evelyn Underhill, 'Introduction', in R. Tagore, *One Hundred Poems of Kabir*, London, 1914.

[14] Helen Bullis, 'Tagore as a Mystic', *New York Times*, 14 February 1915, cited in Sujit Mukherjee, op. cit., p. 49.

[15] Lajpat Rai, 'The Dilemma of Asia', *Independent*, LXXXVIII, 2 October 1916, cited in Sujit Mukherjee, op. cit., p. 46.

[16] Rameshwar Misra, *Madhya-yugin Hindi Sant-sahitya aur Rabindranath*, Banaras, 1989, pp. 84–87, and Appendix no. 4. Pal, *Rabi-jibani*, vol. VI, p. 163, does not accept that the dohas etc. are in Tagore's handwriting.

[17] Tagore to Sharashi Lal Sarkar, 11 October 1931, in Andrew Robinson and Krishna Dutta (eds.), *Selected Letters of Rabindranath Tagore*, Cambridge, 1997, p. 256, (hereafter *Sel. Letters.*)

[18] R.T. to Sturge Moore, 17 February 1914, *Sel.Letters*, p. 138.

[19] R.T. to W. Rothenstein, February 1914, *Sel.Letters*, p. 140.

[20] Rothenstein, *Men and Memories*, p. 301, quoted in *Sel.Letters*, p. 418, emphasis mine, S.B.

[21] Rothenstein to Tagore, 4 November 1932, Marie Lago (ed.), *Imperfect Encounters*, p. 343, cited in *Sel. Letters*, p. 418.

[22] Tagore to Rothenstein, 26 November 1932, *Sel. Letters*, p. 419.

[23] Yeats to Tagore, 20 June 1935; Tagore to Yeats, 16 July 1935; *Sel. Letters*, pp. 455–56.

[24] R.T. to Ezra Pound, 5 January 1913, Noel Stock (ed.), *Ezra Pound: Perspective*, cited in Bikash Chakravarty (ed.), *Poets to a Poet 1912–1940*, Calcutta, 1998, p. 164.

[25] R.T. to Rothenstein, February 1914, and 20 November 1932, *Sel. Letters*, pp. 141, 419.

[26] R.T. to Edward Thompson, 2 February 1921, Uma Dasgupta (ed.), *A Difficult Friendship: Letters of Edward Thompson and Rabindranath Tagore 1913–1940*, p. 128.

[27] R.T. to Sturge Moore, 24 May 1921, Rabindra Bhavan Archives, cited in Chakravarty (ed.), p. 234

[28] R.T. to Rothenstein, 26 November 1932, *Sel. Letters*, p. 419.

[29] R.T., *Poems*, (eds.) Krishna Kripalani et. al., Calcutta, 1942.

[30] Andrew Robinson is sceptical about Tagore's statement that he 'was 'reluctant' to show Rothenstein his translations', Robinson, editorial note, *Sel. Letters*, p. 420.

[31] Bridges to R.T., 7 June 1914, Chakravarty (ed.), pp. 59–61.

[32] Bridges to R.T., 20 October 1914.

[33] Bridges to R.T., 25 June 1915, ibid., p.67.

[34] R.T. to Rothenstein, 20 November 1932, *Sel. Letters*, p. 419.

[35] R.T. to Rothenstein, 26 November 1932, *Sel. Letters*, p. 419.

[36] See Krishna Dutta and Andrew Robinson, *Rabindranath Tagore: the Myriad-Minded Man*, New York, 1996, chapter 17.

[37] This is the view of Andrew Robinson and Krishna Dutta, ibid., p. 164.

[38] R.T. to Rothenstein, 26 November 1932, *Sel.Letters*, pp. 418–420.

[39] R.T. to Sturge Moore, 1 May 1914, *Sel.Letters*, p. 146.

[40] Ibid., p. 146

[41] R.T. to E.J. Thompson, 20 September 1921, in Dasgupta (ed.), p. 132.

[42] R.T. to Rothenstein, 26 November 1932, *Sel.Letters*, p. 420.

[43] R.T. to Sturge Moore, 20 October 1921, Rabindra Bhavan Archives, Santiniketan, in *Sel. Letters*, pp. 281–282.

[44] R.T. to Sturge Moore, 7 February 1923, Rabindra Bhavan Archives, cited Chakravarty (ed.), p. 238.

[45] W.B. Yeats to Rothenstein, 22 September 1931.

[46] Tagore, *The Child*, Allen and Unwin, London, 1931.

[47] *One Hundred Poems of Kabir*, India Society Publication, 1914; reprinted by Macmillan in 1917.

[48] *Poems*, Calcutta, 1942. (The best bibliographic survey of all of Tagore's translations is by Sisir Kumar Das, *The English Writings of Rabindranath Tagore*, Sahitya Akademi, Delhi, 1994, vols. I–III; see specially vol. I, pp. 601–629.)

[49] Mukhopadhyay, *Rabindra Jibani*, vol. II, pp. 546–549; the same point was made in an incisive commentary by Sumit Sarkar, '*Ghare Baire* in its Times', in P.K. Datta (ed.), *Rabindranath Tagore's* The Home and the World: *A Critical Companion*, Permanent Black, New Delhi, 2003, p. 145.

[50] Ashis Nandy, *The Illegitimacy of Nationalism: Rabindranath Tagore and the Politics of the Self*, Oxford University Press, Delhi, 1994, pp. 2, x–xi.

[51] R.T. to Rathindra, August or September 1919, tr. by Dutta and Robinson, *Sel.Letters*, p. 227.

[52] *Gora, R.R.*, vol. III, pp. 663–664.

[53] R.T. to W.W. Pearson, n.d. 1922, *V.B. Quarterly*, 1943, p. 179, cited in Mukhopadhyay, vol. II, p. 284.

[54] R.T., 'On the Purpose of Writing', *Sabuj Patra*, December, 1915, in *R.R.*, vol. IV, pp. 752–756.

[55] There is a translation of *Ghare Baire* by Surendranath Tagore entitled *Home and the World*, Penguin India, Delhi, 1999.

[56] R.T., 'Sahitya Vichar', *Prabasi*, April 1919, in *R.R.*, vol. IV, pp. 756–58.

[57] Dutta and Robinson, *Sel. Letters*, p. 156; Mukhopadhyay, vol. II, p. 419.

58 'Balaka', composed in October 1915, published in *Balaka*, 1916, extracts from translation by Lila Ray, Humayun Kabir (ed.), *Poems of Rabindranath Tagore*, Calcutta, 2005, p. 142.

Chapter 5

1 R.T. to H.E. the Viceroy, Governor General of India, 30 May 1919; for the complete text see Sabyasachi Bhattacharya (ed.), *The Mahatma and the Poet*, National Book Trust, New Delhi, 1997, pp. 187–188.

2 Gandhi to Tagore, 5 April 1919; 11 March 1920; 30 April 1919, R.B. Archives.

3 R.T., 'Letter to a Friend', *Modern Review*, May 1921; 'The Call of Truth', in Bengali entitled 'Satyer Ahvan', *Kalantar*; 'The Cult of the Charkha', *Modern Review*, September 1925; 'Striving for Swaraj', September 1925; full text in Sabyasachi Bhattacharya (ed.), *The Mahatma and the Poet*, pp. 68–86, 99–112, 113–21.

4 M.K. Gandhi, 'The Poet's Anxiety', *Young India*, 1 June 1921; 'The Great Sentinel', *Young India*, 13 October 1921; 'The Poet and the Charkha', *Young India*, 5 November 1925; 'The Poet and the Wheel', *Young India*, 11 March 1926; see Sabyasachi Bhattacharya, op.cit., pp. 87–95, 122–27, 127–31.

5 R.T. in *Visva-Bharati News*, January 1938, pp. 51–53.

6 Gandhi, 'The Poet and the Charkha', *Young India*, 5 November 1925.

7 *Ananda Bazar Patrika*, 20 April 1928; ibid., 19 August 1925.

8 *Bombay Chronicle*, 9 September 1925.

9 See C. Bandyopadhyay (ed.), *Rabindra Prasanga*, Ananda Bazar Patrika, 1922–1932, Calcutta, 1993.

10 'Dharma moha', *Parishesh*, *R.R.*, vol. VIII, p. 206.

11 Although the text of this speech on atheism was not included in the 'Collected Works', we have a verbatim copy made by Kshitimohan Sen; see for details Sabyasachi Bhattacharya, 'The archaeology of a poem', *The Telegraph*, Calcutta, 20 August 1993. The year the Babri Masjid was destroyed, the Vice Chancellor of Visva-Bharati made the poem on communalism, 'Dharma-moha', the theme of the Foundation Day ceremony at Santiniketan. Otherwise the poem has not received the attention it merits.

12 Home Dept. Political Branch, F. 181/1925, 15 May 1925, on R.N. Tagore; also reports from Govt. of Bengal, 24 June 1925, 19 September 1925 on Visva-Bharati, forwarded by L. Birley, Chief Secretary to Govt. of Bengal,

among which L.H. Colson is quite detailed and included possible connection with 'terrorists' i.e. militant nationalist; see S.K. Bagchi 'The Poet and the Raj'; *V.B. Quarterly*, vol. 50, nos. 1–4, May 1985, pp. 94–122.

[13] Erez Manela, *The Wilsonian Moment*, Oxford University Press, New York, p. 92.

[14] R.T. to Sudhindranath Datta, 1 April 1930, *C.P.*, vol. XVI, pp. 30–31, my translation.

[15] G.B. Synge, ICS, Under Secretary, Govt. of Bengal to Royal Mail Service, 2 March 1931, Intelligence Branch, File no. 285A/1925, Part-I, WBSA.

[16] For example, translation of poem 'Chithi' by Tagore, in Home (Political) File no. 181/1925, National Archives of India.

[17] JW House, ICS, India Office to Angus Fletcher, British Library, New York,

[24] February 1925, Intelligence Branch, File no. 285/1925, WBSA.

[18] Home Pol. I/11/1941, National Archives of India.

[19] Superintendent of Police, Birbhum to DIG Police, 2 February 1933, File no. 285/1925, ibid.

[20] DIG of Police, Report of 15 February 1934, Intelligence Branch, File no. 285/1925, WBSA.

[21] R.T. to E.J. Thompson, 20 September 1921, *Sel. Letters*, p. 276.

[22] Ibid., p. 277.

[23] Dutta and Robinson, *Rabindranath Tagore: the Myriad-Minded Poet*, pp. 171–73.

[24] T. S. Eliot was among Wood's students and attended one lecture by Tagore; the quotation *'Om shanti om'* in *Waste Land* has been attributed to Tagore's influence, an unlikely inference, as Dutt and Robinson point out. Ibid., p. 172. *Sadhana* was a great publishing success for there were eight reprints in the first twelve months; see Note by Sisir Kumar Das, *EWRT*, vol. II, p. 770.

[25] Dutta and Robinson, ibid., pp. 203–208.

[26] R.T. to Rathindranath, 11 October 1916, *C.P.*, vol. II, pp.55–56.

[27] R.T. to Harriet Monroe, 4 October 1916, cited in Dutta and Robinson, p. 206.

[28] Dutta and Robinson, p. 301.

[29] Tagore's translation of 'Athithi' in *Purabi*, R.T., *Poems*, p. 108.

[30] 'Shesh Vasanta', or 'The Last Spring', November 1924 in *Purabi*, translated by the poet Samar Sen, in Kabir (ed.), p. 157.

[31] 'Kritagya' or 'Beholden', November 1924, *Purabi*, translated by Hiren Mukherji, Kabir (ed.), pp. 160–161.

[32] R.T. to Victoria Ocampo, 10 July 1940, *Sel. Letters*, p. 523.

[33] R.T. to Ocampo, 14 March 1939, *Sel. Letters*, p. 505.

34 The best collection of the Tagore–Ocampo correspondence is Ketaki Kushari Dyson, *In Your Blossoming Flower-garden*, New Delhi, 1988.

35 R.T. to Ocampo, 13 January 1925, *Sel. Letters*, pp. 316–317.

36 Ibid., p. 317.

37 R.T. to Ocampo, 14 May 1930, *Sel. Letters*, p. 378.

38 R.T. to Ocampo, 9 July 1934, *Sel. Letters*, p. 439.

39 R.T. to Ocampo, 14 March 1939, *Sel. Letters*, p. 505.

40 R.T. to Ocampo, 10 July 1940, *Sel. Letters*, p. 522.

41 *Shesh Lekha*, Poem no. 5, written on 6 April 1941, R.R, vol. XIII, pp. 117–118. There is another poem about the chair gifted by Victoria Ocampo to Tagore in Argentina.

42 Tagore to Indira Devi, 8 March 1895, *Chhinna Patra*, my translation.

43 Tagore to Indira Devi, 7 October 1894, ibid., p. 287.

44 Mary M. Lago (ed.), *Imperfect Encounter: Letters of William Rothenstein and Rabindranath Tagore*, 1911–41, Cambridge, Mass, 1972.

45 Tagore–Elmhirst correspondence in a miscellany, *Purabi*, (ed.), Andrew Robinson, London, 1991.

46 *The Mahatma and the Poet*, Delhi, 1997.

47 R.T. to Indira Devi, July 1893, *Chhinna Patra*, Visva-Bharati, Calcutta, 1960, pp. 184–185, my translation.

48 R.T. to Gaganendra Nath Tagore, 26 October 1928, R.B. Archives, see Gour Saha (ed.), *Rabindra Patrabali: Tathya Panji*, Bolpur, 1984, no. 2521, hereafter cited as *R.P.*, followed by the assigned number of the letter in catalogue.

49 Mukhopadhyay, vol. III, p. 356; Mukul Dey was the first Indian Principal of the Calcutta Art School, after distinguished predecessors like E.B. Havell and Percy Brown; Dey was trained by Abanindranath and he was also protégé of Rabindranath whom he accompanied to Japan in 1916–17.

50 R.T. to Sudhindranath Datta, 2 November 1928, R.B Archives, *R.P.*, no. 2525.

51 R.T. to Nirmal Kumari Mahalanobis, 29 November 1928 and 7 November 1928, R.B Archives, *R.P.*, nos. 2533, 2527.

52 R.T. to Nirmal Kumari Mahalanobis, Letter nos. 23, 27, *Pathe o Pather Prante.*

53 R.T. to Suniti Kumar Chatterji, 20 December 1929, *Sel. Letters*, p. 367, translated by Dutta and Robinson.

54 Dutta and Robinson, *Selected Letters*, mentions Marguerite Milward and some unnamed Japanese artist among those who praised Tagore's paintings, *Sel. Letters*, pp. 373–75.

55 R.T. to William Rothenstein, 30 March 1930, *Sel. Letters*, p. 374.

56 R.T. to Sudhindranath Datta, 1 April 1930, *Sel. Letters*, pp. 375–76, translated by Dutta and Robinson.

[57] R.T. to Rothenstein, 11 June 1937, *Sel. Letters*, p. 478.

[58] R.T. to Jamini Roy, 25 May and 7 June 1941, *R.P.*, nos. 4075, 4080.

[59] See Partha Mitter, 'Tagore's Generation Views his Art.', in *Rabindranath Tagore in Perspective*, Visva-Bharati; Calcutta, 1989, pp. 154–156; Mitter observes that Tagore 'went out of his way to seek the approval of critics' and 'sounded too eager for publicity' and 'anxious to avoid the hostility of Western reviewers' pp. 146–147.

[60] Mitter, op.cit., p. 149; Somendranath Bandyopadhyay, *Rabindra Chitrakala, Rabindra Sahityer Patabhumika*, Santiniketan, 1981, and 'Expressionism and Rabindranath' in Anon (ed.), *Rabindranath Tagore in Perspective*, pp. 167–174, has underlined Tagore's 'expressionist' affinities.

[61] R.T. to Dhirendra Dev Burman, 11 November 1929, R.B. Archives, *R.P.*, no. 2633.

[62] R.T. to Amiya Chakrabarty, 11 October 1931; I owe to Dutta and Robinson, pp. 408–409, data on the scientific study of Tagore's vision, R.W. Pickford and J. Bose, 'Colour Vision and Aesthetic Problems in pictures by Rabindranath Tagore', *British Journal of Aesthetics*, Winter, 1987, pp. 70–75.

[63] R.T. to Jamini Kanta Roy, 7 June 1941, R.B Archives, *R.P.*, no. 4080.

[64] R.T., 'My Pictures', *EWRT*, vol. III, p. 637.

[65] R.T., as above, *EWRT*, p. 635.

[66] R.T., *EWRT*, vol. III, p. 636.

[67] 'What is Art.', *Personality*, *EWRT*, vol. II, pp. 358–62.

[68] 'Construction versus Creation', *EWRT*, vol. III, pp. 401–03.

[69] 'The Meaning of Art', lecture at Dhaka University, February 1926, *EWRT*, vol. III, pp. 586–87.

[70] Krishna Kripalani, *Rabindranath Tagore: a Biography*, pp. 348–349.

[71] Jacob Epstein, *Let there be sculpture*, London, 1940, cited by Kripalani, op. cit., p. 378; Epstein's sculpture of 1926 is in Rabindra Bhavan, Santiniketan.

[72] The persons referred to are Pandit Bhimrao Hasurkar, Buddhimanta Singh, Bidhu Sekhar Bhattacharya and Nandalal Bose.

[73] Krishna Kripalani, op. cit., p. 347.

[74] Leonard Elmhirst (ed.), *Rabindranath Tagore: Pioneer in education*, London, 1961, pp. 22–23.

[75] This band included the poet's son Rathindra, Kalimohan Ghosh (Santidev Ghosh's father), and Suren Kar, the architectural adviser at Santiniketan.

[76] R.T., 'The Cult of the Charkha', *Modern Review*, September 1925, Sabyasachi Bhattacharya (ed.), *The Mahatma and the Poet*, New Delhi, 1997, p. 104.

[77] R.T.'s Note on *Mukta-Dhara* in *Modern Review*, May 1922, *EWRT*, vol. III, p. 767.

[78] R.T., *The Waterfall*, *EWRT*, vol. III, pp. 149–162; Marjorie Sykes, *Three Plays*, Oxford University Press, 1950.

[79] R.T. to Upton Sinclair, 4 September 1923, *Sel. Letters*, p. 304.

[80] Introduction, *Rakta-Karabi*, *R.R.*, vol. VIII, p. 716.

[81] R.T., *Paschim Jatrir Diary*, 28 September 1924, Appendix to *Rakta-Karabi*, *R.R*, vol. VIII, p. 717.

[82] R.T., 'Sanhati', i.e. 'Organisation', in journal entitled *Sanhati*, vol. I, no. 1, 1923, edited by Jnananjan Pal who appears to have interest in the trade union movement; we owe this reference to Prasanta Pal, vol. IX, p. 10.

[83] Professor Radha Kamal Mookerji, Professor of Economics at Lucknow University claims that his conversations with Tagore in Shillong when this play was written provided data to Tagore. Prabhat Mukhopadhyay, vol. III, p. 156.

[84] Elmhirst recorded his memory of these events at the request of Krishna Kripalani for inclusion in the latter's *Rabindranath Tagore: a Biography*, Calcutta, 2008, pp. 353–56.

[85] *Letters from Russia*, tr. by S. Sinha, Visva-Bharati, Calcutta, 1960, pp. 12, 60, 110–11, 113–14.

[86] P. Vinogradov to R.T., 9 May 1922, cited in *R.R.*, vol. X, p. 683.

[87] Ibid., p. 117.

[88] Ibid., p. 12.

[89] R.T. to Radharani Devi, 30 August 1928, R.B. Archives, no. 2479; also cited by Mukhopadhyay, vol. III, p. 372.

[90] R.T., 'The Indian Ideal of Marriage', 1925, in *EWRT*, vol. III, pp. 524–37.

[91] Ibid., p. 527

[92] *Yogayog*, *R.R*, vol. V, p. 457.

[93] Ibid., p. 454.

[94] *Farewell Song*, translation by Radha Chakravarty, Delhi, 2005, p. 43; citations hereafter are from this translation.

[95] p. 51.

[96] p. 117.

[97] p. 105.

[98] pp. 74–75.

[99] pp. 160–61.

[100] pp 10–11.

[101] R.T. to Sudhindranath Datta, 11 July 1928, *C.P.*, vol. XVI, pp. 21–22.

[102] Buddhadeb Bose, *Rabindranath: Kathasahitya*, Visva-Bharati, Calcutta, 1955, p. 126.

[103] 'Kalo Ghora' ('Black Stallion'), *Vichitrita*, *R.R.* vol. IX, p. 30. (my transln.)

Chapter 6

[1] 'Janmadin', in *Nabajatak, R.R.,* vol. XII, p. 134.

[2] R.T. to Andrews, 3 October 1920, *Sel. Letters*, p. 239; Dutta and Robinson comment that 'he adopts the somewhat sanctimonious tone that came easily to him when writing about the USA'. The letter actually shows relief and—indeed he makes a joke of the millions expected—does not justify the comment.

[3] R.T. to Andrews, 30 July 1926, also printed in *Manchester Guardian, Sel. Letters*, p. 333.

[4] R.T. to Nitindranath Gangulee, 31 July 1931, *C.P.,* vol. IV, p. 179.

[5] R.T to NEB Ezra, 17 June 1934, *Sel. Letters*, p. 437.

[6] 'Prayaschitta', *Nabajatak, R.R.,* vol. XII, pp. 108–109; Tagore's translation in Krishna Kripalani (ed.), *Poems*, Calcutta 1942, pp. 187–89.

[7] R.T. to Vincenc Lesny, 15 October 1938, *Sel. Letters*, p. 501; Dutta and Robinson make an important point; Tagore refrained from commenting harshly on Lesny's work on him which he thought was poor in quality because of the enormous tragedy that befell Lesny's country; Ibid., p. 500.

[8] R.T. to Rash Behari Bose, 24 October 1938, *Sel. Letters*, p. 502.

[9] R.T. to J. Nehru, 17 August 1939, *Sel. Letters*, p. 512.

[10] The history of the Cheena Bhavana is recorded by the librarian of the university and the biographer of Tagore, Prabhat Kumar Mukhopadhyay, *Rabindra Jibani*, vol. IV, pp. 94–96. The centre of Japanese students, Nippon Bhavan, was built similarly with individuals' donations, mostly from Japanese alumni of Visva-Bharati; since the Nippon House was founded in 1994 when I happened to be the Vice-Chancellor of Visva-Bharati University, I have personal knowledge of the individual endeavours which led to it.

[11] 'Naginira charidike phaliteche visakta nishwas', *Prantik*, tr. by Chidananda Dasgupta, in Humayun Kabir (ed.), *Poems of Rabindranath Tagore*, UBSPD, Calcutta reprint 2005, p. 222.

[12] 'Alas samaydhara beye mon chale', *Arogya*, tr. by Hiren Mukherji, in Humayun Kabir, op. cit., pp. 246–47.

[13] We owe this nugget of interesting information to Dutta and Robinson, *Sel. Letters*, p. 521. Statement by C. Bossennee, 22.6.40.

[14] R.T. to F.D. Roosevelt, 15 June 1940, published in *New York Times*, 16 June 1940, in *Sel. Letters*, p. 522.

[15] R.T., Address at Annual Convocation, University of Calcutta, 13 February 1937, Calcutta University Press, 1937, p. 11, 13-14, *R.R.,* vol. XVI, p. 351

[16] Ibid., pp. 15–17.

[17] *Crisis in Civilization*, Visva-Bharati, Calcutta, 1st edn., 1941, reprint 1964, pp. 12, 20.

18   R.T., 'Hindu-Musalman', 1931, *Kalantar*, Visva-Bharati, Calcutta, 1937, pp. 323–36,

19   *Kalantar*, pp. 371–82, 389–92.

20   'Mahajati Sadan', 1939, *Kalantar*, p. 391.

21   The objection was to verses such as '*Bahubala-dharinim, namami tarinim*' '*Twam hi Durga dasa-praharana dharini…namami twam*', etc. in the expanded version of 1881.

22   S.C. Bose to R.T., 16 October 1937, R.B. Archives, Santiniketan.

23   R.T. to Jawharlal Nehru, president of Indian National Congress, 26 October 1937, published in *Amrita Bazar Patrika*, 2 November 1937.

24   J. Nehru's note of 30 October 1937, All-India Congress Committee Papers, file no. 31–34 of 1937, Nehru Memorial Museum and Library, New Delhi.

25   A detailed version of the episode appears in Sabyasachi Bhattacharya, *Vande Mataram: the Biography of a Song*, Penguin, Delhi, 2003.

26   R.T. to Buddhadeb Bose, 28 December 1937, in *C.P.*, vol. XVI, p. 135.

27   R.T., Preface, *The Religion of Man*, London, 1930.

28   *The Religion of Man*, *EWRT*, vol. III, p. 89.

29   Ibid., p. 120.

30   Ibid., p. 121.

31   Ibid., pp. 122, 125.

32   Ibid., pp. 87, 90; we have evidence from his correspondence that Tagore was familiar with Henri Bergson's work, *Creative* Evolution, available in English translation from 1911.

33   Ibid., p. 89.

34   Ibid., pp. 89, 91.

35   Ibid., p. 99.

36   Ibid., p. 111.

37   *The Centre of Indian Culture*, Society for Promotion of National Education, Adyar, 1919.

38   Mohit Chakraborti, *Tagore and Education for Social Change*, Calcutta, 1993; Sunil C. Sarkar, *Tagore's Educational Philosophy and Experiment*, Santiniketan, 1961; H.B. Mukherjee, *Education for Fulness*, Bombay, 1962.

39   A more extended treatment of the subject is available in editorial note by Sabyasachi Bhattacharya in Sabyasachi Bhattacharya and Asok Mukerjee (ed.), *The Common Pursuit*, Calcutta, 1995, pp. 13–38.

40   R.T., *Siksha*, Calcutta, 1908.

41   R.T., 'Chatrader Prati', in *Siksha*, 1908.

42   R.T., 'Asantosher Karan', in *Santiniketan*, 1919, in *Siksha* new edition, 1935.

43 *The Centre of Indian Culture*, Adyar, 1919.
44 'My School' in *Personality*, London, 1917.
45 R.T., *Creative Unity*, New York, 1922.
46 R.T., *Creative Unity, EWRT*, vol. II, p. 559.
47 R.T., *Siksha*, new edition 1935, essays entitled 'Sikshar Bikiran' and 'Sikshar Swangikaran'.
48 'Sikshar Swangikaran', *Siksha*, 1935.
49 R.T., 'Palli Seva', speech at Sriniketan, 6 February 1940, reprinted in *Palli Prakiti*, 1961
50 Sabyasachi Bhattacharya, *The Mahatma and the Poet: Letters and Debates Between Gandhi and Tagore*, New Delhi, 2008.
51 'My School', in *Personality*, London, 1917, p. 23.
52 R.T., Chicago, to C.F. Andrews, 5 March 1921, published in *Modern Review*, May 1921, *Selected Letters*, p. 261.
53 R.T., Philadelphia, USA, to Rathindranath Tagore, 31 October 1930, *C.P.*, vol. I, pp. 102–105, tr. by Dutta and Robinson, *Sel. Letters*, pp. 392–93.
54 Amiya Chakravarty, 5 May 1934, *C.P.*, vol. XI, pp. 111–12, tr. by Dutta and Robinson, *Sel. Letters*, p. 436.
55 R.T. to Gandhi, 12 September, 1935, to Jawaharlal Nehru, 9 October 1935, *Sel. Letters*, pp. 457–58.
56 Gandhi to R.T., 19 February 1937; R.T. to Gandhi, 26 February 1937, R.B. Archives; see S. Bhattacharya, *The Mahatma and the Poet*, pp. 162–167.
57 R.T. to Gandhi, 2 February 1940, R.B. Archives; S. Bhattacharya, op. cit. pp. 177–178.
58 Gandhi to R.T., 19 February 1940, ibid., p. 178.
59 *Visva-Parichay*, Dedication to S.N. Bose, *R.R.*, vol. XIII, pp. 519–522.
60 Ibid., p. 521.
61 R.T. to M.K. Gandhi, 28 January 1934, R.B. Archives, full version in Sabyasachi Bhattacharya, *The Mahatma and the Poet*, p. 156.
62 R.T.'s statement published in *Harijan*, 16 February 1934.
63 R.T., 'The Cult of the Charkha', *Modern Review*, September 1925, in S. Bhattacharya, op. cit., pp. 99–112
64 Gandhi, 'Superstition versus Faith', *Harijan*, 16 February 1934; Gandhi, 'The Poet and the Charkha', *Young India*, 5 November 1925, in S. Bhattacharya, op. cit., pp. 122–126, 159–160.
65 For example, debates with Chandranath Basu on Hindu diet, 'Ahar-tatwa', in *Sadhana*, 1891, reprinted in R.T., *Samaj*; and on 'Hindu Marriage', *Hindu Vivaha*, in *Bharati*, reprinted in R.T., *Samaj*, 1887; the latter an important statement against child marriage by Tagore. However, as we noted earlier, circumstances compelled Tagore to marry off two of his daughters at a very early age.

[66] Mukhopadhyay, vol. I, p. 316 on R.T.'s letter to Sris Chandra Majumdar. Tagore's fierce contempt for obscurantism is palpable in the poem 'Hing Ting Chhat'.

[67] Mukhopadhyay, p. 353; the essay 'Brahma-samajer sarthakata', 1910, was included in the collection *Santiniketan* in *R.R.*

[68] R.T. to Indira Devi, 10 January 1930, *C.P.*, vol. V, p. 72.

[69] Dmitri Marianoff, report. in *New York Times,* 10 August 1930, cited in Dipankar Home and Andrew Robinson, 'Einstein and Tagore: Man, nature and mysticism', *Journal of Consciousness Studies*, vol. II, no. 2, 1995, pp. 167–79, reprinted in Dutta and Robinson, *Select Letters*, hereafter cited as Home and Robinson.

[70] Einstein to Romain Rolland, 10 October 1930, Home and Robinson, p. 529.

[71] Ibid., p. 529.

[72] Home and Robinson point to the implications of the debate in terms of the theories of Niels Bohr (1885–1962), Max Born, 1882–1970, et.al.

[73] 'Anmana', *Purabi*, Tagore's translation in Krishna Kripalani (ed.), *Poems*, p. 103.

[74] 'Sangit o Kabita' in the journal *Bharati*, 1881, reprinted in *Samalochana*, 1888, *R.R.*, vol. XV, pp. 75–78.

[75] R.T., 'Sonar Kathi', *Sabuj Patra*, 1915, reprinted in *Parichay*, *R.R.*, vol. IX, pp. 633–35.

[76] 'Sangit', 1912, *Pather Sanchay*, *R.R.*, vol. XIII, pp. 683–87.

[77] R.T., 'Sangit', 1912, *Pather Sanchay*, *R.R.*, vol. XI, p. 684.

[78] Ibid., p. 686.

[79] R.T.'s letters to Dhurjati Prasad Mukherjee, October 1932, began a debate which touched on various aspects of poetry and music, see Mukhopadhyay, vol. III, pp. 481–82.

[80] R.T., *Jiban Smriti*, *R.R.*, vol. IX.

[81] Subhas Chowdhury, *Gitabitaner Jagat*, Calcutta, 2004, pp. 565–593. For example from Guru Nanak, *'Gaganer thale, rabi chandra dipak jwale'*— translation is also attributed to Jyotirindranath Tagore; from Haridas Swami, *'Bipul taranga re'*; from Meera, *'kakhon dile paraye'*; from Thyagaraja, *'Nilanjana-chhaya'*; from Dikshitar, *'Basanti, hey bhubanamohini'*. These evidence from sources have been assembled by Subhas Chowdhury, op. cit., pp. 556–593.

[82] There are many commentators and interpreters of *Rabindra Sangit*, e.g. Santidev Ghosh, Kanika Bandyopadhya, as well as reminiscences throwing light on the subject by disciples of Tagore at Santiniketan, e.g. Amita Sen, *Santiniketan Ashram Kanya*, Calcutta, 1977; or Pramatha Nath Bishi, *Rabindranath o Santiniketan*, Calcutta, n.d. A recent exposition of the subject in English is by Reba Som, *Rabindranath Tagore: the singer and his song*, Delhi, 2009.

[83] In the early scores published the song was classified as *Khambaj-dhumali*; later scores dropped the specification. See Subhas Chowdhury, op. cit., p. 448.

[84] R.T. to Pulin Behari Sen, 20 November 1937, R.B. Archives, Letter no. 3659.

[85] R.T.'s own translation, *Poems*, p. 75.

[86] *Gitabitan*, 2nd edition, 1941, Visva-Bharati, Calcutta.

[87] The songs are '*Tumi rabe nirabe*', 1896; '*Hriday amar nuchhichhe ajike*', 1900; '*Klanti amar kshama karo*', 1914; '*Kabe tumi ashbe bolay*', 1918; '*Akash bhara surya tara*', 1922; '*Swapane dohe chhinu ki mohay*', 1931; all in *Gitabitan*.

[88] Mukhopadhyay, *Gitabitan: Kalanukramik Suchi*, Calcutta, 1964, revised edn. 1992, p. 31; Subhas Chowdhury, *Gitabitaner Jagat*, Calcutta, 2004, pp. 170–204.

[89] R.T. on 25 May 1941, in conversation with Rani Chanda, *Alapchari Rabindranath*, Visva-Bharati, Calcutta, 1942, 1970, pp. 125–126, 128.

[90] Letter to Lokendra Palit, 1892, *Sahitya*, *R.R.*, vol. IV, p. 706.

[91] 'Bankimchandra', *Adhunik Sahitya*, *R.R.*, vol. V, p. 807.

[92] 'Sahityer Tatparya' 1903, 'Sahityer Samagri', *Sahitya*, *R.R.*, vol. IV, pp. 619–24.

[93] 'Sahityer Vicharak', *Sahitya*, *R.R.*, vol. IV, p. 627.

[94] Ibid., pp. 638–40.

[95] 'Visva-sahitya', ibid., p. 648.

[96] Krishna Kripalani, *Rabindranath Tagore*, p. 349.

[97] Gadya-Kavya, *Sahityer Swarup*, *R.R.*, vol. XIV, pp. 190–92.

[98] 'Sahitye Nabatva', i.e. Modernism in Literature, *Sahityer Pathe*, *R.R.*, vol. XIV, pp. 455–58.

[99] 'Adhunik Kavya', *Sahityer Pathe*.

[100] Talk at seminar in Vichitra Bhavan, Jorasanko in 1937, *Sahityer Pathe*, *R.R.*, vol. XIV, pp. 511–14.

[101] 'Rater Gadi', 1940, *Nabajatak*, Kabir, 2005, p. 230.

[102] 'Anek hazar bachharer', 1935, *Sesh Saptak*, Kabir, p.185.

[103] 'Ami', 1937, *Shyamali*, my translation.

[104] 'Bismay', 'A wonder', 1932, *Parisesh*, R.T., Poems, p. 136, Tagore's translation

[105] For example, Sudhindranath Datta, Buddhadeb Bose, Bishnu De, and Sanjay Bhattacharya, in R.T., *C.P.*, vol. XVI, Calcutta, 1995.

[106] Samar Sen, *Babu Brittanta*, 1978, cited by editor Sutapa Bhattacharya, in *C.P.*, vol. XVI, p. 268.

[107] Krishna Kripalani *Rabindranath Tagore: a Biography*, p. 438.

[108] *Char Adhyay*, *R.R.*, vol. VII, pp. 403–404.

[109] Tagore's 'Explanation', *Char Adhyay*, *R.R.*, vol. VII, p. 744.

[110] 'Introduction to *Char Adhyay*, my translation, Appendix, *R.R.*, vol. VII, pp. 743–44.

[111] Chinmohan Sehanovis, *Rabindranath o Biplabi Samaj*, Calcutta, 1988, pp. 135–140.

[112] This was the protest on 26 September 1931 against police firing upon prisoners in Hijli Detenu Camp and police atrocities in Chittagong to avenge the Chittagong Armoury Raid by Surya Sen's group of revolutionaries, the Indian Republican Army.

[113] 'Nishithere lajja dilo . . . Pinjare bihanga bandha, sangit na manilo bandhan', *Parishesh*, *R.R.*, vol. VIII, p. 143.

[114] *Parishesh*, p. 145.

[115] Sahanovis, op. cit., p. 73.

[116] R.T., Introduction to *Punascha*, *R.R.*, vol. VIII, p. 228.

[117] 'Kopai', 'Ak jon lok', *Poems*, translated by Tagore, Kripalani (ed.), pp. 140–148.

[118] Tr. by Tagore, *Poems*, Kripalani (ed.), p. 159.

[119] 'Hatat dekha', in *Shyamali*, *R.R.*, vol. X, pp. 169–71.

[120] 'Amrita', in *Shyamali*, *R.R.*, vol. X, pp. 173–178.

[121] 'Africa', poem no. 16, *Patraput*, tr. by R.T., *Poems*, Kripalani (ed.), pp. 164–166.

[122] 'Chira-Jatri', *Shyamali*, tr. by R.T., in *Poems*, pp. 160–163.

[123] '25 Vaisakh', written in May 1936, *Sesh Saptak*, tr. by Sisir K. Ghosh in Humayun Kabir (ed.), 2005, pp. 191–94.

[124] Poem no. 1, R.T., translation, Kripalani (ed.), *Poems,* p.175.

[125] '*Abasanna chetanar godhuli-belay...*' in *Prantik*, tr. by Sisir K. Ghosh in Kabir (ed.), p. 221.

[126] '*Jakhan rabo na ami....*', in *Senjuti*, *R.R.*, vol. XI, p. 134.

[127] 'Janmadin', *Senjuti*, tr. by Tagore, *Poems*, Kripalani (ed.), p. 180.

[128] 'Janmadin', in *Senjuti*, tr. by Tagore, *Poems*, Kripalani (ed.), p. 168.

[129] 'Parichay', in *Senjuti*, tr. by Humayun Kabir (ed.), p. 227.

[130] R.T. wrote 'Keno' in *Nabajatak* both as prose and rhymed verse, and published the latter. *R.R.*, vol. XII, pp. 111, 693.

[131] 'Ishteshan', tr. by Buddhadeb Bose, *Nabajatak*, in Kabir (ed.), p. 228.

[132] 'Romantic', *Nabajatak*, RB, vol. XII, p. 136.

[133] 'Bhalobasa esechilo nihshabda charane', 28 March 1940, *Sehnai*, *R.R.*, vol. XII, p. 154, my translation.

[134] 'Bhumika', *Akash-pradip*, *R.R.*, vol. XII, p. 63.

[135] 'Kankal', in *Purabi;* this translation, made by Tagore, was published posthumously in *Poems*, Kripalani (ed.), pp. 109–110. K.K. Dyson, 2011, p. 295.

[136] Rogsajya, translation by Samar Sen in Kabir (ed.), 1966, p. 239.

[137] *Rogsajyay*, tr. by Krishna Kripalani, *Rabindranath Tagore: a Biography*, p. 484.

[138] Rogsajya, tr. by Abu Sayyid Ayub, in Kabir (ed.), p. 235.

[139] 'Janmadin', tr. by Amalendu Dasgupta, Kabir (ed.), pp. 241–242.

[140] 'Jabar samay holo bihanger', 1934, *Prantik*, *R.R.*, vol. XI, p. 217, my translation.

[141] *Prantik*, 1937, Kabir (ed.), p. 221.

[142] Rogsajya, tr. by Amiya Chakravarty, *Poems*, Kripalani (ed.), ibid., p. 195.

[143] Ibid., p. 208.

[144] K. Kripalani, *Rabindranath Tagore: a Biography*, 1st edn. 1962, p. 349.

[145] M.K. Gandhi, in Ramananda Chatterjee (ed.), *The Golden Book of Tagore*, 1933, quoted by Kripalani, ibid., p. 422.

[146] Gandhi to R.T., 2 May 1933, Sabyasachi Bhattacharya, *The Mahatma and the Poet*, New Delhi, 1997.

[147] R.T. to Gandhi, 19 February 1940, Gandhi to R.T., 19 February 1940, S. Bhattacharya, ibid., pp. 177–178.

[148] Gandhi to R.T., 13 April 1941, R.T. to Gandhi, 13 April 1941, S. Bhattacharya, ibid., p. 181.

[149] Gandhi to R.T., 1 October 1940, S. Bhattacharya, ibid., p. 180.

[150] The poem cited is '*Sammukhe santi parabare*', which was written in 1939 and designated by him as the song to be sung at his funeral, Prabhat K. Mukhopadhyay, *Gitabitan: Kalanu-kramik Suchi*, Calcutta, 1992, p. 378.

[151] *Sesh Lekha*, no. 13, translated by Amiya Chakravarty, *Poems*, Kripalani (ed.), p. 214; needless to say here there is a play on the word 'Rabi', his own name.

[152] *Sesh Lekha*, poem no. 28, *Poems*, tr. by Amiya Chakravarty, in *Poems*, Kripalani (ed.), ibid., p. 215.

[153] Poem no. 11, *Sesh Lekha*, tr. by Amiya Chakravarty, in *Poems*, Kripalani (ed.), ibid., p. 213.

[154] '*Tomar srishtir path....*', Poem no. 15, *Sesh Lekha*, tr. by Amiya Chakravarty, in R.T., *Poems*, Kripalani (ed.), pp. 216–217.

Epilogue

[1] Pal, vol. III, p. 62.

[2] Martin Kämpchen, *Rabindranath Tagore and Germany: a documentation*, Max Mueller Bhavan, Calcutta, 1991; also see Kämpchen, *Tagore in Germany: Four Responses to a Cultural Icon*, Indian Institute of Advanced Study, Shimla, 1999.

[3] Ray Monk, *Ludwig Wittgenstein: The Duty of a Genius*, London, 1990, pp. 243, 408–12; I am indebted for information on Wittgenstein to Dr Basudev Chatterjee of Delhi University.

[4] Mrs. Susan Owen, Mother of Poet Wilfred Owen, to R.T., 1 August 1920, quoted in Dutta and Robinson, *Rabindranath Tagore*, p. 2.

[5] Dutta and Robinson, 1995, p. 208.

[6] Pound to Iris Barry, 25 January 1917, Dutta and Robinson, 1995, p. 208.

[7] Dutta and Robinson, 1995, pp. 226–27.

[8] Rothenstein to Max Beerbohm, 5 August 1920, Dutta and Robinson, 1995, p. 227.

[9] Yeats to Rothenstein, 22 September 1931, in Bikash Chakravarty, *Poets to a Poet*, Visva-Bharati, Calcutta, 1998, p. 176.

[10] Dutta and Robinson, 1995, p. 349.

[11] Dutta and Robinson, 1995, p. 178.

[12] Krishna Kripalani, *Rabindranath Tagore: a Biography*, Visva-Bharati/UBS, Calcutta, p. xxi.

[13] For details in respect of Hindi and Urdu writers and translators I am indebted to Soma Bandyopadhyay and Shafe Qidwai's research papers in 'Proceedings of National Seminar on the Impact of Rabindranath Tagore on Other Indian Literatures', National Library (NLI), Calcutta, 20–21 January 2011, with Introduction by Swapan Chakraborty, Director, NLI, hereafter cited as National Seminar Proceedings, 2011; I have drawn upon the above collections of papers in the following pages in respect of several other languages, as well as *The Encyclopaedia of Indian Literature*, Amaresh Datta et al. (eds.), vols. I to VI, Sahitya Akademi, Delhi, 1987–94.

[14] Vinod Joshi, 'Tagore and Gujarati Literature', Biplab Chakraborty, 'Tagore and Contemporary Marathi Literature', C.N. Ramchandran, 'Impact of Tagore on Kannada Literature', in National Seminar Proceedings, mimeo, 2011.

[15] I have drawn upon, apart from the previously cited Amaresh Datta et al. (eds.), *The Encyclopaedia of Indian Literature*, vols. I–VI, the essays by Subramaniam Krisnamoorthy, Akkiraju Ramapati Rao and R. Surendran on the impact of Tagore on literature in Tamil, Telugu and Malayalam in previously cited 'Proceedings of National Seminar, National Library, Calcutta, mimeo, 2011.

[16] Sheldon Pollock, *The Language of the Gods in the World of Men: Sanskrit, Culture and Power in Pre-Modern India*, Berkeley, University of California Press, 2006; Sheldon Pollock (ed.) 'Introduction', *Literary Cultures in History: Re-constructions in South Asia* Oxford University Press, Delhi, 2003; P.P. Ravindran, 'Genealogies of Indian Literature', *Economic and Political Weekly*, vol. XLI, no. 25, June 2006, pp. 2558–63.

A Chronology of Tagore's Life and Contemporary Historical Events

1861–1890: Chapter Two

Chronology of Life

Rabindranath Tagore born, 7 May 1861, the eighth son, and fourteenth child of Debendranath (1861).

Enrols at age four in Oriental Seminary, and soon after in Normal School, Calcutta (1868).

Regime of rigorous teaching at home: languages, classical music, drawing, gymnastics, wrestling (from 1868).

At age ten begins raiding family library to read Bengali literature (from 1871).

Enrols in new school, Bengal Academy. (1872 ?)

At age eleven, *upanayana*, i.e. Brahmin's sacred thread ceremony (1873).

On tour with father in Dalhousie hills; lessons from father in Sanskrit, English, Astronomy (1873).

Enrols in St Xavier's School (1874).

'Irregular' according to school record, drops out (1876).

Publishes verses in journals; 'forgettable' writings according to R.T. (1875–77).

Composes verses, pseudonym Bhanu Singha (1877–78).

Spends eighteen months as a ward of elder brother Satyendranath, I.C.S., in Ahmedabad and Bombay (1877–78).

R T sent off by family to England (September 1878).

R T admitted to a school in Brighton and then to London University College (1878–79).

Publishes *Europe-Prabasir Patra* (Letters on a Sojourn in Europe) serialized in '*Bharati*'; it did not please family elders (1879–80).

Father recalls R.T. to Calcutta (February 1880).

Musical drama on Valmiki by R.T. staged at the family seat in Calcutta (September 1881).

Publishes several books of verse, *Kabi-Kahini, Bana-Phul, Valmiki-Pratibha, Bhagna-Hriday, Rudrachanda,* and prose *Europe-Prabasir Patra* (1878–1881).

Publishes *Sandhya-Sangeet* and *Kal-Mrigaya*; Bankim Chandra Chatterjee recognizes R.T. as a promising poet of the next generation (1882); R.T. writes '*Nirjharer Swapnabhanga*' in an ecstatic moment.

Family arranges R.T.'s marriage with Bhabatarini (re-named Mrinalini), daughter of a functionary working in the Tagore Estates in Jessore, East Bengal (9 December 1883).

Publishes *Prabhat Sangit, Bau-thakuranir Hat* (1883).

Kadambari, sister-in-law, wife of R.T.'s elder brother Jyotirindranath, companion to Tagore since he was seven years of age, commits suicide; R.T. writes many poems in her memory and dedicates five books to her (April 1884).

R.T. is appointed secretary to Adi Brahma Samaj, and publishes *Bhanu Singha Thakurer Padabali* as well as *Prakitir Pratishodh, Nalini, Shaishab Sangeet* (1884).

R.T. takes charge of family journal *Balak* and fills it up with poems, essays, stories; publishes essay on *Rammohan Roy* and his first book of songs, *Rabi-Chhaya* (1885).

First child born to R.T. and Mrinalini, daughter Madhurilata (nickname Bela) (October 1886).

Indian National Congress session in Calcutta. R.T. presents a song to delegates— or perhaps to a section of them (December 1886).

R.T.'s essay condemning Hindus child marriage leads to controversies with conservative Hindu leaders (1887).

R.T. represents family at the Foundation Laying Ceremony, Santiniketan Ashram

R.T.'s second child, son Rathindranath born (November 1888).

Publishes and stages dance-drama *Mayar Khela* (1888).

R.T.'s *Raja-o-Rani* is published and staged at Satyendra's house, his wife and Mrinalini participating (1889).

In England, also tours Italy and France (August to November 1890).

Publishes drama *Bisarjan* and a collection of poems *Manasi*, a turning point; R.T. considered these poems his first mature work (1890).

Contemporary Historical Events

Birth of Motilal Nehru, Bhikaji Cama (1861),
Election of President Lincoln, beginning of American Civil War (1861).
First romantic novel in Bengali, *Durgesh Nandini*, by Bankim Chandra
   Chatterjee (1865).
Birth of Gopal Krishna Gokhale (1866).
Publication of Karl Marx's *Das Kapital*, vol. 1 (1867).
Meiji Restoration gives birth to new Japan (1868).
Birth of Mohandas Karamchand Gandhi (1869).
Unification of Germany by Bismarck (1871).
Charles Darwin publishes *Descent of Man* (1871).
Birth of Aurobindo Ghosh (1872).
Death of John Stuart Mill (1873).
Foundation of Mohamedan Anglo-Oriental School by Sir Sayed Ahmed
   Khan (1875).
Arya Samaj founded by Dayananda Saraswati (1875).
Foundation of Indian Association, Calcutta by Surendranath Banerjea
   (1876).
Birth of Mohammad Ali Jinnah (1876).
Victoria is declared Empress of India (1877).
England occupies Khyber Pass (1879).
Boers declare independence in South Africa (1880).
Birth of Kemal Ataturk (1881).
Birth of Subramania Bharathi (1882).
Britain occupies Egypt (1883).
P. Ananda Charlu establishes Madras Mahajana Sabha (1884).
Indian National Congress first session in Bombay (1885).
Death of Bharatendu Harishchandra (1885).
Birth of Abul Kalam Azad (1888).
Birth of Jawaharlal Nehru (1889).

1891–1908: Chapter Three

Chronology of Life

Birth of third child, second daughter, Renuka (January 1891).
Appointed literary editor of journal *Hitabadi* (1891).
R.T. given new responsibility by father Debendranath: begins tour of estates
   of North Bengal and Orissa (1891).

First major public speech in Calcutta on Eastern and Western Civilizations (April 1891.)

In anticipation of his role in Santiniketan, R.T. organizes foundation of Prayer Hall or Mandir (1891).

Publications: *Europe-Jatrir Diary* (1891), stylistic innovation of writing in Bengali that is spoken; late 1891 or early 1892 he writes the poem 'Sonar Tari', a turning point in his literary life (1891–92).

Writes and publishes *Chitrangada*, the first version of several of this work, and *Goday-galad*, a comedy (1892).

Major public speech on 'Indians and the British' at meeting chaired by Bankim Chatterjee (1893).

Third daughter, Mira, born (January 1894).

Death of Bankim Chatterjee, R.T. organizes and addresses a public meeting to pay tributes to him (April 1894).

Foundation of Bengal Literary Academy, later known as Bangiya Sahitya Parishad, with R.T. as vice-president (1894).

Editor of journal *Sadhana* (1894–95).

Publications: *Sonar Tari, Biday Abhishap* (1894); the poem 'Sonar Tari' written in late 1891 or early 1892 was first published in 1893 and later in the book bearing the same title (1894).

R.T. involved in an abortive commercial enterprise Tagore and Co with nephew Surendranath (1895).

Major public speech on future of Bengali literature at Sahitya Parishad, Calcutta (1895).

Father Debendranath rewards R.T. for his diligent supervision of his estate and vests in him overall powers (August 1896).

Birth of youngest child, son Samindranath (December 1896).

Indian National Congress session in Calcutta, reception at Tagore family residence, R.T. sings 'Vande Mataram' (December 1896).

Publications: *Chitra, Nadi* (1896).

Bengal Provincial Conference, offshoot of Congress, addressed by R.T. (1897).

Publication: *Panch-bhuta* (1897).

R.T. establishes 'Swadeshi Bhandar' near his house in Calcutta to market Indian handicrafts (1897).

Protests Sedition Bill in public meeting at Calcutta Town Hall (March 1898).

Editor of journal *Bharati* (1898–99).

'Tagore & Co.', due to poor supervision by the Tagores, near bankruptcy, R.T. has to cope with financial liabilities (1899).

Publication: *Kanika* (1899)

R.T. borrows from Sir T.N. Palit a huge sum of money to meet his liabilities on account of Tagore & Co., till 1918 repayment had to be made in instalments (1900).

Publications: *Katha, Kahini, Kalpana, Kshanika, Galpa-Guchha* (1900).

R.T. assumes editorship of literary journal *Bangadarshan*, new series (1901–05).

Arranged marriage of daughters Madhurilata and Renuka (1901).

School started in Santiniketan with five students and about the same number of teachers (1901).

Publications: *Naibedya, Galpa-Guchha*, vol. II (1901).

R.T. has to sell off some of his land property and his wife's ornaments to meet expenses of his school (1902).

Publication of essay 'History of Bharatvarsha', emphasizing the unity of Indian civilization within diversity (1902).

R.T.'s wife Mrinalini passes away (November 1902).

Daughter Renuka victim of tuberculosis, passes away (1903).

Publications of the year: *Shishu* (written for ailing Renuka), *Smaran* (written in memory of wife Mrinalini), *Chokher Bali* (1903).

Major public speech, 'Swadeshi Samaj' in Calcutta (July 1904).

Writes textbook for Bengali students of English Language, as a means of meeting financial liabilities (1904).

Father Debendranath dies at age eighty-eight (January 1905).

R.T. writes his first protest against Partition of Bengal (August 1905).

R.T.'s national songs sung by processionists protesting partition and observing *Rakhi-bandhan*, symbol of the bond between the two Bengals being created by partition (October 1905).

R.T. involved in boycott and non-cooperation against partition, but realizes the greater need for rural construction and self-development of capabilities (1905).

Collaborates with National Education movement (1905).

Publications: *Atma-sakti, Swadesh* (1905).

R.T. sends son Rathindranath to Illinois, USA, to study agricultural science (1906).

Publications: essays collected in *Bharatvarsha, Kheya*, novel *Nauka-dubi* (1906).

First Spring Festival, Vasantutsava, in Santiniketan (1907).

R.T.'s daughter Meera's arranged marriage takes place (June 1907).

Commences writing the novel *Gora* (1907).

R.T.'s son Samindranath dies while vacationing in Mungher (1907).

Publications of the year: *Prachin Sahitya, Loka-sahitya, Adhunik Sahitya, Charitra Puja* (1907).

Practical experiment in rural reconstruction in Patisar (1908).

Presides over Bengal Provincial Committee, of Congress (1908).

Path o Patheya, critical of secret societies and political assassination as strategy of freedom struggle, opens new phase in political thinking (1908).

R.T. composes spiritually oriented 'Gitanjali' and songs, and four political essays (1908–09).

Publications: *Raja Praja, Samuha, Swadeshi Samaj, Shiksha, Path o Patheya* (1908)

Contemporary Historical Events

Age of Consent Bill enacted in India (1891).

Birth of Bhimrao Ambedkar (1891).

Death of Ishwarchandra Vidyasagar (1891).

Death of Alfred Tennyson (1892).

Vivekananda attends Chicago Parliament of Religions (1893).

Annie Besant comes to India (1893).

Death of Bankim Chandra Chatterjee (1894).

M.K. Gandhi initiates Congress in Natal (1894).

Lumière Brothers invent cinematography (1894).

Marconi begins radio communication (1895).

Death of Alfred Nobel, inventor of dynamite and founder of Nobel Prize (1896).

Birth of Subhas Chandra Bose (1897).

Bal Gangadhar Tilak imprisoned for sedition (1897).

Birth of Bengali poets Jibanananda Das and Nazrul Islam (1899).

Boxer Rebellion in China (1900).

Max Planck propounds Quantum Theory (1900).

Death of Mahadev Govind Ranade (1901).

Bengal Revolutionaries establish Anushilan Samiti (1902).

Death of Vivekananda (1902).

Ibn Saud begins consolidation of Saudi Arabia (1902).

Edward VII at Delhi Durbar (1903).

Bolshevik Party led by Vladimir Ilyich Lenin founded (1903).

Henry Ford starts his automobile factory (1903).

Russo-Japanese War begins (1904).

Bengal partition leading to Swadeshi Movement (1905).

Japan's victory in war with Russia (1905).

Uprising in Russia against Tsar (1905).

Albert Einstein propounds Special Theory of Relativity (1905).

Aurobindo Ghosh and friends begin revolutionary cell in Bengal (1906).

Death of painter Ravi Varma (1906).

Death of Henrik Ibsen (1906).

Sarat Chandra Chatterjee publishes his first novel (1907).

Sun Yat-sen proclaims plan of Republican Government (1907).

Henri Bergson publishes *Creative Evolution* (1907).

M.K. Gandhi Leads passive resistance against apartheid and anti-Asiatic policy in South Africa (1907–08).

Aurobindo Ghosh and group are arrested for Bomb Conspiracy (1908.)

Kshudiram Bose hanged for attempted assassination of European officers (1908).

B.G. Tilak exiled to Mandalay for sedition (1908).

1909–1919: Chapter Four

Chronology of Life

R.T. writes in 1909 poems later to be published in *Gitanjali*, no political tracts, and his opinion against the cult of violence in Indian politics is expressed in *Prayaschitta*, a play which proved to be unpopular when published in 1909.

Son Rathindranath completes B.Sc in Illinois University (1906–09) and tours Europe (1909).

Publications: *Prayaschitta, Shabda-tattwa, Dharma,* and poems for children *Shishu,* (1909).

Son Rathindranath married to Pratima Devi, first widow marriage in Tagore family (1910).

R.T.'s fiftieth birthday celebrated in Santiniketan, first public celebration (1910).

William Rothenstein and Count Keyserling visit Rabindranath Tagore (1910).

Publications: *Gora, Gitanjali* (in Bengali), *Raja* (1910).

Ananda Coomaraswamy visits Santiniketan (1911).

Death of Vivekananda's Irish disciple Sister Nivedita, obituary written by R.T. (October 1911).

At Congress session in Calcutta, R.T.'s *'jana-gana-mana'* is sung (December 1911).

R.T. travels to England with Rathindra and Pratima, a leisure time spent in translating poems for the English version of 'Gitanjali' (May–June 1912).

William Rothenstein, W.B.Yeats, Bertrand Russell, A.C. Bradley, Sturge Moore and India Society members in England appreciate R.T.'s *Gitanjali* in translation; manuscript edited by Yeats, Rothenstein. (June–October 1912).

R.T. departs for USA (28 October 1912), visits Urbana, Illinois; introduced by Ezra Pound to Harriet Monroe, published in journal *Poetry*, invited to lecture at Chicago; also lectures at Harvard University, later text published as *Sadhana*. (November 1912–January 1913).

India Society, London, publishes *Gitanjali* (Eng.) favourably reviewed by *Times Literary Supplement* on 7 November 1912.

Publications: *Gitanjali* (English), *Dakghar, Jivan-smriti, Chhinna Patra, Achalayatan* (1912)

R.T. returns to England to a huge welcome from litterateurs due to appreciation of *Gitanjali* (April, 1913).

Philosophical lectures at Caxton Hall and drama *The King of the Dark Chamber* staged in Albert Hall (May–June 1913).

R.T. continues to translate his works into English under contract with MacMillan publishing house. (May–November 1913).

Departure from England for India (4 September 1913).

W.W. Pearson and C.F. Andrews visit Santiniketan (1912–13).

R.T. informed of Nobel Prize award (15 November 1913).

R.T. at a felicitation ceremony recalls the slight and humiliation he had earlier received from those who now felicitated him after Nobel Prize award. (23 November 1913).

Calcutta University confers DLitt honoris causa on R.T., decision made prior to Nobel Prize. (26 December 1913).

Publications: *Gitanjali* (Eng.), *Chitra, The Gardener* (Eng.), *The Crescent Moon* (Eng.), *Sadhana* (Eng.) (1913).

R.T. joins literary group of *Sabuj Patra*, literary journal (1914).

M.K. Gandhi visits Santiniketan (November 1914), leaves to attend G.K. Gokhale's last rites in Poona, returns on to meet R.T. (March 1914).

Gandhi's students of Phoenix School stay in Santiniketan for four months (1914).

Publications: *The King of the Dark Chamber* (Eng.), *One Hundred Poems of Kabir* (Eng.), *Post Office* (Eng.), *Utsarga, Smaran, Giti-malya, Gitali.* (1914).

R.T. awarded Knighthood by British Government (3 June 1915).

R.T. visits Kashmir where the title poem of *Balaka* begins to be written. (October 1915).

Shakespeare Tercentenary celebrated by Shakespeare Society of England, R.T. composes poem as tribute (November 1915).

Lecture in Calcutta Rammohan Library on 'The Medium of Education', on the essential role of the mother tongue (December 1915).

Publications: 6 volumes of Collection of Poems, *Santiniketan* sermons, *Kavyagrantha completed* 1916 (1915).

Leaves for Japan on way to USA (3 May 1916).

In Japan for three months, lecture tour; resentment in Japan against R.T.'s criticism of Japan's aggression in China (May–August 1916).

Departs Japan for USA (7 September 1916).

R.T. begins his lecture tour in USA arriving at Seattle, Washington State (18 September 1916).

Publications: *Phalguni, Ghare Baire, Sanchay, Parichay, Chaturanga, Balaka, Fruit Gathering* (Eng.) *Hungry Stones* (Eng.), *Stray Birds* (Eng.) (1916).

A professional agent organizes R.T.'s lectures at 25 major cities in USA including the west coast; earnings from lecture fees are high but R.T. cancels the last few scheduled lectures due to exhaustion (September 1916–January 1917).

Leaves USA on 21 January 1917, via Japan to reach India after ten months of tour (17 March 1917).

Vichitra Club set up in R.T.'s Calcutta residence, *'Dakghar'* staged with Gandhi, Tilak, Annie Besant among spectators (September1917).

Writes essays protesting internment of Annie Besant, condemning communal riots in Bihar, etc. (1917).

R.T. requested to be President of Calcutta Congress Reception Committee by C.R. Das, B.C. Pal, Fazlul Haque (8 September 1917).

Sadler Committee on Calcutta University visits Santiniketan (December 1917).

R.T. attends Congress session in Calcutta and recites poems (December 1917).

Publications: *Kartar Ichhaye Karma, Jiban Smriti* (*My Reminiscences* in Eng.), *Nationalism* (Eng.), *Personality* (Eng.) (1917).

R.T. writes to Gandhi approving of Hindi as national language, provided it is not imposed from above (January 1918).

R.T.'s eldest daughter, Bela dies (16 May 1918).

Foundation laying of Visva-Bharati Bhavan (23 December 1918).

Publications: *Palataka* (Eng.), *Lover's Gift and Crossing* (Eng.), *The Parrot's Training* (Eng.), (1918).

R.T. on lecture tour to Bangalore, Ootacamund, Palghat, Salem, Trichinopoly, Kumbakonam, Tanjore, Madura, Adyar (January to March 1919).

Martial law imposed upon Punjab as a result of disturbances during movement started by M.K. Gandhi; R.T. sends C.F. Andrews to Punjab but he is not allowed entry (April–May 1919).

R.T. goes to Calcutta, to organize a public meeting on the Punjab situation, and he fails to mobilize support (28 May 1919).

A Chronology of Tagore's Life 277

Contemporary Historical Events

Sigmund Freud publishes *Interpretation of Dreams* (1909).

M.K. Gandhi publishes *Hind Swaraj* (1909).

Madanlal Dhingra hanged in London for political assassination (1909).

Morley-Minto Reform legislation towards representative government and communal representation (1909).

Aurobindo Ghosh renounces politics, retreats to Pondicherry (1910).

Japanese aggression in Korea (1910).

M.K. Gandhi leads passive resistance in Transvaal in South Africa against anti-Asiatic policy and apartheid (till 1914).

At 27th session of Congress in Calcutta (December 1911) Rabindranath Tagore's song *Jana-gana-mana* is sung.

At the Delhi Durbar of King, George V declares revocation of partition of Bengal; India's capital shifts from Calcutta to Delhi (December 1911).

End of rule of emperor in China, foundation of Republic (1911).

Ghadr Party formed by Hardayal in USA (1912).

Andrews and Pearson, teachers at Santiniketan, travel to South Africa to aid Gandhi's movement (30 November 1913).

Ship *Kamagata maru* returns to India leading to a massacre (1914).

World War I begins with British declaration of war 4 August (1914).

Special legislation in India for Defense of India against sedition in the context of World War I (1915).

Death of G.K. Gokhale (1915).

Albert Einstein publishes General Theory of Relativity (1915).

Banaras Hindu University founded by M.M. Malaviya (1916).

D.K. Karve establishes SNDT University for Women (1916).

Indian National Congress session in Lucknow to frame a constitution and ensure Hindu-Muslim unity (December 1916).

Foundation of Justice Party in Madras (1917).

Death of Dadabhai Naoroji (1917).

Beginning of Mahatma Gandhi's Champaran Satyagraha (1917).

USSR revolution (1917).

Secretary of State in London, Montague, declares in Parliament the policy of conceding self-governance in successive stages (20 August 1917).

Tagore writes against government repression and in defence of Annie Besant and others prosecuted (1917).

Congress session, Calcutta, President Annie Besant, Rabindranath Tagore attends, recites his poems (1917).

The Montague-Chelmsford Report declares the new policy on India, self governance by slow stages (12 July 1918).

Sedition Committee or Rowlatt Committee Report (July 1918) recommends strong measures against political agitators.

World War II ends (November 1918).

Rowlatt Bill passed despite opposition from Indian members of Imperial Legislative Council Gandhi declares agitation (23 March 1919).

Agitation from 30 March 1919 leads to declaration of Martial law in Punjab (10 April 1919).

Tagore writes to Gandhi on 12 April 1919 expressing concern about Martial law to suppress unarmed people.

Jallianwala Bagh massacre the next day (13 April 1919).

1919–1929: Chapter Five

Chronology of Life

R.T. begins to live in a thatched cottage, later called Uttarayan in Santiniketan (November 1919).

R.T. gathers members of the faculty at Santiniketan, including Nandalal Bose, C.F. Andrews, Bidhu Sekhar Bhattacharya, Marathi musician Bhimrao Hasurkar Shastri, Manipuri dance-teacher Buddhimanta Singh, et al. (1919).

Publications: *Home and the World* (Eng.), *The Centre of Indian Culture* (Eng.), *Mother's Prayer* (Eng.) (1919).

Invited by Gandhi, R.T. visits Ahmedabad (April 1920).

R.T. travels to England with William Rothenstein and Ernest Rhys as social sponsors, but meets with a cold reception due to the renunciation of Knighthood the previous year (May–July 1920).

Escapes from England to France to meet at Autors de Monde in Paris intellectuals like Henri Bergson, Sylvain Levi (August 1920).

Lecture tour to Rotterdam, Amsterdam, the Hague, Leiden, Utrecht (September, October 1920).

Lecture tour in USA, from 28 October 1920; meets Helen Keller and Leonard Elmhirst and Poetry Society members in New York and also lectures in Houston and Chicago (November 1920–March 1921).

Publication: *Arupratan* (1920).

R.T. returns to England (March 1921) disappointed with his USA tour; apprehended that Americans regarded him as pro-German.

Travels by aeroplane, London to Paris, his first flight; meets Romain Rolland and Patrick Geddes(16 April 1921).

Proceeds to Strasburg to lecture at university, then to Geneva, Lucerne, Zurich.

Next leg of journey trip to Hamburg, Copenhagen and Stockholm (Nobel Prize recipient's Address to Swedish Academy delivered by R.T.)

Thereafter lectures at Berlin, Munich, Vienna, Prague; among German and Czechoslovak intellectuals he meets Thomas Mann, Count Keyserling, and Indologists, Moritz Winternitz and V. Lesny (May 1921).

Departs for India (July 1921).

Santiniketan affected by Non-Cooperation movement; connection with Calcutta University for entrance examinations cut off by Santiniketan faculty, C.F. Andrews obtains R.T.'s approval but R.T. is sceptical (1921.)

Engages in debate with Gandhi on nationalist agenda of action (July–September 1921).

'Varsha Mangal' (rain festival) celebrated for the first time (July 1921).

Gandhi visits R.T. in Calcutta, and they agree to disagree on most political issues; Bengal public opinion against R.T. (September 1921).

Leonard Elmhirst joins rural reconstruction work at Sriniketan, then called Surul (September 1921).

French Indologist Sylvain Levi, Visiting Professor arrives (November 1921).

Foundation Ceremony of Visva-Bharati Society (22 December 1921).

Publications: *The Fugitive* (Eng.), *The Wreck* (Eng.) (1921).

Statement against violent actions in course of Non-Cooperation (February 1922).

R.T. suspends dramatic performance on receiving news of Gandhi's imprisonment (March 1922).

Observes centenary of death anniversary of Percy Bysshe Shelley (August 1922).

Tribute to B.G. Tilak in speech at Puna Sarvajanik Sabha (September 1922).

Lecture tour in South India: Bangalore, Madurai, Coimbatore, Mangalore, Colombo, Quilon, Cochin, etc. (October–November 1922).

Visits Sabarmati Ashram, speech in honour of Gandhi who was then in prison (December 1922).

Indologist Moritz Winternitz, Visiting Professor at Santiniketan (December 1922).

Publications: *Lipika, Mukta-Dhara, Shishu Bholanath, Creative Unity* (Eng.) (1922).

Death of elder brother and a mentor Satyendranath (January 1923).

Musical drama *Basanta*, dedicated to Nazrul Islam (then in prison), staged by R.T. in Calcutta (February 1923).

Presides over the first All India Bengali Literary Conference in Benaras; warns against Bengal's parochialism (March 1923).

Visits Karachi, Hyderabad, Porbandar, Bombay (March–April 1923).

Indologist Vincene Lesny, Visiting Professor at Visva-Bharati (March 1923).

Ratan Kuthi Guest House at Santiniketan built with donation from Lady Ratan Tata (1923).

First of the nine drafts of play *Rakta-Karabi* composed in Shillong (April 1923).

Expresses to media his views on the Swarajya Party (June 1923).

R.T. addresses the Malaria Prevention Association, on a topic that concerned him deeply (August 1923).

R.T.'s colleague W.W. Pearson dies in an accident in Italy (September 1923); new faculty members included F. Benoit, from France, Stella Kramrisch from Germany (1923)

Tours several western Indian princely states to collect funds for Kala Bhavan of Visva-Bharati (November 1923).

Publications: *Basanta, The Visva-Bharati* (Eng.) (1923).

Tours Burma, China, Japan; lectures on the civilizational unity of Asia; unwelcome to radical Left political groups; meets Rash Behari Bose (March–June 1924).

Contests the comments of Lord Lytton, Government of Bengal, on Indian women (July 1924).

Departs via Paris for Peru, then celebrating centenary of her independence day (September–October 1924).

On board the ship R.T. falls gravely ill, accepts in Buenos Aires invitation of litterateur and grand-dame Victoria Ocampo (7 November 1924).

R.T. a guest of Ocampo, cancels trip to Peru and stays in Argentina (November–December 1924).

Publications: *Gora* (Eng.), *Talks in China* (Eng.), *Letters from Abroad* (Eng.) (1924).

Returns to India via Geneva (17 February 1925).

Gandhi visits Santiniketan and discusses with R.T. his objection to Gandhian programme (May 1925).

Professor Carlo Formichi visits R.T. along with Indologist Giuseppe Tucci of Italy (November 1925).

Publications: *Purabi*, E.J. Thompson's translations of R.T.'s poems (1925).

Visits Dhaka and East Bengal (Bangladesh) (February 1926).

Visits Italy at Mussolini's invitation (May 1926).

Retracts statement in praise of Mussolini after being informed of the true state of affairs by Romain Rolland and others (July–September 1926).

Visits Zurich, Oslo, Stockholm, Copenhagen, Berlin, meets Albert Einstein (July–September 1926).

Visits several German cities on the way to Prague, Vienna, Budapest, Athens (September–November 1926).

Returns to India via Cairo and Alexandria (December 1926).

Statements against communalism apropos of condemnation of the assassination of Swami Sraddhananda (December 1926).

Publications: *Rakta-Karabi, Natir Puja, Chirakumar Sabha* (1926)

Statement against government's policy of imprisoning without trial political activists under Bengal Ordinance (February 1927).

Presides over All-India Hindi Literary Conference at Bharatpur (March 1927).

Begins writing novel *Yogayog*, earlier entitled *Tin Purush* in Shillong (May–June 1927).

Trip to South-East Asia via Singapore; visits Bali, Java, Bangkok (August–October 1927).

Publications: *Lekhan, Ritu Ranga* (1927).

Addresses Vichitra Club on the occasion of Poetry festival of modern, i.e. post-Tagorean poets (March 1928).

Visits Adyar, Aurobindo's ashram in Pondicherry, Colombo, Bangalore (May–July 1928).

Begins festival of Vriksha-ropona (tree planting) and Hala-Karshana (ploughing) at Santiniketan and Sriniketan (July 1928).

Takes lessons in drawing and painting while residing in the Government Art College, Calcutta (August 1928).

Film version of one of Tagore's short stories prepared but withdrawn by Censor Board (1928).

Publications: *Fire Flies* (Eng.), *Letters to a Friend* (Eng.) (to C.F. Andrews), *A Poet's School* (Eng.) (1928).

Addresses All-Bengal Cooperative Society on cooperation as the means of development, independent of government support (February 1929).

Visits North America: Lectures at Vancouver, stops at Los Angeles, having met with discourtesy at Immigration Office, R.T. cancels lectures in California and sails for Japan (April–May 1929).

Returns to India via Yokohama and Saigon (June 1929).

R.T.'s play 'Tapati' filmed by Dhirendra Ganguly, but the movie remained unexhibited (1929).

A turning point in R.T.'s literary life, novel *Yogayog*, remarkable for its earthy portrayal of affective relationship and *Sesher Kabita*, for having outdone 'modernist' writers (1929).

Publications: *Yogayog, Sesher Kabita, Tapati, Mohua, Jatri* (1929).

Contemporary Historical Events

Mahatma Gandhi starts journal *Young India* (8 October 1919).

Khilafat Conference in Delhi (23 November 1919).

Versailles Conference for post-world war settlement (1919).

Government of India Act restructures Indian governance (1919).

Death of B.G. Tilak (1920).

India becomes member of League of Nations (1920).

Congress leaders adopt principle of Non-cooperation (August 1920).

Non-cooperation movement sweeps India leading to boycott of foreign goods, government schools, courts of law (1921)

Chittaranjan Das abandons legal practice and joins Non-cooperation movement in Bengal (1921).

Japan quits China under international pressure (1921).

Reza Khan, Head of Army, takes over power in Iran (1921).

Violent incident at Chauri Chaura leads Gandhi to call off Non-cooperation Movement (February 1922).

Gandhi arrested (10 March 1922).

Mussolini establishes Fascist rule in Italy (1922).

T.S. Eliot publishes *The Waste Land* and James Joyce *Ulysses* (1922).

Kemal Ataturk establishes Republic in Turkey (1923).

Swaraj Party founded by C.R. Das and Motilal Nehru (1923).

First Communist Party conference at Kanpur (1924).

Hindu-Muslim communal riots break out intermittently, Gandhi observes fast (1924).

Death of V.I. Lenin (1924).

Death of C.R. Das (1925).

Death of Sun Yat-sen (1925).

Adolf Hitler publishes *Mein Kampf* (1925).

Communal riots in Calcutta (1926).

Rash Behari Bose founds Independence League in Japan (1926).

All India Women's Conference meets (1926).

Trotsky expelled from Communist Party of USSR (1926).

Soekarno assumes leadership of national struggle against Dutch rule in Indonesia (1926).

Simon Commission meets with rejection in India (1927.)

C.V. Raman publishes findings called 'Raman Effect' (1928).

Hindustan Socialist Republican Army led by Bhagat Singh gathers strength (1928).

Death of Lajpat Rai from injury in police action (1928).

Women get right to vote in Britain (1928).

Gandhi renews movement for upliftment of Harijans (1929).
Death of Jatindranath Das, on hunger strike for five weeks (1929).
Attempt on life of Viceroy Irwin fails (1929).

1930–1941: Chapter Six

Chronology of Life

Elmhirst expands work at Sriniketan then known as Surul (February 1930).
R.T.'s paintings exhibited at Paris, curated by Andrée Karpelès, funded by
   Victoria Ocampo (May 1930).
Hibbert Lectures at Oxford University; subject of 3 lectures *Religion of Man*.
   (May 1930).
R.T. meets Albert Einstein in Berlin (July 1930).
Passion Play at Oberammergau seen by R.T.; inspired to write *The Child*
   (July 1930).
Visits USSR for 15 days (September 1930).
Visits New York and Philadelphia, meets President Hoover, Helen Keller
   (October–December 1930).
Returns to England and holds abortive discussion with Indian leaders assembled
   for Round Table Conference (December 1930).
During R.T.'s tour his paintings are exhibited in many cities: Paris,
   Birmingham, London, Berlin, Copenhagen, Moscow, New York, Boston
   (March–December 1930).
Major publications: *Bhanu Singher Patrabali, Sahaj Path* (1930).
Letters from Russia published (May 1931).
Buxar Jail prisoners felicitate R.T. on his birthday, R.T. responds in verse
   (June 1931).
Protests at public meeting in Calcutta against firing on prisoners at Hijli Jail
   (September 1931).
First exhibition of R.T.'s paintings in India at Town Hall, Calcutta (December
   1931).
Publication of *Golden Book of Tagore*, tributes to him, and felicitation ceremony
   by Calcutta citizens (December 1931).
Publication: *The Religion of Man* (Eng.), *The Child, Russiar Chithi. Shap-
   Mochan, Banabani* (1931).
Protest letter to Ramsay MacDonald against imprisonment of Gandhi (January
   1932).
Exhibition of R.T.'s paintings at Government Art School, Calcutta (February
   1932).

Visit to Persia at the invitation of Reza Shah (April 1932).

R.T. goes to Yervada Jail to meet Gandhi on hunger-strike (September 1932).

Publications: *Mahatmaji and the Depressed Humanity* (Eng.), *Kaler Jatra, Punascha* (1932).

'Religion of Man' (*Manusher Dharma*), professorial lecture at Calcutta University (January 1933).

Writes to Gandhi dissuading him from undertaking another hunger-strike, and to Government of India demanding release of unconvicted political prisoners (May–June 1933).

Uday Shankar and dance troupe perform in Santiniketan (July 1933).

Statement critical of Poona Pact (July 1933).

Tagore Festival in Bombay organized by Sarojini Naidu; R.T.'s philosophical lectures, *Price of Freedom* (November 1933).

Lecture on philosophy of education at Osmania University, Hyderabad (December 1933).

Lecture on ideas of Rammohan Roy on his hundredth death anniversary (December 1933).

Address to All India Women's Conference in Calcutta (December 1933).

Publications: *Manusher Dharma* (Religion of Man), *Bharat Pathik Rammohun, Chandalika, Tasher Desh*, (1933).

Debate with Gandhi on latter's statement on Bihar earthquake (January–February 1934).

Nehru visits R.T. to see daughter Indira, a student at Santiniketan (January 1934).

R.T. condemns anti-Gandhi propaganda occasioned by Poona Pact (February 1934).

Visit to Ceylon (Sri Lanka) (May 1934).

Khan Abdul Ghaffar Khan visits Santiniketan (August 1934).

R.T. tours Madras, Waltair, etc. (November 1934).

Publications: *Char Adhyay, Malancha* (1934).

Bengal Governor Anderson visits Santiniketan, a campus devoid of faculty and students since they were sent away during visit (February 1935).

DLitt conferred on R.T. by M.M. Malaviya at Banaras Hindu University (February 1935).

Visits Punjab, R.T. awarded Sikh saropa at Dera Sahib Gurdwara (February 1935).

Lecture on Buddha at Mahabodhi Society, Calcutta (May 1935).

Death of Dinendranath Tagore, editor and score-writer of Tagore songs (21 July 1935).

R.T. vilified in Bengal media due to his statement against animal sacrifice at Kalighat temple (September 1935).

Japanese poet Yone Noguchi visits R.T. (November 1935)

Publications: *Sesh Saptak* (The Last Chords), *Bithika, Shabda-tattwa, Chansons de Rabindranath Tagore* (French) (1935).

R.T. lectures on People's Education (*Loka-shiksha*) at New Education Fellowship Conference in Calcutta (February 1936).

R.T.'s school being in debt he tours north India to collect funds; Gandhi objects to such a 'begging mission' and obtains donation from G.D. Birla (March 1936).

Government stalls Delhi municipality plan to felicitate R.T., Asaf Ali organizes independent public ceremony (March 1936).

R.T.'s granddaughter Nandita marries Krishna Kripalani (April 1936).

R.T. protests Communal Award at meeting in Calcutta (July 1936).

Loka-siksha Samsad for popular education founded (July 1936).

Addresses to All India Women's Conference at Albert Hall, Calcutta (October 1936).

Jawaharlal Nehru visits R.T. (November 1936.)

Dramatic versions of two major novels staged in Calcutta, *Gora* and *Yogyog* (December 1936).

Publications: *Shyamali, Chitrangada* (dramatized version), *Chhanda, Sahityer Pathe* (1936).

Convocation Address at Calcutta University, in Bengali language for the first time in eighty years (February 1937).

Lecture on 'religion of the spirit and sectarianism' at conference on birth centenary of Ramakrishna, the spiritual leader (March 1937).

China Bhavan inaugurated in Santiniketan (April 1937).

Statement in support of Bengal jute mill workers, on strike since February 1937 (April 1937).

Visits Almora writes introduction to *Visva-Parichay* (May–June 1937).

Presides over meeting in Calcutta in sympathy with Andaman prisoners on hunger strike (August 1937).

Gravely ill, loses consciousness for two days (10–11 September 1937).

Meets Gandhi and AICC members in Calcutta (October 1937).

Intimate friend, scientist Jagadish Chandra Bose, passes away. (November 1937).

Poems of *Prantik* are composed (December 1937).

Publications: *Kalantar, Visva-Parichay, Khapchara, Shay* (1937).

Hindi Bhavan founded at Santiniketan (January 1938).

Osmania University confers DLitt on R.T. (March 1938).

R.T. and Gandhi hold a discussion in Calcutta on action to obtain release of political prisoners (March 1938).

Artist Gaganendranath Tagore passes away, one of few relatives close to R.T. (19 July 1938).

Tagore's school observes a day of mourning on the day the news of death of Kemal Ataturk was received (November 1938).

Publications: *Prantik* (Terminal), *Senjuti*, *Bangla Bhasha Parichay* (1938).

Felicitation meeting for Subhas Chandra Bose, President of the Congress (January 1939).

Nehru inaugurates Hindi Bhavan, Santiniketan (February 1939).

R.T. fails in attempt to bring about reconciliation between Bose and Nehru (February 1939).

Rajendra Prasad visits R.T. (February 1939).

Malayalam poet Vallathol and Kerala Kalamandalam artists visit Santiniketan (March 1939).

R.T. visits Orissa (April–May 1939).

Invited by Subhas Bose R.T. lays the foundation stone of Mahajati Sadan, Calcutta (August 1939).

Nehru meets R.T. on the eve of leaving for China, both enthusiastic about building relationship with China (August 1939).

Outbreak of World War II (3 September 1939).

First volume of R.T.'s 'Collected Works' published by Visva-Bharati (September 1939).

Chinese artist Zhu Peong visits R.T. (December 1939).

Publications: *Akash-Pradip*, *Shyama*, *Pather Sanchay* (1939).

R.T. writes in condemnation of Russian aggression in Finland (January 1940).

Gandhi and Kasturba's last visit to Santiniketan in R.T.'s lifetime (17–19 February 1940).

R.T. appeals to Gandhi to remain the guardian of Visva-Bharati; 'My life's best treasure', Gandhi assures R.T. 'of doing all I can in the common endeavour'. (19 February 1940).

Death of C.F. Andrews in Calcutta (April 1940).

Death of Surendranath Tagore, son of R.T.'s elder brother and mentor Satyendranath (3 May 1940).

Death of Kalimohan Ghosh, who served both Sriniketan and Santiniketan since 1907 (12 May 1940).

Oxford University confers on R.T. DLitt honoris causa at special convocation held in Santiniketan (April 1940).

R.T. moved from Santiniketan to Calcutta for medical treatment, and to Kalimpong to recuperate, and back to Calcutta for further treatment (September–November 1940)

Gandhi writes to R.T.: 'Stay yet a while.' (10 October 1940).

Publications: *Nabajatak, Sehnai, Chhelebela, Tinsangi, Rogsajya* (1940)

R.T.'s last birthday celebration at Santiniketan; his address entitled 'Crisis in Civilization' is his last public pronouncement (14 April 1941).

R.T. writes a reply to denigration of Indian people by Mrs Rathbourne, M.P. (?) (4 June 1941).

Gravely ill, R.T. is removed from Santiniketan to Calcutta for treatment for urinary problem and erysipelas (25 July 1941).

R.T. composes his last two poems (29, 30 July 1941).

Death at 12.10 p.m. (7 August 1941).

Publications: *Arogya, Janmadine, Sabhyatar Sankat, Sesh Lekha* ('Last Writings') 1941.

Contemporary Historical Events

World Depression spreads from New York globally causing unemployment (1929).

Gandhi's Dandi March to defy Salt Law (1930).

Surya Sen leads attack on Chittagong Armoury (1930).

Revolutionaries Binoy, Badal and Dinesh kill Inspector General of Prisons in battle at Bengal Government secretariat (1930).

Bhagat Singh, Rajguru and Sukhdev sentenced to death after Lahore Conspiracy trial (1930).

First Round Table Conference in London, Congress boycotts (1930).

Government ban on Congress and its activities (2 December 1930).

Muslim League and M.A. Jinnah declare aim to establish sovereign Muslim state (1930).

Shooting of political prisoners in Hijli jail leading to nationalist protest (1931).

Japan captures Manchuria (1931).

Electoral success of Nazi Party in Germany (1932).

Death of Bipin Chandra Pal (1932).

Centenary of Goethe's death observed worldwide, including Santiniketan (1932).

Unemployment causes economic distress during World Depression (1929–32).

The term 'PAKISTAN' is invented by Chowdhuri Rahamat Ali (1932).

Gandhi starts journal *Harijan* (1933.)

Death of Bengali nationalist Jatindra Mohan Sengupta (1933).

Controversy regarding Poona Pact on caste representation (1933).

Hitler assumes dictatorship in Germany (1933).

Development of concentration camps in Germany for Jews, political suspects, etc (1933).

Surya Sen of Chittagong Armoury Raid hanged (1934).

Bihar earthquake kills 20,000 (1934).

Foundation of Congress Socialist Party by Jayaprakash Narayan (1934).

Hitler takes the title of Fuhrer (1934).

Government of India Act of 1935 allows limited powers to elected provincial government (1935).

Mussolini's Italy attacks Abyssinia i.e. Ethiopia (1935).

Chiang Kai-Shek elected President of Republic of China (1935).

Death of revolutionary Bhikaji Cama (1936).

Death of Hindi writer Munshi Premchand (1936).

Success of Vaikom Satyagraha to end caste distinction in temple admission (1936).

Italy scores victory in Abyssinia (1936).

Beginning of Civil War in Spain and assumption of power by General Francisco Franco (1936).

Berlin–Rome Axis formed by Hitler and Mussolini (1936).

Chiang Kai-Shek declares war on Japan (1936).

Trotsky expelled from USSR, migrates to Mexico, to be assassinated later (1936).

Congress wins election to form government in about all but two provinces (1937).

Scientist Jagadish Chandra Bose dies (1937).

In Spanish Civil War Franco's forces are defeated in many cities (1937).

Treaty of Belgrade between Italy and Yugoslavia (1937).

Neville Chamberlain, infamous for his appeasement policy towards Germany, becomes prime minister of Britain (1937).

Japan returns to policy of territorial expansion in China (1937–40).

Mao-Tse-Dong and Chiang Kai-Shek join hands to save China from foreign invasion (1937).

Egypt adopts new constitution but remains under British protection (1937).

Naval Pact between Germany and USSR (1937).

Death of Sarat Chandra Chatterjee (1938).

Death of Mohammad Iqbal (1938).

Subhas Chandra Bose elected President of Congress (1938).

Neville Chamberlain's appeasement policy is climaxed by Munich Pact with Hitler (1938).

Subhas Bose compelled to resign from presidentship of Congress due to opposition of leading Congress members (1939).

Franco's Fascist government in Spain recognized by Britain and France (1939.)

Germany invades Poland (1 September 1939).

Britain and France declare war on Germany, beginning of World War II (1939).

Muslim League pass Karachi Resolution demanding Pakistan (23 March 1940).

Udham Singh kills Michael O' Dyer infamous for Jallianwala Bagh massacre (March 1940).

Germany invades Denmark and Norway (9 April 1940).

Winston Churchill becomes Prime Minister of Britain (May 1940).

France falls and Battle of Britain begins (June 1940).

Germany invades Yugoslavia (6 April 1941).

Axis powers attack USSR (22 June 1941).

Bibliographic Note

This bibliographic note is intended to bring together the main sources which have been used in writing this book, to provide details of books mentioned in the text and references, and to suggest further readings, particularly for readers who do not have access to the Bengali language. It does not aim to be a comprehensive bibliography because that would be too long for the average reader and too brief for the scholarly. There is in print as of now no comprehensive bilbliography of the kind that is demanded by Tagore's huge corpus of writings, a considerable body of published correspondence, and a vast number of works containing commentaries and literary appreciation by Tagore scholars. In the English language one has to make do with a bibliography now out of date, Katherine Henn, *Rabindranath Tagore: A Bibliography*, Metuchen (New Jersey) and London, 1985, published by the American Theological Library Association. In Bengali, one can use the scholarly compendium prepared by Swapan Majumder, *Rabindra-grantha-suchi* (Calcutta, 1988).

The most frequent reference in the previous pages and the most important source in this book is obviously the *Rabindra Rachanabali* ('Collected Works of Tagore'). The oldest collection is the Visva-Bharati publication series since 1939, *Rabindra Rachanabali*, vols. I to XXXI, published by the Visva-Bharati Granathan Vibhag, Calcutta. This is to be supplemented by *Rabindra Rachanbabali: Achalita Sangraha* ('Commonly Unavailable Works Collected'), vols. I and II, Visva-Bharati, Calcutta, 1940, !941. Visva-Bharati has also published what the above two publications contain in *Rabindra Rachanabali*, in sixteen volumes, published in imprints by Visva-Bharati Granthan Vibhag, Calcutta, from the year 1986 onwards. Of these two editions I have preferred to use the latter, the sixteen-volume edition, because it is more handy and contains more up-dated bibliographic notes than the thirty-one volume edition of earlier date. There is a third series of *Rabindra Rachanabali*, which was published by the government of West Bengal on the occasion of the 125th birth anniversary of Tagore; that too is serviceable but it is not the edition I have cited in this book; in any event, it is going to be replaced by a new edition now under preparation on the occasion of the 150th birth anniversary. Some private publishers have started publishing collections of Tagore's works, parallel to the Visva-Bharati publications. Thereby hangs a tale. Tagore's copyright was due to expire in 1991 because the copyright law then prescribed fifty years after the death of the author as the time limit of copyright. As the Vice Chancellor of Visva-Bharati University my first task was not to let that happen in 1991 because the university depended heavily on the large income from the sale of Tagore's works; he had gifted the royalty income from publication rights to the university. The Government of India was eventually persuaded to extend the copyright time limit by ten more years. The university's interest was protected for the time being, at the cost of the interest of private publishers. The reprieve thus obtained ran out in 2001. Since the termination of Tagore's copyright private publishers have produced Tagore's works on a large scale but the accuracy and authenticity might vary and the reader has to check that himself or herself. In this work I have depended on the imprints from Visva-Bharati exclusively.

As regards the writings of Tagore in English as well as translations done by himself the consolidated edition published by the Sahitya Akademi, New Delhi, is the best: Sisir Kumar Das (ed.) *English Writings of Rabindranath Tagore* (New Delhi, 1994–96), vol. I, 1994; vol. II, 1996; vol. III, 1996. The scholarly bibliographic notes are commendable in this edition. There is a fourth volume in the series which brings together fragments not included earlier.

A major source used in this work is Tagore's correspondence. The best selection from that in the English language is: Krishna Dutta and Andrew Robinson (eds.), *Selected Letters of Rabindranath Tagore* (Cambridge University Press, 1997). Something of a classic is the collection of Tagore's letters to his confidant, Andrews: Charles Freer Andrews (ed.) *Letters to a Friend* (London, 1928). Some more letters in English are available in: Mary M. Lago (ed.), *Imperfect Encounter: Letters of William Rothenstein and Rabindranath Tagore, 1911–1941*, Cambridge (Massachusetts), 1972; Bikash Chakravarty, *Poets to A Poet, 1912–1940* (Visva-Bharati, Calcutta, 1998); Uma Das Gupta, *A Difficult Friendship: letters of Edward Thompson and Rabindranath Tagore, 1913–1940* (Oxford University Press, Delhi, 1993); Krishna Dutta and Andrew Robinson (eds.), *Purabi: The Miscellany in Memory of Rabindranath Tagore, 1941–1991* (London, 1991); Ketaki Kushari Dyson, *In Your Blossoming Flower-Garden: Rabindranath Tagore and Victoria Ocampo,* (New Delhi, 1988); Sabyasachi Bhattacharya (ed.), *The Mahatma and the Poet: Letters and Debates Between Gandhi and Tagore, 1915–1941* (National Book Trust, Delhi, 1997).

When one turns to Tagore's letters in Bengali the problem is the embarrassment of riches. About four thousand letters of Tagore have been published in various imprints, and a sort of index is available, the letters arranged in chronological order, in: Gour Chandra Saha, *Rabindra-Patrabali* (Bolpur, 1984). Some of Tagore's letters which constitute a main source in this biography have been published in *Chithi-Patra*, vols. I to XVIII (Visva-Bharati, Calcutta, 1942, 1943, 1945, 1957, 1960, 1963, 1967, 1974, 1986, 1992, 1995, 1998, 2000, 2002, 2004). Among these for our purposes the particularly important series are: vol. I, rev. edn., 1993, letters to wife Mrinalini; II, to son Rathindranath; IV, to his daughters and grandchildren; V, to his brothers and niece Indira and her husband; V, 1945; VI, to friend Jagadish Chandra Bose; VIII, to his friend of youth Priyanath Sen; XI, to his secretary Amiya Chakravarty; XII to friend, editor

Ramananda Chattopadhyay; XIII, to Manoranjan Bandyopahyay and teachers at Santiniketan School; XVI to Sudhindranath Datta, Jibanananda Das, Buddhadeb Bose and other young Bengal poets; XVIII, to young admirer Ranu Adhikari. Tagore's letters in the literary vein are widely read: to niece Indira Devi, in *Chhinna Patra* (Calcutta, 1912) and *Chhinna patrabali* (1960); to Nirmal Kumari Mahalanobis, *Path o Pather Prante* (Calcutta, 1938).

The Rabindra Bhavan archives at Santiniketan contain many yet unpublished letters, including the letters in English, a few of which I have cited in this book. Founded in 1942, the Rabindra Bhavan is the largest depository of not only Tagore's correspondence in about 1470 files but also his manuscripts in over a thousand volumes. There are also Tagore family estate papers, accounts of expenditure, etc. which have been used adroitly by Prasanta Pal, *Rabi-Jibani,* cited below, a work of research unique for its thorough documentation.

The National Archives of India, New Delhi, contain some material relating to Tagore in the Home Department, Political Branch, from the 1920s when he came under surveillance of the intelligence branch of the police because his loyalty was in question due to his renunciation of his knighthood, his contact with nationalists, his frequent trips abroad, his tendency to employ Jewish and other émigrés from Europe, etc. The West Bengal State Archives holds more papers ranging from Tagore's letter to the Government of Bengal requesting an age certificate in 1878, to various reports on him and his school from officials in the departments of education, police etc. up to the 1930s. A recent collection of some of these papers is: Directorate of State Archives, eds. Madhurima Sen, Atish Dasgupta, Government of West Bengal, *A Tribute to Rabindranath Tagore: glimpses from archival records* (Calcutta, 2011).

While Tagore's writings and letters have been my major source, I must acknowledge my indebtedness to the works of many distinguished predecessors in writing Tagore's biography. The substantial, source-based biographies are the following: Prabhat Kumar Mukhopadhyay, *Rabindra-jibani o Rabindra-Sahitya*

Prabeshak, vols. I to IV, (Visva-Bharati, Calcutta, rev. edns, 1946–2008), an indispensable classic; Krishna Kripalani, *Rabindranath Tagore: a Biography* (Calcutta, 1980, now in an annotated edition of 2008, edited by Supriya Roy), an insightful observer who studied at Santiniketan and married Tagore's granddaughter; Krishna Dutta and Andrew Robinson, *Rabindranath Tagore: the Myriad-Minded Man* (New York, 1996), notable for pioneering research into archival depositories abroad on Tagore's international contacts and experiences; there is recent reprint of a contemporary biographer's work, which Tagore himself did not approve of: E.J. Thompson, *Rabindranath Tagore: Poet and Dramatist,* New Delhi, 1991 (introduction by Harish Trivedi; also see E.P. Thompson, *Alien Homage: Edward Thompson and Rabindranath Tagore,* New Delhi, 1993). The most well-documented and detailed biography of Tagore unfortunately remains unfinished since the author's demise: Prasanta Kumar Pal, *Rabi-Jibani* (Ananda Publishers, Calcutta) vols. I, (1861–1871), rev. edn, 1993; II, (1878/9–1884/5), 1984; III, (1885/6–1893/4, 1986; IV, (1894/5–1900/1), 1988; V, (1901/2–1907/8), 1990; VI, (1908/9–1913/14), 1993; VII (1914–1920), 1997; VIII (1920–1923), 2001; IX, (1923–1926), 2003.

The reminiscences of contemporaries form a different category of source. William Rothenstein, *Men and Memories: Recollections, 1900–1922,* London, 1932, is a sympathetic account. Some of those who studied or taught in Santiniketan: e.g. Alex Aronson, *Brief Chronicles of the Time: Personal Recollections of My Stay in Bengal 1937–1946,* (Calcutta, 1991); or Pramathanath Bisi, *Rabindranath o Shantiniketan,* (Calcutta 1975); W.W. Pearson, *Shantiniketan: The Bolpur School of Rabindranath Tagore,* London, 1917; *Rabindranath Tagore: Pioneer in Education,* London, 1961 (essays and exchanges between R.T. and Leonard K. Elmhirst). Among many memoirs written by Tagore's relatives the important one is: Rathindranath Tagore: *On the Edges of Time,* (2nd edn, Calcutta, 1981).

There are several useful surveys of contemporary opinion, newspaper reports, etc. which supplement internal sources of Santiniketan. Martin Kampchen, *Rabindranath Tagore and Germany:*

A Documentation, (Calcutta, 1991) broke new ground in exploring German sources; Sujit Mukherjee, *Passage to America: The Reception of Rabindranath Tagore in the United States, 1912–1941* (Calcutta, 1964); Kalyan Kundu et. al., eds, *Rabindranath Tagore and the British Press (1912–1941),* (London, 1990). Two earlier insightful works were by Alex Aronson, *Rabindranath Tagore Through Western Eyes,* 2nd edn, (Calcutta, 1978); Stephen N. Hay, *Asian Ideas of East and West: Tagore and His Critics in Japan, China and India,* Cambridge (Massachusetts), 1970. Two collections of contemporary material are: Ramananda Chatterjee, (ed.), *The Golden Book of Tagore,* Calcutta, 1931; *Calcutta Municipal Gazette,* (Tagore Memorial Special Supplement), 13 September 1941.

In putting together this bibliographic note, I have excluded secondary works, literary appreciations, etc. very few of which have been used in this work for reasons I have explained in the Introduction. The following selective list of works by Tagore in translation may be useful for readers without access to the Bengali language. When no translator is named, the author himself was the translator.

Among recent translations the notable ones are in the Oxford Tagore Translations series, the outcome of a collaboration established by a memorandum in 1994 that Neil O'Brien signed on behalf of Oxford University Press and I on behalf of Visva-Bharti; as of now the following volumes, edited by Sukanta Chaudhuri, are available: *Selected Short Stories* (2001), *Selected Writings on Language and Literature* (2001), *Selected Poems* (2004) with introduction by Sankha Ghosh, *Selected Writings for Children* (2006), and the novel *Relationships* ('*Yogayog*'), translated by Supriya Chaudhuri.

The Child, London, 1931 (poem).
Chitra, London, 1914 (drama).
Creative Unity, London, 1922 (essays).
The Crescent Moon, London, 1913 (poems).
Crisis in Civilization, Calcutta, 1941 (essay).
The English Writings of Rabindranath Tagore, Sisir Kumar Das, (ed.), cited above.

Farewell, My Friend, Krishna Kripalani trans., London, 1946 (novel); *Sesher Kavita*, also translated by Radha Chakravarty, *Farewell Song*, (Delhi, 2005).

Four Chapters, Surendranath Tagore trans., Calcutta, 1950 (novel).

Fruit-Gathering, London, 1916 (poems).

The Gardener, London, 1913 (poems).

Gitanjali (*Song Offerings*), London, 1913 (introduction by W.B. Yeats, poems).

Gora, W.W. Pearson and Surendranath Tagore trans., London, 1924 (novel).

The Home and the World, Surendranath Tagore trans., London, 1919; London, 1985, (introduction by Anita Desai), (novel).

I Won't Let You Go: Selected Poems, Ketaki Kushari Dyson trans., Newcastle-upon-Tyne, 1991.

The King of the Dark Chamber, Kshitis Chandra Sen trans., London, 1914 (drama).

Letters from Russia, Sasadhar Sinha trans., Calcutta, 1960.

Lover's Gift and Crossing, London, 1918 (poems).

Nationalism, London, 1991, (introduction by E.P. Thompson), (essays).

Personality, London, 1917.

Poems, (anthology), Krishna Kripalani (ed.), Calcutta, 1942.

Poems of Rabindranath Tagore, Calcutta, 1966, reprint 2005, Humayun Kabir (ed.), trans. by Buddhadeb Bose, Samar Sen, Amiya Chakravarty, Bhabani Bhattacharya, Abu Syed Ayub, Tarak Sen, et al.

The Religion of Man, London, 1931 (essays).

Sadhana: The Realisation of Life, London, 1913 (essays).

Selected Poems, William Radice trans., rev. edn, London, 1987.

Songs of Kabir, Rabindranath Tagore trans., New York, 1915.

Talks in China, Calcutta, 1925.

Three Plays, Marjorie Sykes trans., Bombay, 1950.

Index